THE MEANING OF SPENSER'S FAIRYLAND

THE MEANING OF
SPENSER'S FAIRYLAND

BY

ISABEL E. RATHBORNE

NEW YORK

RUSSELL & RUSSELL · INC

1965

COLUMBIA UNIVERSITY STUDIES IN ENGLISH
AND COMPARATIVE LITERATURE
NUMBER 131

PRINTED IN THE UNITED STATES OF AMERICA

To

ISABEL STURGES

and

THOMAS T. STURGES, JR.

FOREWORD

THIS study was undertaken in the belief that a clearer understanding of Spenser's fairy mythology would necessarily shed light upon the meaning of his poem. In particular, I have tried to answer three questions. What did Spenser mean by "Fairyland"? What was the basis for his distinction between fairies and Britons? And why did he celebrate Elizabeth in the character of Fairy Queen?

No one of these questions can, of course, be answered simply. Yet light is thrown upon all of them by the interpretation of Fairyland which is defended in the following chapters. This may be summarized as follows: Spenser's Fairyland is a land of fame, resembling the classical Elysium. The fairies are the race of gods and heroes who in their earthly lives anticipated the fame of Arthur and the future worthies who were destined to revive it. Arthur's visit to Fairyland, like the similar visits of classical epic heroes to the lower world, is preparatory to his accomplishment of his earthly mission and the *Faerie Queene*, like the *Divine Comedy*, is a literary descendant of the Sixth Book of the *Aeneid*.

The main thesis of this book is thus concerned primarily with Spenser's "fable" or "historicall fiction," and only secondarily with his allegory. Yet the two cannot profitably be separated; and a closer study of the "fable" must necessarily lead to a clearer understanding of the meaning. This principle is exemplified in some of the most fruitful modern work on Spenser, that inspired by the late Professor Greenlaw. Professor Millican, for example, has greatly increased our understanding of Spenser's political allegory by recreating for us the Elizabethan concept of Arturus Rex. Similarly, I have tried to show what Fairyland could mean to a

learned Elizabethan poet, and to do for the setting and hero-
ine of Spenser's "historicall fiction" what Professor Millican
has done for its hero.

In formulating my theory I have therefore considered the
probable sources of Spenser's fairy mythology with a view to
discovering the symbolic meaning which was already attached to it, or which could most easily be read into it by a
poet of Spenser's habit of mind. These sources I have found
not only where previous investigators have sought them, in
medieval romance, but also in the allegorical poetry of Spenser's predecessors and in the mythology of Greece and Rome.
And I have tried to indicate how this literary mythology,
which Spenser created out of such varied materials, became
the vehicle for a message which was derived both from
his studies and from his personal experience, and which
summed up the most vital ideas of the English Renaissance.

The cultivated Englishman of the Renaissance worshipped Fame, Beauty, and the State. In Spenser's *Faerie
Queene* this trinity becomes a unity. The individual's thirst
for glory, the Platonist's cult of love and beauty, and the
patriot's devotion to his country are all expressed through
Arthur's love for Gloriana. Many scholars have discussed
Spenser's use of these three themes. I have tried to show that
his ability to fuse them into a single artistic whole was
largely due to his use of the fairy mythology. The identification of the fairies with gods and heroes of classical mythology
and with ancestors of noble European families made them
worthy occupants for a land of fame. The traditional beauty
of the fays and their habit of seeking the love of famous
knights made the fairy-mistress story a suitable vehicle for
the characteristic Renaissance philosophy of Platonic love.
And the peculiar position of Queen Elizabeth as donor of
fame, inspiration of love, and embodiment of the State furnished Spenser with a living symbol of the tri-natured Re-

naissance goddess whom he celebrated as Gloriana, the Fairy Queen.

The theory advanced in the following pages is the result of a careful examination of Spenser's probable sources, including the "famous poets historical," whose example he professedly followed. In view of the unfinished state of the *Faerie Queene*, however, this theory cannot be proved, and it may not seem equally probable to all students of Spenser. In attempting to defend it I have been able to make some additions to the body of Spenser commentary, which may perhaps justify this work to those who are unconvinced by its main argument. Some traditional interpretations of the allegory have been challenged or qualified, and additions have been made to the list of sources and analogues for Spenser's Gloriana, Cleopolis, and Panthea. In particular, the identification of the Elfin emperors in Chapter II depends upon material which has not previously been brought forward in connection with Spenser, but which seems to me of considerable importance for the complete understanding of his mind.

My obligations to other writers are indicated in the footnotes and bibliography. In addition I acknowledge the courtesy of the following publishers for permitting me to quote from copyrighted material: the Yale University Press, American publishers of Edward Thompson's *Sir Walter Ralegh;* the Oxford University Press, publishers of Gough's edition of *Faerie Queene, Book V;* Harper & Brothers, publishers of *Selections from Lucian,* translated by Emily J. Smith; Ginn & Company, publishers of Lucy Paton's *Studies in the Fairy Mythology of Arthurian Romance;* Edwin Arnold & Company, publishers of Janet Spens's *Spenser's Faerie Queene;* E. P. Dutton & Company, New York, publishers of *Socratic Discourses by Plato and Xenophon,* containing the Reverend J. S. Watson's translation of Xenophon's *Memo-*

rabilia; and the Houghton Mifflin Company, publishers of the Cambridge edition of Chaucer's *Complete Works.*

I wish to express my thanks also to Professor Harry Morgan Ayres, Professor Dino Bigongiari, Professor Thomas Ollive Mabbott, and Dr. Henry Wells for reading the manuscript and making helpful suggestions, to Mrs. Mendelsohn for typing the greater part of the manuscript, to my mother and my sister for assistance with proofreading, and to my fellow members of Professor Fletcher's seminar during the past four years for listening patiently to different formulations of my argument and helping me to clarify both thought and expression.

To Professor Fletcher himself, under whose supervision this work has been written, I owe an inestimable debt. At every stage of my task, I have benefited by his searching yet sympathetic criticism. If I have managed to avoid at least some of the pitfalls which await the unwary traveler through Spenser's "wandering wood," I have my guide to thank for it; and if I have not avoided them all, I have no one but myself to blame.

ISABEL E. RATHBORNE

Scarborough, N. Y.
August 3, 1937

CONTENTS

ABBREVIATIONS

CCCHA	Colin Clouts Come Home Againe
Daph.	Daphnaida
EETS	Early English Text Society
ELH	ELH, a Journal of English Literary History
FQ	Faerie Queene
GL	Gerusalemme liberata
HB	Hymne of Beautie
HHB	Hymne of Heavenly Beautie
JEGP	Journal of English and Germanic Philology
MLN	Modern Language Notes
MP	Modern Philology
Mui.	Muiopotmos
OF	Orlando furioso
OI	Orlando Innamorato
PMLA	Publications of the Modern Language Association
RR	Ruines of Rome
RT	Ruines of Time
SAB	Shakespeare Association Bulletin
SC	Shepheardes Calender
SP	Studies in Philology
TM	Teares of the Muses
VB	Visions of Bellay

A Footnote on Footnotes

In the footnotes I have aimed at clearness, brevity, and consistency, in the order named. Thus I have included the abbreviations for "volume," "book," "stanza," and so forth, only when they could not readily be supplied by the common sense of the reader. For instance, in citations of the form "Holinshed, *Chronicles*, I, 5," the numbers ordinarily refer to volume and page, but where this meaning is clearly impossible, I have used the same form for book and line, or for sonnet and line (*e.g.*, Chaucer, *House of Fame*, III, 5, *RR*, II, 7, but Lydgate, *Fall of Princes*, Bk. VIII, l. 12).

Except in classical and Biblical references, I have consistently used Roman capitals for the largest division of the work cited (volume, book, canto) Arabic numerals for the smallest, (page, line), and lower-case Roman for intermediate divisions (chapter, stanza). In references to the *Faerie Queene* and to the *Orlando innamorato* I have used Roman capitals for book and canto, lower-case Roman for stanza, and Arabic numerals for lines (*e.g.*, *FQ*, I, X, xv, 1–2).

I

THE GLORY OF THIS WORLD

The god hath made of hire an ende,
And fro this worldes faierie
Hath take hire into compaignie.
—GOWER, *Confessio amantis.*

Quivi è colei che l'alte menti infiamma,
E che de' petti ogni viltà disgombra.
—POLIZIANO, *Stanze.*

Yet is *Cleopolis,* for earthly frame,
The fairest peece, that eye beholden can.
—SPENSER, *Faerie Queene.*

IN THAT Faery Queene," wrote Spenser, "I meane glory." It was a word of power in the Renaissance. Synonymous with fame and honor, and carrying implications of the tangible symbols of power, "the sweet fruition of an earthly crown," as well as of the unfading laurels bestowed by the muses of history and epic poetry, it summed up the aspirations of an epoch which was equally fascinated by the bright possibilities of the future and the vanished splendors of the past.[1] Poets coveted for themselves the undying fame which they promised—for a consideration —to their patrons. Masque and pageant presented the triumph of fame, and the worthies of the world looked down from tapestried wall or lived in song and story to inspire the emulation of their descendants. The antiquarian interests fostered by humanism in Italy and by the rising national patriotism of France and England revealed the earth as a vast temple of fame, full of monuments and trophies of the past. Even the starry heavens became a Pantheon to declare the glory of man. Therein was inscribed the fame of those great worthies whom the ancients had honored with deification, a practice which reminded English Harrison unpleasantly of the Romish method of canonizing saints, "but yet," he tells us, "so esteemed, that everie prince would oft hazard and attempt the uttermost adventures, thereby to win such fame in his life, that after his death he might by merit have such place in heaven, among the shining starres."[2] There, too, were set the trophies of Christian worthies. Spenser

---

[1] The classic treatment of this subject is in Burckhardt, *Kultur der Renaissance in Italien*, pp. 113 *et sqq.* For a criticism of Burckhardt's view, with examples of a similar cult of glory in the later Middle Ages, see Huizinga, *Waning of the Middle Ages*, pp. 58–62. For Renaissance definitions of glory and honor as the reward of virtue in the courtesy books, see Kelso, *Doctrine of the English Gentleman in the Sixteenth Century*, pp. 97 *et sqq.*

[2] Holinshed, *Chronicles*, I, 38.

speaks of "*Charlemaine* among the starres seven,"[3] and Lydgate tells us that Arthur was translated

> Up to the riche sterri briht dongoun—
> Astronomeeres well reherse kunne—
> Callid Arthuris constellacioun.[4]

The exemplary value of these stellified worthies is emphasized in Chapman's *Hymnus in noctem*.

> to thy virtue-famed train,
> All the choice worthies that did ever reign
> In eldest age, were still preferr'd by Jove,
> Esteeming that due honour to his love.
> There shine they: not to seamen guides alone,
> But sacred precedents to every one.[5]

The desire to attain such a glory, to write one's name
among the very stars, was surely the noblest of human
aspirations, most worthy of the "gentle spirits" to whom the
poetry of an aristocratic age ostensibly addressed itself. Before the desire of fame all lesser ambitions should fade, all
ignoble desires give way. Poliziano summed up this classical
ideal of glory, calling her

> colei che l'alte menti infiamma,
> E che de' petti ogni viltà disgombra.[6]

Writing in the Florence of Lorenzo de' Medici, Poliziano
exhibits that serene paganism which characterizes the Italian
Renaissance at its height. To him, as to the ancients,[7] the
thirst for glory could not but seem the noblest of all human
desires. But for the Italians of the previous century, over

---

[3] *TM*, l. 462.   [4] *Fall of Princes*, Bk. VIII, ll. 3103–5.
[5] *Poems*, p. 7. Cf. the *Somnium Scipionis* where the souls of famous men
return to the stars from which they came. Cicero *Republic* vi. 13.
[6] *Stanze*, II, xxxi, 3–4.
[7] For a collection of passages in praise of glory from ancient literature
see Blondus, *De Roma triumphante*, Lib. V, fol. lxxi.

which the shadow of the Christian Middle Ages still brooded, as for the later poets of the northern nations in whom the spirit of the Renaissance was modified by the sterner doctrines of the Reformation, the golden trumpet of fame sounded less clearly. They were troubled by doubts. Was not this Fame after all a pagan goddess, sister to Fortune, as Chaucer indeed pictures her,[8] bestowing her favors indifferently upon the just and the unjust? Were not the lamentable falls of famous princes and mighty empires a warning that earthly glory is rooted in the sin of pride, and doomed to a swift decay? Even if we distinguish between ill-gotten power or the mere reputation which may be acquired by fraud and the true honor which is the reward of virtue, what is mortal righteousness in the sight of God? Are we not all sinners, doomed to die for our sins? Is not this earth, covered with the ruins of temples and palaces built by the ancients, who were so much wiser than we, itself a vast *memento mori?* And should not these ruins remind us that the earth itself and its fair vault of heaven shall themselves disappear before God makes all things new? To trust in earthly glory, to seek fame as the earnest of immortality, is not this to set up the Earthly City against the City of God?

These questions, which St. Augustine had answered for the Middle Ages, continued to haunt the mind of the Renaissance and help to explain the vacillation of many of its characteristic writers between pagan exaltation and Christian depreciation of earthly fame. The outstanding example of this is perhaps Petrarch, who followed the *Triumph of Fame* with the *Triumph of Time* and the *Triumph of Eternity,* and who partly admitted in his *Secretum* that his own desire for glory was a sin. Likewise Boccaccio wrote his

[8] *House of Fame,* III, 1547.

enormously popular and influential *De casibus virorum illustrium* to exhibit the vicissitudes of fortune, and thus to warn princes against the sin of pride. The *ubi sunt* motif, which echoes through the French, English, and Spanish poetry of the fifteenth century, sounds also in the sixteenth. Du Bellay, champion of the ancients though he was, could sing of the ruins of Rome as a mirror of the world's vanity, and his work was translated and imitated by Edmund Spenser, poet of the *Faerie Queene*.

In his greatest work, also, Spenser is influenced by medieval as well as classical notions of fame. This becomes clear when we compare the ideas of glory in the *Faerie Queene* with those in the *City of God*. Augustine admits that the desire of fame was for the pagans a stimulus to virtue. The disinterested patriotism of the early Romans, who were responsible for the growth of the Empire, sprang from their great love of honor and glory, which suppressed all base affections and enabled them to sacrifice all for their country.[9] This desire for glory, says Augustine, is quite different from desire for rule. Those who desire "true human glory" wish "to be pleasing to good judgments. . . . Those who desire rule without desiring glory care not by what villainy they reach their goal." Men like Nero, who despise glory but love domination, are worse than beasts.[10] The highest type of pagan virtue, on the other hand, is found in Cato, who sought for glory by the right path, that is, by virtuous action.[11]

Midway between the man who seeks domination by open villainy and the man who seeks glory by preëminence in virtue is the ambitious man, who seeks to obtain by fraud an honor which he does not deserve. The substitution of

[9] *De civitate Dei*, Lib. V, cap. xii; Healey's translation, Vol. I, pp. 159, *et sqq.*
[10] *Ibid.*, cap. xix; Healey, Vol. I, p. 171.
[11] *Ibid.*, cap. xii, D; Healey, Vol. I, p. 161.

ambition for a lofty desire for fame was the first step in the deterioration of Roman character under the later republic and the Empire. On this point St. Augustine quotes Sallust:

At first men's hearts gave place to ambition, rather than covetousness, because that was more near to virtue; for the industrious and the slothful have both one desire of honour, glory and sovereignty. But the first . . . goes the true way to work, the latter by craft and false means, because he has not the true course. The true are these, to come to honour by virtue, not by ambition: which honour, empire, and glory, good and bad wish alike. But the good goes the true way, that is, by virtue leading him directly to his possession of honour, glory, sovereignty.[12]

This conception of ambition as superior to covetousness, but inferior to the virtuous pursuit of honor, appears in Spenser's picture of Philotime, daughter of Mammon. Guyon has already shown himself superior to covetousness by rejecting Mammon's offer of wealth.

All that I need I have; what needeth mee
To covet more, then I have cause to use?
With such vaine shewes thy worldlings vile abuse:
But give me leave to follow mine emprise.[13]

In refusing the hand of Philotime, Guyon rejects ambition, a subtler temptation because it is "more near to virtue." Philotime is in effect an imitation Gloriana. The room in which she sits is a temple of earthly honor.

The rowme was large and wide,
As it some Gyeld or solemne Temple weare:
Many great golden pillours did upbeare
The massy roofe, and riches huge sustayne,
And every pillour decked was full deare
With crownes and Diademes, and titles vaine,
Which mortall Princes wore, whiles they on earth did rayne.

[12] *Ibid.*
[13] *FQ*, II, VII, xxxix, 3–6. Cf. also *ibid.*, xxvii.

> A route of people there assembled were,
>   Of every sort and nation under skye,
>   Which with great uprore preaced to draw nere
>   To th' upper part, where was advaunced hye
>   A stately siege of soveraigne maiestye;
>   And thereon sat a woman gorgeous gay,
>   And richly clad in robes of royaltye,
>   That never earthly Prince in such aray
> His glory did enhaunce, and pompous pride display.[14]

She seems to be the glory that all men seek, but she is really the counterfeit, undeserved honor obtained by fraud.

> Her face right wondrous faire did seeme to bee,
>   That her broad beauties beam great brightnes threw
>   Through the dim shade, that all men might it see:
>   Yet was not that same her owne native hew,
>   But wrought by art and counterfetted shew,
>   Thereby more lovers unto her to call;
>   Nath' lesse most heavenly faire in deed and vew
>   She by creation was, till she did fall;
> Thenceforth she sought for helps, to cloke her crime withall.[15]

In thus presenting Philotime as in origin heavenly, like Gloriana herself,[16] Spenser seems to be expressing the same idea as that of Sallust and Augustine. In its origin the bad man's desire for glory is divine, but the honor he gains is tarnished by being sought through ambition rather than through virtue. This latter idea is clearly expressed in Spenser's image of Philotime's golden chain, borrowed from Natalis Comes.[17]

> There, as in glistring glory she did sit,
>   She held a great gold chaine ylincked well,
>   Whose upper end to highest heaven was knit,
>   And lower part did reach to lowest Hell;
>   And all that preace did round about her swell,

---

[14] *FQ*, II, VII, xliii, 3–xliv, 9.   [15] *Ibid.*, xlv.   [16] Cf. I, X, lix, 9.
[17] Lotspeich, *Classical Mythology in the Poetry of Edmund Spenser*, p. 64.

To catchen hold of that long chaine, thereby
To clime aloft, and others to excell:
That was *Ambition,* rash desire to sty,
And every lincke thereof a step of dignity.

Some thought to raise themselves to high degree,
By riches and unrighteous reward,
Some by close shouldring, some by flatteree;
Others through friends, others for base regard;
And all by wrong wayes for themselves prepard.[18]

Mammon tries to persuade Guyon that Philotime is true glory, goal of heroic aspiration and reward of virtue.

Honour and dignitie from her alone
Derived are, and all this worldes blis
For which ye men do strive: few get, but many mis.

And faire *Philotime* she rightly hight,
The fairest wight that wonneth under skye,
But that this darksome neather world her light
Doth dim with horrour and deformitie,
Worthy of heaven and hye felicitie,
From whence the gods have her for envy thrust:
But sith thou hast found favour in mine eye,
Thy spouse I will her make, if that thou lust,
That she may thee advance for workes and merites iust.[19]

Guyon refuses this offer for two reasons. He does not desire or deserve any higher station than that to which it has pleased God to call him; and his love is already engaged.

Gramercy *Mammon* (said the gentle knight)
For so great grace and offred high estate;
But I, that am fraile flesh and earthly wight,
Unworthy match for such immortall mate
My selfe well wote, and mine unequall fate;
And were I not, yet is my trouth yplight,

18 *FQ,* II, VII, xlvi–xlvii, 5.   19 *Ibid.,* xlviii, 7–xlix, 9.

> And love avowd to other Lady late,
> That to remove the same I have no might:
> To chaunge love causelesse is reproch to warlike knight.[20]

Upton believed that the "other lady" was Gloriana, whose picture Guyon bears on his shield,[21] and to whose service he is especially vowed as a knight of Maydenhead. If this interpretation be correct, the decisive factor in Guyon's rejection of the counterfeit glory sought by ambition is his devotion to the true glory attained only by virtue.

Yet even this glory was to St. Augustine unworthy of a Christian's devotion. An incentive to virtue in the Earthly City, the love of glory is a vice for citizens of the heavenly. For the saints desire no glory for themselves but give all glory to God. Despised in this world, the Christian hopes for immortal bliss in heaven.

But the others, living in an earthly city, wherein the end of all their endeavours was by themselves propounded to themselves, the fame (namely) and domination of this world, and not the eternity of heaven, not in the everlasting life, but in their own ends, and the mouths of their posterity; what should they desire but glory, whereby they desired to survive after death in the memories and mouths of such as commended them.[22]

To Augustine the desire of glory is essentially pride. Hence he declares "that virtue is as much disgraced in serving human glory as in obeying the pleasures of the body."[23] In developing this idea, he suggests two allegorical pictures which directly or indirectly may have influenced Spenser.

The philosophers that make virtue the scope of all human good, do use in disgrace of such as approved virtue and yet applied it all to bodily delight (holding this to be desired for itself, and virtue to be sought only for respect to this pleasure) to

---

[20] *Ibid.*, II, VII, 1, 1–9.   [21] *Variorum Spenser*, II, 262.
[22] *Op. cit.*, Lib. V, cap. xiv, F; Healey, Vol. I, p. 165.
[23] *Ibid.*, cap. xx (title); Healey, Vol. I, p. 172.

delineate a picture (as it were with their tongues) wherein Pleasure sits on a throne, like a delicate queen, and all the Virtues about her, ready at a beck to do her command. There she commands Prudence to seek out a way whereby Pleasure may reign in safety: Justice must go do good turns, to attain friends, for the use of corporal delights, and injury none: Fortitude's task is, that if any hurt (not mortal) invade the body, she must hold Pleasure so fast in the mind, that the remembrance of delights past, may dull the touch of the pain present. Temperance must so temper the nourishment, that immoderation come not to trouble the health, and so offend lady Pleasure, whom the Epicures do say is chiefly resident in the body's soundness. Thus the Virtues being in their own dignities absolute commanders, must put all their glories under the feet of Pleasure; and submit themselves to an imperious and dishonest woman. Than this picture, there cannot be a sight more vile, deformed, and abominable to a good man, say the philosophers; and it is true.[24] Nor think I that the picture would be so fair as it should be *if human glory* were painted in the throne of Pleasure: for though it be not a nice piece [liceat ipsa gloria delicata mulier non sit] as the other is, yet it is turgid [inflata], and full of empty air, so that it should ill beseem the substantial Virtues to be subject to such a shadow that Prudence should foresee nothing, Justice distribute nothing, Fortitude endure nothing, Temperance moderate nothing, but that which serveth at the pleasing of men and serving of windy glory.[25]

The picture of the virtues serving Pleasure suggests Spenser's treatment of Acrasia, who seeks to enslave the subjects of Gloriana. And the Fairy Queen herself, in whose service the personifications of virtue overthrow their opposed vices, bears a certain likeness to Augustine's companion picture of the virtues in the service of glory. In the two antitypes of Gloriana, Acrasia and Philotime, Spenser expresses a view of the relations between pleasure, ambition, and earthly glory which is quite in accord with Augustine. But where

[24] The original of this "picture" is from the Stoic Cleanthes, preserved in Cicero *De finibus* ii. xxi. 69. Welldon's ed. of *De civ. Dei*, Vol. I, p. 233 n.

[25] *Op. cit.*, Lib. V, cap. xx, A–C; Healey, Vol. I, pp. 172–73.

Augustine makes earthly glory synonymous with pride,
Spenser separates the two conceptions, presenting them in
the two sharply contrasted figures of Gloriana and Lucifera.

Lucifera is clearly an antitype of Gloriana, and the House
of Pride, which is balanced in its own book by the House of
Holiness, was probably intended also as a foil to Panthea,
Gloriana's dwelling, which should naturally be described
near the end of the poem. As Professor Nottcutt has pointed
out, it was Spenser's habit to place a striking allegorical
representation of the opposite vice near the beginning of his
exposition of a virtue in each book of the *Faerie Queene*.[26]
It is reasonable to suppose that he intended to use the same
narrative device in defining the subject of his poem as a
whole, and that Lucifera is the opposite not only of Cœlia
but also of Gloriana.

Like Philotime, Lucifera is also an imitation of Gloriana.
Just as the House of Pride is really of brick, but is overlaid
with golden foil,[27] its mistress appears as a "Mayden Queene,
that shone as *Titans* ray." But where Gloriana is a true sun,[28]
Lucifera is like Phaeton,

> That did presume his fathers firie wayne,
> And flaming mouthes of steedes unwonted wilde
> Through highest heaven with weaker hand to rayne;
> Proud of such glory and advancement vaine.[29]

Since pride is essentially self-love, Lucifera holds a mirror
in her hand

> Wherein her face she often vewed fayne,
> And in her selfe-lov'd semblance tooke delight.[30]

---

[26] "The Faerie Queene and Its Critics," in *Essays and Studies by Members of the English Association*, XII (1926), 73.
[27] Gloriana's city, Cleopolis, has a golden wall. *FQ*, II, X, lxxii, 9.
[28] *Ibid.*, VI, X, xxviii, 1–2.   [29] *Ibid.*, I, IV, ix, 2–5.
[30] *Ibid.*, x, 7–8.

Unlike Philotime, Lucifera is not of heavenly birth.

> Of griesly *Pluto* she the daughter was,
>   And sad *Proserpina* the Queene of hell;
>   Yet did she thinke her pearelesse worth to pas
>   That parentage, with pride so did she swell,
>   And thundring *Iove* that high in heaven doth dwell,
>   And wield the world, she claymed for her syre.[31]

In the dungeons of Lucifera are the famous men and women who in the past have gained "great place," only to lose it through impious pride. The conception goes back to the *De casibus* of Boccaccio, but Spenser regards the fall of these famous men not as the result of adverse fortune, which attacks good and bad alike, but solely as a punishment for sin. Typical of this view is his stern exultation over the fall of Alexander.

> There also was that mightie Monarch layd
>   Low under all, yet above all in pride,
>   That name of native syre did fowle upbrayd,
>   And would as *Ammons* sonne be magnifide,
>   Till scorned of God and man a shamefull death he dide.[32]

Spenser's House of Pride thus resembles Augustine's Earthly City, whose true founder was the devil, since his fall divided the angels into powers of light and powers of darkness, thus inaugurating the "two societies, the one enjoying God, the other swelling in pride,"[33] which were later to divide mankind. These two cities originate in two loves, and each seeks a different glory.

Fecerunt itaque civitates duas amores duo, terrenam scilicet amor sui usque ad contemtum Dei, caelestem vero amor Dei usque ad contemtum sui. Denique illa in se ipsa, haec in Domino

---

[31] *Ibid.*, xi, 1–6.   [32] *Ibid.*, I, V, xlviii, 5–9.
[33] *Op. cit.*, Lib. XI, cap. xxxiii, B; Healey, Vol. I, p. 340.

gloriatur. Illa enim quaerit ab hominibus gloriam; huic autem
Deus conscientiae testis maxima est gloria. Illa in gloria sua ex-
altat caput suum; haec dicit Deo suo: *Gloria mea et exaltans
caput meum.*[34]

In view of this likeness between the House of Pride and
Augustine's Earthly City, one might assume that Gloriana,
the opposite of Lucifera, was intended to represent, not
earthly, but celestial, glory, the heavenly beauty which is
the object of Christian love and aspiration. Such a suggestion has in fact been made. In her recent book on the *Faerie
Queene* Miss Spens remarks:

In both preface and poem . . . Prince Arthur from the moment
of his vision of the Faerie Queene is possessed by an inextin-
guishable desire for her. 'In that Faerie Queene,' writes Spenser,
'I mean glory in my general intention,' and it cannot be doubted
that she stands for the supreme loveliness—the Sapience of the
Hymn of Heavenly Beauty, the 'Principle' of Soul.[35]

I do not know what Gloriana may have represented in the
hypothetical original version of the *Faerie Queene* which
Miss Spens is attempting to reconstruct, but as an interpretation of the *Letter to Raleigh* and of the fragment of the
poem which we actually possess her explanation seems to me
untenable. In the first place, it ignores the Renaissance cult
of fame as the reward of virtue, which is naturally suggested
by Spenser's use of the word "glory" in the *Letter to
Raleigh*. I have already said something about the importance of this classical notion of fame as earthly immortality
in the European literature which formed the mind of Spen-

[34] *Ibid.,* Lib. XIV, cap. xxviii, A; Welldon's ed., Vol. II, p. 128. I quote
the Latin because Healey's translation of this passage is so free as to be misleading.
[35] *Spenser's Faerie Queene,* p. 50. J. W. Bennett, "Spenser's Muse," *JEGP,*
XXXI (1932), 217, also identifies Gloriana with the Celestial Venus or
Heavenly Wisdom (Sapience).

ser's generation. Examples might be multiplied.[36] Those which follow have been chosen because they may well have been known to Spenser and because they present analogues to his Gloriana.

Allegorical and emblematic pictures of fame are common in Renaissance literature. Petrarch's *Trionfi* depicts Fame as a beautiful lady mounted in a chariot and followed by a throng of those who have deserved her favors. Similarly Boccaccio in the *Amorosa visione* is guided by a nymph representing virtue, who herself bears the symbols of earthly honor, the scepter and ball, into an allegorical castle where he sees "La Gloria del Popolo Mondano" pictured on the wall. Like Petrarch's goddess of fame, she is a beautiful lady, seated in a triumphal chariot, surrounded by the crowd of the famous, all seeking to approach her. That similar representations of Lady Fame surrounded by the worthies of the past and present were common in tapestry we learn from the opening sentences of John Coke's *Debate between the Heralds of England and France* (1549). The speaker is Prudence.

You have sene depycted in tapisteries th' ymage of Honour fygured in hygh Magnifycence, sytting in a chayre adourned with golde, and appareiled in habyte royall, havyng upon her head dyvers crownes, and in th'one hand a round apple of golde, and in the other the sworde of honour, on the one syde of her sytting kyng David, Judas Machabeus, duke Josue, Hector of Troy, Alexander, Julius Caesar, Brute, Ebranke, Cassibilane, Belinus, Brenius, Constantyne the great, Malgo, Athelston, Guy of Warwyke, Roland, Olyver, and Ogier le danois. And on the other syde, the mighty Arthur, Charlmayne, Godfrey of Byllion, Wyllyam Conquerour, Richard Coeur de lyon, Edward the fyrst, Edmond earle of Lancastre and of Leycetour, his brother, Richard duke of Cornwall, Edward the thyrde with his fyve sonnes, Henry the V, Henry the VII, Henry the VIII, syr John Chandos, Charles duke of Suffolke, and syr Edward Poynynges,

[36] Cf. the interpretation of the Hercules myth by Natalis Comes discussed in chap. II, below.

with many other representyng the persons of the valiant kynges, prynces, knyghtes that have ben in tymes past, for whose noble actes the chronicles be made; and all the sayde noble parsonages gyve themselves to come to Honour.[37]

The conception of Fame, Glory, or Honor as a beautiful lady made it easy to associate her with the idea of love, recognized in the chivalric and Platonic codes alike as the spur to noble action. Since none but the brave deserve the fair, the winning of fame might be identified with the winning of a lady, as the love of a lady might be represented as the first step in the acquisition of fame. An example of this relation between love and glory is found in Poliziano's *Stanze,* a poem which bears certain resemblances to Spenser's story of Arthur.[38] Like Arthur, Troilus, and other heroes, young Julio (Giuliano de' Medici) has always scorned love as a waste of time, until Cupid sends him a magic white stag which leads him, not as in medieval romance to a fairy mistress, but to a human "nymph," the beautiful Simonetta, with whom he falls in love. Later Venus sends him a dream in which he sees his lady overcome Cupid with the chaste arms of Minerva. Cupid calls upon Julio for help. He protests that he can do nothing against the gorgon-headed shield. Cupid's answer is, in effect, "Become famous, and she will yield to you." This idea is developed by means of an allegorical vision of glory, to which Cupid directs the lover's attention.

> —Alza gli occhi, alza, Julio, a quella fiamma
> che come un sol col suo splendor t'adombra.
> Quivi è colei che l'alte menti infiamma,
> e che de' petti ogni viltà disgombra.

[37] Pages 56–57.
[38] The same connection of ideas might be illustrated by Petrarch's conception of Laura as *il lauro* (the laurel of fame). Cf. *Sonetti,* "Arbor vittoriosa trionfale" and "L'aura e l'odore."

Con essa, a guisa di semplice damma,
prenderai questa, che or nel cor t'ingombra
tanta paura e t'invilisce l'alma;
che sol ti serba lei trionfal palma.—

Così dicea Cupido: e già la Gloria
scendea giù folgorando ardente vampo:
con essa Poesia, con essa Istoria
volavan tutte accese del suo lampo.[39]

Glory despoils Simonetta of her armor and crowns Julio with olive and laurel.[40]

Upon Spenser's Prince Arthur, also, Cupid is avenged for former slights. He, too, yields to love while he is out hunting, and he, too, sees a vision of Glory in a dream. But she comes to him, not as an assistant in attaining his heart's desire, but as the object of desire itself, the fairy mistress who promises him her love. It is through the "glorious fire" thus kindled in his heart that Arthur is to become the greatest of Christian Worthies.[41] By making Glory herself the object of his hero's love, Spenser was able to combine in his central story of Arthur's quest for Gloriana two popular Renaissance themes, the desire for earthly immortality through fame, and the cult of love as a stimulus to noble actions. The triumph of Gloriana as goddess of fame was presumably to be reserved for the end of the poem, which Spenser never wrote, but it is far more likely that his general conception of her is related to the goddesses of fame we have been describing than that she is to be identified with the Sapience of the fourth *Hymne*.

A second and stronger reason for rejecting the idea that Gloriana represents heavenly glory appears in the tenth canto of Book I, where the Red Crosse Knight compares

---

[39] *Op. cit.*, II, xxxi–xxxiii, 4. [40] *Ibid.*, xxxiii, 1–4.
[41] *FQ*, I, Proem, iii, 4.

Cleopolis, city of Gloriana, with the New Jerusalem, City of God.

> Till now, said then the knight, I weened well,
>   That great *Cleopolis*, where I have beene,
>   In which that fairest *Faerie Queene* doth dwell,
>   The fairest Citie was, that might be seene;
>   And that bright towre all built of christall cleene,
>   *Panthea*, seemd the brightest thing, that was:
>   But now by proofe all otherwise I weene;
>   For this great Citie that does far surpas,
> And this bright Angels towre quite dims that towre of glas.[42]

Surely this implies also that the glory of the "great king," "quite dims," the glory of the fairy queen. The same implication appears in the answer of Heavenly Contemplation, which expresses the typical compromise of the Christian Renaissance between pagan and patristic ideas of earthly glory.

> Most trew, said then the holy aged man;
>   Yet is *Cleopolis*, for earthly frame,
>   The fairest peece, that eye beholden can:
>   And well beseemes all knights of noble name,
>   That covet in th' immortall booke of fame
>   To be eternized, that same to haunt,
>   And doen their service to that soveraigne Dame,
>   That glorie does to them for guerdon graunt:
> For she is heavenly borne and heaven may iustly vaunt.

> And thou faire ymp, sprong out from English race,
>   However now accompted Elfins sonne,
>   Well worthy doest thy service for her grace,
>   To aide a virgin desolate foredonne.
>   But when thou famous victorie hast wonne,
>   And high emongst all knights has hong thy shield,
>   Thenceforth the suit of earthly conquest shonne,
>   And wash thy hands from guilt of bloudy field:
> For bloud can nought but sin, and wars but sorrowes yield.

[42] *Ibid.*, I, X, lviii.

Then seeke this path, that I to thee presage,
  Which after all to heaven shall thee send;
  Then peaceably thy painefull pilgrimage
  To yonder same *Hierusalem* do bend,
  Where is for thee ordained a blessed end:

. . .

Unworthy wretch (quoth he) of so great grace,
  How dare I thinke such glory to attaine?[43]

In other words, fame is the noblest of earthly rewards, and her "immortall booke," in which the citizens of Cleopolis are "eternized" is inferior only to the Book of Life, which registers the saints of the New Jerusalem. Nor is there any enmity between the two cities. The queen of Cleopolis is "heavenly borne," and unlike her antitype, Philotime, has never lost her heavenly citizenship, for fame, rightly pursued, is a divinely implanted stimulus to moral action on earth. The love of fame, indeed, has inspired St. George to undertake the defense of true religion. Yet the service of Gloriana is only a stage upon the road to the celestial glory. After St. George has won Gloriana's favor by serving her in just war, the typical activity of the Christian knight and Renaissance gentleman, he must "wash his hands from guilt of bloudy field." War is the road to earthly, not to heavenly glory. To the soldier, even though he be a Christian, this is a hard saying. St. George himself, though he has seen the difference between earthly and heavenly glory, yet questions the difference in their means of attainment. Must he really give up love and war, the twin joys of chivalric life?

But deeds of armes must I at last be faine,
  And Ladies love to leave so dearely bought?
  What need of armes, where peace doth ay remaine,
  (Saith he) and battailes none are to be fought?
  As for loose loves are vaine, and vanish into nought."

---

[43] *Ibid.*, lix, *et sqq.*   " *Ibid.*, I, X, lxii, 5–9.

But this renunciation should be postponed until the claims of the active life have been satisfied. St. George is not allowed to renounce the world immediately, as he wishes to do when once he has seen that its joys are vanity. The sage reminds him of his quest. Undertaken originally in the desire for fame, it is to be completed in obedience to God's will. Henceforth St. George will serve Gloriana not "for her grace," but for the sake of the greater glory, beside which her own is but a shadow, "So darke are earthly things compard to things divine."[45]

No doubt as a Christian Platonist Spenser conceived Gloriana as in some sense a mirror of heavenly glory. Some such relation between the two kinds of glory is suggested by St. Augustine. The fame of the Roman Empire, he says, was not only a just reward for the disinterested patriotism of its founders but also an example to Christian men.

And therefore the Roman Empire had that glorious increase, not only to be a fit guerdon to the virtues of such worthies as we forenamed, but also that the citizens of heaven in their pilgrimage upon earth, might observe those examples with a sober diligence, and thence gather how great care, love, and respect ought to be carried to the heavenly country for life eternal, if those men had such a dear affect to their earthly country for glory so temporal.[46]

But to admit that Gloriana may be in some sense a mirror of heavenly glory is not to say that she represents heavenly glory in the continued allegory of the *Faerie Queene.* For the main action of Spenser's poem was to be Arthur's quest for Gloriana, and this must terminate, not in the New Jerusalem, though no doubt he has a place there, too, but in Cleopolis, capital of Fairyland.

The name "Cleopolis" apparently means "city of fame."

[45] *Ibid.,* lxvii, 9.
[46] *De civ. Dei,* Lib. V, cap. xiv–xvi; Healey, Vol. I, p. 166.

Mrs. Bennett connects it with Clio, muse of history, whose name was commonly derived from *kleos*, "fame."[47] This derivation is perhaps reflected in Chaucer's invocation of this muse as "Lady myn, that called art Cleo."[48] In the *Teares of the Muses*, Spenser celebrates Clio as "eldest sister" of the "brood of blessed Sapience," and indicates that the glory she bestows is the same as that granted by the Fairy Queen to her faithful servants. The muse is lamenting the degeneracy of the present race of "mightie peeres," who neglect wisdom and virtue, and

> onely strive themselves to raise
> Through pompous pride, and foolish vanitie;
> In th' eyes of people they put all their praise,
> And onely boast of Armes and Auncestrie:
> But vertuous deeds, which did those Armes first give
> To their Grandsyres, they care not to atchive.
>
> So I, that doo all noble feates professe
> To register, and sound in trumpe of gold;
> Through their bad dooings, or base slothfulnesse,
> Finde nothing worthie to be writ, or told:
> For better farre it were to hide their names,
> Than telling them to blazon out their blames.
>
> So shall succeeding ages have no light
> Of things forepast, nor moniments of time,
> And all that in this world is worthie hight
> Shall die in darknesse, and lie hid in slime:
> Therefore I mourne with deep harts sorrowing,
> Because I nothing noble have to sing.[49]

If we discount the extreme pessimism of this, which is certainly not the prevailing mood of the *Faerie Queene,* we

---

[47] JEGP, XXXI, 214–15.
[48] *Troilus and Criseyde,* II, 8. Cf. Lyndsay, *Ane Dialog betwix Experience and ane Courteour,* Bk. II, l. 2159, where Cleo is named in a list of principal pagan goddesses.
[49] *TM,* ll. 91 *et sqq.*

can discern an instructive parallel between Clio and Gloriana. Both are opposed to pride, which seeks dominion through "bad dooings," and to slothfulness, which seeks undeserved glory in the "eyes of the people" through ambition. Both are concerned with the celebration of virtuous actions, which are a light to "succeeding ages." This likeness between Clio and Gloriana strengthens the interpretation of Cleopolis in Spenser's general intention as an ideal city of earthly fame, spiritual motherland of all those whose deeds make them worthy of Clio's ministrations. Cleopolis, as its name implies, is the city of earthly glory, the heaven of virtuous pagans.

Spenser has generally been credited with inventing the name of his fairy capital.[50] The name had been used, however, by the Italian humanist, Quintianus Stoa, in the title of a Latin poem published in 1514.[51] Stoa's *Cleopolis* is a conventional encomium on the city of Paris, which is described in the Preface as the greatest of all cities by virtue of its all-inclusive excellence. Babylon, Rome, Carthage, and Florence may have surpassed Paris in one kind of fame, but Paris is to be preferred before them as the man of encyclopedic knowledge is preferred before the specialist. This idea is carried out in the poem by constant comparisons of the monuments of Paris with the wonders of the ancient world, so that Stoa's Cleopolis, like Spenser's, is in effect a generalized type of a famous city. Thus the river Seine, by virtue of its commercial importance, is declared to be more precious than Hermus or Pactolus[52] and as deserving of fame as the Eridanus, the Hebrus, the Ister, the Nile, and the Hydaspes.[53] Notre Dame vies in splendor with the temple of

[50] Bennett, JEGP, XXXI, 214.

[51] *De celeberrimae Parrhisiorum urbis laudibus sylva cui titulus Cleopolis.* My attention was called to this work by the late Professor C. S. Baldwin.

[52] Page biiii verso. Cf. Spenser's "wealthy Thamis," *FQ,* III, IX, xlv, 2.

[53] *Op. cit.,* p. ci recto.

Diana at Ephesus and the temple of Jupiter Capitolinus.[54]
The largest of the Parisian bridges is compared to the
bridges of Xerxes and Trajan,[55] and the walls of Paris to
those of Rome and Mantua.[56] To this praise of the river,
bridge, buildings, and fortifications of Paris are joined
praise of its inhabitants, distinguished for loyalty, valor,
and religion, a long eulogy of the university, and an account
of the beauty and fertility of the surrounding countryside.
The main idea, expressed in the Preface, is reiterated in a
passage near the close of the poem, which hails Paris as the
greatest of all cities.

> Roma armis/Carthago manu/curvamine Memphis/
> Imperiis Babylon/Lacadaemon classe/theatris
> Parthenope/musis Parnassia/Pella tyaris/
> Troia viris/Epiros equis/animalibus Argos/
> Inda ebore/argento Sardinia/et Attica melle/
> Fertilitate Samos/Paros insula marmore/ferro
> Norica/principibus Nilotica/Thracia Marte/
> Nobilitate Pharos/Phoenicia murice/cultu
> Sidonis/infectu plaga Bethica: & aere Corynthos/
> Frumentis Libya/& dulci campana Lyeo/
> Vatibus Italia/& medicato castore Pontus/
> Cariaque excultis semper memoranda sepulchris.[57]

Besides the likeness in name and general character of
Stoa's Cleopolis to Spenser's fairy capital, there is no clear
indication of a connection between the Latin poem and the
Faerie Queene. A description of the view of Paris from a
hill outside the city walls does indeed suggest St. George's
vision of the New Jerusalem and his description of Cleopolis.

> Egredere hanc urbem paulum: celsumque parumper
> Scande iugum: spectesque excelsa cacumine rerum:
> Invenies maiora fide. pinacula fulvis
> Culminibus caput extollunt sub nubila: & omnem

[54] *Ibid.*, p. ci.   [55] *Ibid.*, p. ciii recto.   [56] *Ibid.*, p. iiii recto.
[57] *Ibid.*, p. kiiii recto.

Luminis humani rapiunt cervice colurum
Urbs tota adridet monstrans curvamina tectis
Convexis: quaecunque domus conspecta cacumen
Erigit: aspectu cernentem invitat amoeno.
Nam sic nobilium splendent fastigia Phoebo
Tectorum lucente velut circumlita vitro
Splendicat in longum radiis cratera coruscis.[58]

The last lines in particular remind us of Spenser's tower of glass, but the comparison of the splendor of a city to glass or crystal goes back to the *Apocalypse,* and appears also in the description of Oberon's city in *Huon of Burdeux.*[59] There is no evidence, therefore, that Spenser's fairy city owes anything to Stoa's poem except its name, and even that may possibly have been coined independently by the English poet and the Italian humanist. If Spenser did have Stoa's poem in mind in naming Gloriana's city "Cleopolis," we have further evidence not only for the usual identification of Cleopolis with London in Spenser's particular intention, but also for our interpretation of the fairy capital in his general intention as an ideal city of earthly fame, combining the ancient glories of Babylon, Troy, and Rome.

As a foil to the New Jerusalem, Spenser's Cleopolis is a modification of St. Augustine's Earthly City, which in turn goes back to the *Apocalypse.* Before John saw the holy city descending from heaven,[60] he heard an angel crying, "Babylon the great is fallen," and saw the merchants standing afar off lamenting for "that great city, that was clothed in fine linen, and purple and scarlet, and decked with gold and precious stones, and pearls."[61] For Augustine the city of pride was symbolized concretely by Babylon and Rome, the two imperial capitals which successively stood for earthly dominion and persecution of the saints. But while Babylon

[58] *Ibid.,* p. hiii recto.   [59] See below, p. 194.   [60] Rev. 21:2.
[61] *Ibid.,* 18:15–16.

never lost its bad reputation, Rome came to be regarded with mixed feelings. Hints for a more favorable attitude could be derived from Augustine's qualified praise of the early Roman virtues, which would naturally appear less like "splendid vices" as classical ideals reasserted themselves. Unlike Babylon, Rome was not completely destroyed. Its monuments remained, and the tale of its wonders grew. Even before the Italians of the Renaissance exalted the civilization of pagan Rome into an ideal of humane living, there were stirrings of not unfriendly interest in the antique glories of the eternal city.

This spirit is reflected in a very popular medieval guide-book dating apparently from the twelfth century.[62] The *Mirabilia urbis Romae* and its later recension, the *Graphia urbis aureae* pictured classical Rome as a true fairy city, full of marvelous buildings, many of them the work of the enchanter Virgil, all gleaming with gold, crystal, and precious stones as though to emulate the New Jerusalem itself.

The Colosseum, for instance,

was the temple of the Sun, of marvellous greatness and beauty, disposed with many diverse vaulted chambers, and all covered with a heaven of gilded brass, where thunders and lightnings and glittering fires were made, and where rain was shed through slender tubes. Besides this there were the signs supercelestial and the planets Sol and Luna, that were drawn along in their proper chariots. And in the midst abode Phoebus, that is the god of the Sun, which having his feet on the earth reached unto heaven with his head, and did hold in his hand an orb, signifying that Rome ruled the world.[63]

[62] For accounts of the influence of this work see H. Jordan, *Topographie der Stadt Rom im Alterthum*, II, 357 *et sqq.;* A. Graf, *Roma del medio evo*, I, 58 *et sqq.;* and the introduction and notes to F. M. Nichols's translation, *Mirabilia urbis Romae, The Marvels of Rome or a Picture of the Golden City*, from which the following quotations are taken. Versions of the Latin text are to be found in Jordan, *op. cit.*, pp. 607–43, and L. Urlichs, *Codex urbis Romae topographicus*.
[63] *Mirabilia*, pp. 62–64.

Another marvel was a round temple "that was called *Holovitreum,* being made of glass and gold by mathematical craft, where was an astronomy with all the signs of heaven."[64] The *Mirabilia* duly tells us that the roof of the Colosseum was destroyed by St. Sylvester because its marvels distracted pilgrims from their devotions, and the Holovitreum by St. Sebastian, but there is no apocalyptic exultation over their destruction.

Enthusiasm for the glories of pagan Rome is also evidenced in the Mirabilian description of the Capitol,

so-called, because it was the head of the world, where the consuls and senators abode to govern the Earth The face thereof was covered with high walls and strong, rising above the top of the hill, and covered all over with glass and gold and marvellous carved work. And in the Capitol were molten images of all the Trojan kings and of the Emperors. Within the fortress was a palace all adorned with marvellous works in gold and silver and brass and costly stones, to be a mirror to all nations.[65]

The same tendency to exalt the Earthly City which is evidenced by the *Mirabilia* appears in Dante's attitude toward pagan Rome. The noble castle of Limbo, shining by its own light in the darkness of the Inferno,[66] is a temple of earthly glory, the highest reward of pagan or purely human aspiration and virtue. In a recent article[67] Professor Fletcher has very plausibly interpreted the castle of Limbo as a symbol of Rome. If this interpretation be correct, Dante's noble castle may be linked with Spenser's Cleopolis as a humanistic modification of Augustine's Earthly City, symbolized concretely in that "mirror to all nations" which is the "golden city" of the *Mirabilia.*

There is no direct proof that Spenser knew Dante, but he must certainly have been familiar with the Mirabilian conception of Rome. The book itself remained popular even

[64] *Ibid.,* p. 114.   [65] *Ibid.,* pp. 86–87.   [66] *Inferno,* IV, 106 *et sqq.*
[67] "Dante's School of the Eagle," *Romanic Review,* XXII (1931), 191–209.

after its information had become obsolete, and was several times printed during the fifteenth and sixteenth centuries.[68] Moreover, as the standard work on ancient Rome from the twelfth to the fifteenth centuries, the *Mirabilia* was a source for descriptions of Rome in works of general reference like Higden's *Polychronicon*. Higden describes in succession the Pantheon, the Holovitreum, and the Capitol,[69] all of which suggest features of Spenser's Panthea. Lydgate, in the lament for the past glories of Rome which he introduced into his *Fall of Princes*, mentions several of the Mirabilian monuments, among them the Holovitreum.

> Where is thy temple of christal bright shewing,
> Made half of gold, most richely moustrying
> The heavenly spheres, by compasse wrought & line,
> Which that long processe hath brought unto ruine?[70]

The influence of the *Mirabilia* is also evident in Du Bellay's *Songe,* where the gold and crystal Capitol is used as a symbol of the city itself. I quote Spenser's translation.

> On high hills top I saw a stately frame,
> An hundred cubits high by iust assize,
> With hundreth pillours fronting faire the same,
> All wrought with Diamond after Dorick wize:
>   Nor brick, nor marble was the wall in view,
>   But shining Christall, which from top to base
>   Out of her womb a thousand rayons threw,
>   On hundred steps of *Afrike* golds enchase:
> Golde was the parget, and the seeling bright
> Did shine all scaly with great plates of golde;
> The floore of *Iaspe* and *Emeraude* was dight.
> O worlds vainesse. Whiles thus I did behold,
>   An earthquake shooke the hill from lowest seat,
>   And overthrew this frame with ruine great.[71]

In another "vision" Du Bellay compares Rome to the

---

[68] *Mirabilia*, Preface (Nichols), pp. v–vi.
[69] *Polychron.*, Rolls Series, I, 214–16.
[70] Bk. II, ll. 4484–87.   [71] *VB*, II.

New Jerusalem in terms which recall both Gloriana's Cleopolis and Lucifera's House of Pride.

> Long having deeply gron'd these visions sad,
> I saw a Citie like unto that same,
> Which saw the messenger of tidings glad;
> But that on sand was built the goodly frame:
>   It seem'd her top the firmament did rayse,
> And no lesse rich than faire, right worthie sure
>   (If ought here worthie) of immortall dayes,
> Or if ought under heaven might firme endure.[72]

Les Antiquitez de Rome reflect the mingling of humanistic and Augustinian views of earthly glory in the mind of a poet whom Spenser admired and imitated at the outset of his poetic career.[73] An analysis of the *Antiquitez* as Spenser read and translated them may therefore well serve as a summary of the ideas we have been attempting to develop, and as a point of departure for further exploration of Spenser's "general intention" in making Gloriana the ruler of a purified earthly city, inferior but not hostile to the City of God.

Du Bellay is fascinated by the splendor of Rome. In his first sonnet he sets the keynote of the whole, when he invokes the spirit of the ancient Roman poets.

> Thrice unto you with lowd voyce I appeale,
> And for your antique furie here doo call,
>   The whiles that I with sacred horror sing
> Your glorie, fairest of all earthly thing.[74]

The last three words, which are Spenser's own addition to his original,[75] are almost an echo of the sage's characterization of Cleopolis as

>   for earthly frame,
>   The fairest peece, that eye beholden can.[76]

---

[72] *VB*, XIV, 1–8.
[73] For a discussion of Spenser's use of the "ruin literature" see Hughes, *Virgil and Spenser*, pp. 340 *et sqq.*
[74] *RR*, I, 11–14.
[75] The last line in French is: "Je vays chantant vostre gloire plus belle."
[76] *FQ*, I, X, lix, 2–3.

This likeness in phrasing suggests a likeness between Rome
and Cleopolis as symbols of earthly glory.

In the *Antiquitez* the physical glories of Rome surpass all
the wonders of the ancient world, and her citizens are like
the gods in fame. Following Virgil, Du Bellay compares the
city to Cybele, to whom the Pantheon was believed to be
dedicated.

> Such as the *Berecynthian* Goddesse bright
> In her swift charret with high turrets crownde,
>   Proud that so manie Gods she brought to light;
>   Such was this Citie in her good daies fownd:
>   This Citie, more than that great *Phrygian* mother
>   Renown'd for fruite of famous progenie.[77]

She was great not in arms alone, but in virtue,[78] yet her history exemplified the evil, as well as the good, of this world
which is subject to time.

> All the mishap, the which our daies outweares,
> All the good hap of th' oldest times afore,
> *Rome* in the time of her great ancesters,
> Like a *Pandora,* locked long in store.
>   But destinie this huge *Chaos* turmoyling,
>   In which all good and evill was enclosed,
>   Their heavenly vertues from these woes assoyling,
>   Caried to heaven, from sinfull bondage losed:
>   But their great sinnes, the causers of their paine,
>   Under these antique ruines yet remaine.[79]

Among the sins of Rome it was the civil wars that particularly impressed Du Bellay. Just as Jason sowed the dragon's
teeth, which engendered men of arms,

> So this brave Towne, that in her youthlie daies
> An *Hydra* was of warriours glorious,
> Did fill with her renowmed nourslings praise

[77] *RR*, VI. Cf. *Aeneid* vi. 784 *et sqq.*   [78] *RR*, VIII.
[79] *Ibid.*, XIX, 5-14.

> The firie sunnes both one and other hous:
>   But they at last, there being then not living
> An *Hercules,* so rank seed to represse;
> Emongst themselves with cruell furie striving,
> Mow'd downe themselves with slaughter mercilesse;
>   Renewing in themselves that rage unkinde,
>   Which whilom did those earthborn brethren blinde.[80]

But the chief sin of Rome was impious pride. The Goths were thus instruments of justice, inspired by Mars to rebuke the *hybris* of his offspring.[81] Yet in the next line Du Bellay calls the Goths "th' earths new Giant brood," and he harks back regretfully to the divine origin of Rome. In the next sonnet he again emphasizes the pride of Rome, using the simile of the war between the gods and giants, this time with the Romans as the giants, piling "hils on hils, to scale the starrie skie."[82]

The most persistent theme, however, in the *Antiquitez de Rome* is not the virtues of Rome or its sins, but the triumph of time, the inevitable passing of all earthly glory, of which the fall of Rome is the most dramatic example. The decay of earthly glory is sometimes contemplated with regret.

> Ye cruell starres, and eke ye Gods unkinde,
> Heaven envious, and bitter stepdame Nature,
> Be it by fortune, or by course of kinde
> That ye doo weld th' affaires of earthlie creature;
>   Why have your hands long sithence traveiled
> To frame this world, that doth endure so long?
>   Or why were not these Romane palaces
> Made of some matter no lesse firme and strong?[83]

The answer is: as Rome goes, so goes the world. "All this whole shall one day come to nought."

Regret for the triumph of time is mitigated by a personal

---

[80] *RR,* X, 5–14. Cf. also *RR,* XXI.   [81] *Ibid.,* XI, 1–8.
[82] *Ibid.,* XII, 2.   [83] *Ibid.,* IX, 1–8.

application. Time puts an end to all things, sorrow as well
as joy. The glorious monuments of Rome are falling to
decay.

> Alas, by little ye to nothing flie,
> The peoples fable, and the spoyle of all:
>> And though your frames do for a time make warre
> Gainst time, yet time in time shall ruinate
> Your workes and names, and your last reliques marre.[84]

But this triumph of time brings romantic comfort to the
poet,

>> For if that time make ende of things so sure,
>> It als will end the paine, which I endure.[85]

He derives comfort also, perhaps, from the notion of cyclical
regeneration. From the foundation of Rome to the Rome
of the popes there is a cyclical movement.[86] Shepherds became kings; kings were succeeded by consuls, who gave way
to dictators and finally to emperors. But the power of the
Empire passed to "Peter's successor,"

>> Who shepheardlike, (as fates the same foreseeing)
>> Doth shew, that all things turne to their first being.[87]

The chief consolation, however, against the melancholy in-
duced by contemplation of the triumph of time was for Du
Bellay, as for other Renaissance poets, the immortality of
literature. Rome is dead,

> But her brave writings, which her famous merite
> In spight of time, out of the dust doth reare,
> Doo make her Idole through the world appeare.[88]

Chief among these "brave writings" was the *Aeneid*, and
Spenser, as we know, aspired to be the English Virgil. As

[84] *Ibid.*, VII, 7–11.   [85] *Ibid.*, ll. 13–14.   [86] *Ibid.*, XVIII.
[87] *Ibid.*, XVIII, 13–14.   [88] *Ibid.*, V, 12–14.

such he was the singer of an ideal empire, the British Empire that was to be, the third Troy which was to rival the glories of the first and second, and to avoid their sins. Spenser puts the sins of Rome in the House of Pride. Like Du Bellay, he emphasizes her fatal civil strife and her overweening ambition.

> And in another corner wide were strowne
> The antique ruines of the *Romaines* fall:
> Great *Romulus* the Grandsyre of them all,
> Proud *Tarquin,* and too lordly *Lentulus,*
> Stout *Scipio,* and stubborne *Hanniball,*
> Ambitious *Sylla,* and sterne *Marius,*
> High *Caesar,* Great *Pompey,* and fierce *Antonius.*[89]

Unlike Catholic Du Bellay, Protestant Spenser saw in papal Rome the continuation of the sinful pagan empire. To him, as to St. Augustine, the city of the seven hills was the new Babylon, the Scarlet Whore seated upon the seven-headed beast. Duessa sits at the right hand of Lucifera in the House of Pride, while Gloriana's Cleopolis sends forth Una's champion, the Christian hero for whom a place is prepared in the heavenly city. Pagan Rome was compact of good and evil. The evil remained with the papacy, but the good lived on in twofold immortality, ideally in "brave writings," concretely in the third Troy, heir to the virtue and glory of its predecessors.

This twofold immortality of Rome is symbolized in Cleopolis, which represents both the ideal city of fame, in a sense the Idea of Rome, and London, capital of the British Empire. The meaning of Cleopolis in Spenser's particular intention and its relation to Troy, Rome, and London will be discussed in the following chapter. Of Cleopolis as city of fame we have already spoken, recognizing it as a humanistic modification of Augustine's Earthly City, drawn in the

[89] *FQ,* I, V, xlix, 3–9.

spirit of the Mirabilian picture of Rome. The same two
elements enter into the symbolism of Panthea, the crystal
tower, chief ornament of the city "in which that fairest
Faerie Queene doth dwell."

Panthea is apparently a temple of earthly glory. It had
seemed "the fairest thing that was" to St. George before he
saw the "bright angels towre" in the New Jerusalem. This
tower does not appear in the *Apocalypse,* which states explicitly that there was no temple in the heavenly city, "for
the Lord God Almighty and the Lamb are the temple of
it."[90] Spenser seems to have created his angels' tower as a
symbol of the glory of God and as a deliberate foil to Panthea. The suggestion may have come from the opening
verses of the description of St. John's vision.

And he carried me away in the spirit to a great and high
mountain and shewed me that great city, the holy Jerusalem,
descending out of heaven from God.
Having the glory of God: and her light was like unto a stone
most precious, even like a jasper stone, clear as crystal.[91]

If this glory is concentrated in the "angels towre" we can
readily see why it should quite dim "that towre of glas"
which housed the glory of Cleopolis.

This glory, symbolized by the Fairy Queen herself, is, as
we have seen, an earthly glory, sought and won by virtuous
action in the active life, particularly by warfare in a just
cause. It is just this element of war, even in the service of an
empire founded on justice and devoted to the cause of truth,
which makes Cleopolis inferior to the heavenly city. Similarly St. Augustine had regarded the glory of the Roman
Empire as unworthy the admiration of a Christian because
it was founded and enlarged by war.[92] He points out that

[90] *Rev.* 21:22.   [91] *Ibid.,* 21:10–11.
[92] *De civ. Dei,* Lib. IV, cap. iii; Healey, Vol. I, pp. 116–17.

war is inseparable from sin and suffering, since both sides cannot win, and one of them must be wrong. Empires obtained by wars of aggression are simply "thievish purchases." Ninus and Alexander were no better than pirates.[93] It is true that an empire may be built up not by unprovoked aggression but by the defeat of would-be aggressors. Such an empire is just, but it owes its existence, not to the justice of its rulers, but to the sins of its enemies, on account of which they are justly subdued. All worldly empire, according to St. Augustine, is thus based on sin.

What reason, then, or what wisdom shall any man show in glorying in the largeness of empire, all their joy being but as a glass, bright and brittle, and evermore in danger of breaking?[94]

Possibly this passage was in Spenser's mind when he set his goddess of earthly glory in a city whose principal building was a tower of glass.[95]

For actual analogues to Panthea, however, we must turn from the *City of God* to the *Mirabilia*. The name of Spenser's fairy palace suggests the Pantheon, temple of Cybele and all the gods. According to the common euhemeristic explanation of mythology, which reduced the gods to famous men of old, this temple would become a hall of fame. In this sense Godfrey of Viterbo, in the twelfth century, used the word "Pantheon" as a title for his universal history. As temple of Cybele the Pantheon might also be considered a symbol of the Roman Empire, which Virgil had compared to the Berecynthian goddess crowned with towers. I have already quoted Du Bellay's adaptation of this well-known passage. Augustine tells us that Cybele represented the earth,[96] and this, too, would make her temple an appropriate

---

[93] *Ibid.*, cap. iv, B; Healey, Vol. I, pp. 117–19.
[94] *Op. cit.*, Lib. IV, cap. iii, A; Healey, Vol. I, p. 116.
[95] Cf. Horace *Serm.* ii. iii. 222: "Quem cepit vitrea fama."
[96] *De civ. Dei*, Lib. VII, cap. xxiv, B; Healey, Vol. I, p. 218.

symbol for the Roman Empire, which included the whole world, and was itself an epitome of earthly glory. Cybele was also identified with Proserpina, goddess of the dead,[97] who, as we shall see later, may have been one of the literary ancestors of Spenser's Gloriana.[98]

Another symbol of Roman glory was the Mirabilian Capitol with its walls of glass and gold and its palace containing statues of the Trojan kings and Roman emperors "to be a mirror to all nations."[99] Du Bellay's description of this "stately frame" may well have furnished one of the principal models for Spenser's Panthea.

Another was probably the Holovitreum, the round temple of glass and gold which contained the symbols of the heavenly bodies. This temple, obviously a symbol of the crystal spheres of heaven, would become a pantheon by virtue of the common belief in stellification. The heavenly spheres were often called temples. Chapman speaks of them as "Heaven's crystal temples."[100] In the *Visions of Bellay* the same figure appears in a context which suggests Spenser's Panthea as a symbol of earthly glory. The poet tells how a ghost appeared to him

> On that great rivers banck, that runnes by *Rome,*
> Which calling me by name, bad me to reare
> My lookes to heaven whence all good gifts do come,
> And crying lowd, loe now beholde (quoth hee)
> What under this great temple placed is:
> Lo all is nought but flying vanitee.[101]

[97] *Blondus, De Roma triumphante,* Lib. I, fol. xi.

[98] The Proserpina who suggests Gloriana is the heavenly Proserpina, who presides over the Elysian Fields in the air, not the "Queen of Hell" who is the mother of Lucifera. See below, pp. 162–63.

[99] The *speculum* or *spectaculum* of the *Mirabilia* meant a "marvel" rather than a "mirror" in the modern sense. But the modern meaning would probably suggest itself to a Renaissance poet like Spenser who was particularly fond of the Platonic "mirror" image.

[100] *Poems,* p. 4.   [101] *VB,* I, 6–11.

The curious description of the heavens in the *Hymne of Heavenly Beauty* may also throw light upon the symbolism of Panthea. Spenser is proceeding from

> th' easie vew
> Of this base world, subiect to fleshly eye,
> From thence to mount aloft by order dew,
> To contemplation of th' immortall sky,[102]

in order at last to reach the vision of God's glory, which is only mirrored in the beauty of His works. The final experience described is parallel to that of St. George on the mount of Heavenly Contemplation, and should help to explain his contrasted vision of the two cities. Spenser first directs our attention to the beauty of the visible universe.

> Then looke who list, thy gazefull eyes to feed
> With sight of that is faire, looke on the frame
> Of this wyde *universe,* and therein reed
> The endlesse kinds of creatures, which by name
> Thou canst not count, much lesse their natures aime:
> All which are made with wondrous wise respect,
> And all with admirable beautie deckt.

> First th' Earth, on adamantine pillers founded,
> Amid the Sea engirt with brasen bands;
> Then th' Aire still flitting, but yet firmely bounded
> On everie side, with pyles of flaming brands,
> Never consum'd nor quencht with mortall hands;
> And last that mightie shining christall wall,
> Wherewith he hath encompassed this All.[103]

"That shining christall wall," the sky or visible heaven,[104] reminds us not only of Panthea, but also of the Mirabilian

---

[102] *HHB*, ll. 22–25.   [103] *Ibid.*, ll. 29 *et sqq.*

[104] Cf. the "crystal battlements" of heaven in *Paradise Lost,* I, 742, and the "thousand Crystal Pillors" which uphold the palace of Cynthia, *FQ,* VII, VI, x, 4. Mrs. Bennett takes the crystal wall of *HHB* as "the Crystalline sphere located between the fixed stars and the Empyrean." "The Theme of Spenser's *Fowre Hymnes,*" *SP,* XXVIII (1931), 40. But the context seems to indicate that the sky as a whole is meant.

Capitol. The beauty of the heavens is further described in
a later stanza.

> Looke thou no further, but affixe thine eye,
> On that bright shynie round still moving Masse,
> The house of blessed Gods, which men call *Skye,*
> All sowd with glistring stars more thicke then grasse,
> Whereof each other doth in brightnesse passe;
> But those two most, which ruling night and day,
> As King and Queene, the heavens Empire sway.
>
> And tell me then, what hast thou ever seene,
> That to their beautie may compared bee,
> Or can the sight that is most sharpe and keene,
> Endure their Captains flaming head to see?
> How much lesse those, much higher in degree,
> And so much fairer, and much more than these,
> As these are fairer then the land and seas?
>
> For farre above these heavens which here we see,
> Be others farre exceeding these in light,
> Not bounded, not corrupt, as these same bee,
> But infinite in largeness and in hight,
> Unmoving, uncorrupt, and spotlesse bright,
> That need no Sunne t' illuminate their spheres,
> But their owne native light farre passing theirs.[105]

These invisible heavens, whose beauty can only be perceived by contemplation, are also arranged in ascending
series, beginning with the heaven of happy souls, and ending with that which contains God and Sapience. Spenser's
picture of these supercelestial heavens is curious, reversing
the traditional order of the angelic hierarchies, and arrang-
ing them in twos instead of threes.[106] We are not here concerned, however, with the problems raised by this arrangement, interesting as they are. For our present purpose it is
sufficient to note that these supercelestial heavens, contem-

---

[105] *HHB,* ll. 50 *et sqq.*
[106] The traditional arrangement is preserved in *FQ,* I, XII, xxxix, 3-5.

plated together (as the lower heavens may be considered as forming one "sky"), correspond to the New Jerusalem, which had "no need of the sun, neither of the moon to shine in it: for the glory of God did lighten it, and the Lamb was the light thereof."[107] And if this glory of the supercelestial heavens is represented by the "bright angels towre" of St. George's vision, the glory of the crystal sky may well be symbolized in Panthea, which as the fairest of all objects perceptible to the senses, is a fitting shrine for earthly fame, the highest ideal possible to the man who lives under the law of nature.[108] The Christian, aided by grace and revelation, can pass through and beyond these earthly beauties of the senses and the carnal mind, to the higher beauty of the invisible heavens.

The visible heavens below may be immortal in comparison with the earth, but they are not eternal, for they belong to the realm of time and change.[109] This idea is expressed in the speech in which Mutabilitie claims dominion not only over the gods, or planets, but also over the whole universe.

> Then are ye mortall borne, and thrall to me,
> Unlesse the kingdome of the sky yee make
> Immortall, and unchangeable to bee.[110]

But the sky is not unchangeable, for as the planets are subject to change in their nature and influence, and in the movements of the planetary spheres,[111] the "starrie skie" is likewise inconstant.

---

[107] *Rev.* 21:23.

[108] The law of nature was commonly identified with the moral law as expounded by "Aristotle and the rest." Cf. Hooker, *Ecclesiastical Polity*, Bk. i. chap. viii, sec. 9.

[109] Cf. Williamson, "Mutability, Decay, and Seventeenth Century Melancholy," *ELH*, II (1935), 121–50.

[110] *FQ*, VII, VII, liv, 1–3.   [111] *Ibid.*, lv, 1–4.

Yet do the Starres and Signes therein still move,
And even itself is mov'd, as wizards saine.
But all that moveth, doth mutation love:
Therefore both you and them to me I subiect prove.

Then since within this wide great *Universe*
Nothing doth firme and permanent appeare,

. . .

What then should let, but I aloft should reare,
My Trophee, and from all, the triumph beare?[112]

The triumph of Mutabilitie suggests the Petrarchan triumph of Time, which eclipses the triumph of Fame, and is itself eclipsed by the triumph of Eternity. Spenser himself connects Mutabilitie with Time,[113] and declares that she must at last yield to Eternity. He does not mention fame here, but he allows Mutabilitie to claim as her final conquest the heavenly spheres, which, as we have seen, were often a temple of fame. To be sure the claim of Mutabilitie is not allowed, and the heavens are left in the possession of a qualified immortality. Since the changes they undergo are a dilation and perfection of their "being," the heavens are said to "raigne over change."[114] Spenser takes this as a reassertion of the traditional idea that change reigns only beneath the moon.

When I bethinke me on that speech whyleare,
    Of Mutability and well it way:
    Me seemes, that though she all unworthy were
    Of the Heav'ns Rule; yet very sooth to say,
    In all things else she beares the greatest sway.[115]

But though the sky can thus still be called "immortal," its immortality is obviously different from that of the super-

---

[112] *Ibid.*, lv, 6–lvi, 5.   [113] *Ibid.*, VIII, i, 9.   [114] *Ibid.*, VII, lviii, 9.
[115] *Ibid.*, VIII, i, 1–5.

celestial spheres of the *Hymne of Heavenly Beautie,* not only because the sky includes change now, but because it is at last to be changed permanently in the triumph of eternity.

The *Mutabilitie Cantos,* like the *Hymne of Heavenly Beautie,* then, present the visible heavens as in some sense corruptible, and link them to the rest of the visible universe rather than to the incorruptible, invisible heavens of which it is a shadow. The *Hymne* presents the starry heavens as the highest type of beauty which can be perceived by the senses. The *Mutabilitie Cantos,* while reaffirming the traditional belief in "th' immortall skye," in effect present the visible heavens as the least changeable and most enduring elements in a changing universe. The crystal sky is thus doubly appropriate as a symbol of the fame bestowed by literature, which is not only the fairest but the most enduring of earthly things, outlasting the material monuments of architecture and sculpture, and prolonging man's life in the memory of posterity by a sort of pagan shadow of Christian immortality.

It seems likely, therefore, that Spenser's Panthea, like the Holovitreum in Rome, was an image of the "crystal temple" of heaven. But this was possibly the model also for the Mirabilian Capitol and certainly for the Colosseum, temple of the Sun; and these latter buildings were symbols of the power of Rome. The likeness may reflect the astrological notion that all things on earth had a counterpart among the stars. Augustine quotes Hermes Trismegistus as saying:

> Know you not, Asclepius, that Egypt is heaven's image, or rather the place whereunto all the celestial graces descend, the very temple of the whole world.[116]

Still more might Rome be regarded as an image of the

---

[116] *De civ. Dei,* Lib. VIII, cap. xxiii, D. Healey, Vol. I, p. 250.

heavens or of the whole universe. We have already seen examples of the latter identification in the work of Du Bellay.

Spenser's Panthea, then, may be regarded as a symbol either of Rome or of the starry heaven, crown and citadel of the visible universe, since both are symbols of earthly glory, fairest and most enduring of transitory rewards. The connection of Panthea with Rome will be further discussed in the following chapter. Its connection with the starry heaven is strengthened by a consideration of other temples of fame in the poetry of Spenser's predecessors.

Most often suggested as an analogue to Panthea is the temple of glass in Chaucer's *House of Fame*.[117] Mrs. Bennett works out the comparison in some detail.

The crystal tower, Panthea, which seems to be the chief ornament of Cleopolis, is commonly identified with Westminster Abbey. . . . But it has a more important affinity with the temple of glass described by Chaucer in *The Hous of Fame* (Bk. I) as having the story of the *Aeneid* engraved on its walls. Chaucer's purpose in introducing this description is not clear. It serves as a sort of prelude, or false start, to his main description of the House of Fame, which takes its central conception from Ovid (*Met.* XII, 39–63) and treats fame as synonymous with rumor. Spenser puts the widest distance between good fame which is eternal glory, the true reward of virtue, and this rumor which, in its more malevolent form, he symbolizes in the Blatant Beast. It is quite possible that Spenser interpreted Chaucer as dealing first with true fame, in the house of glass episode, and second with false fame, in the passage enlarged from Ovid. The "table of bras" which preserved the story of Aeneas in Chaucer's temple would be equally suitable as an ornament for Panthea, since Aeneas was looked upon by Spenser as a famous example of virtue; and the proper reward of virtuous deeds was good fame secured through the services of a poet.[118]

While I agree with Mrs. Bennett that Spenser's view of fame was quite different from Chaucer's, I doubt her theory

[117] *Eg.* Kitchin in his edition of *FQ, Bk. I*, p. 208.   [118] *JEGP*, XXXI, 215.

of Spenser's interpretation of the two temples in the *House of Fame*. That the temple of glass in Book I is a temple of Venus is clear from Chaucer's own words and from Lydgate's imitation,[119] which Mrs. Bennett herself rules out as an analogue to Panthea.[120] As a decoration for either type of temple, and indeed for Spenser's Panthea, the story of Aeneas would certainly be appropriate, but its presence in Chaucer's temple of glass is sufficiently explained by the connection between Aeneas and Venus. Chaucer probably began his poem with this vision to symbolize his own character as a poet of love, which is specifically mentioned by the eagle as a reason for the later visit to the House of Fame, where new tidings of love are to be revealed.[121] In the House of Fame proper this promise is not kept, but it is repeated when the poet is led into the small whirling house especially devoted to rumors. Just before the poem breaks off there is a "gret noyse"

> In a corner of the halle,
> Ther men of love-tydynges tolde,[122]

and a "man of gret auctorite" appears, probably as a messenger of the promised tidings. There is no need to assume, therefore, that Spenser read the *House of Fame* in the manner suggested by Mrs. Bennett. To me it seems far more likely that he saw the three "houses" in Chaucer's poem as dedicated, respectively, to love, fame, and rumor.

While the temple of glass may have contributed slightly to Spenser's idea of Panthea, a far more likely analogue is the House of Fame itself. The temple of glass is not a temple of fame. It is located on earth, since from it the poet ascends to the House of Fame in the heavens. At first he fears that he is to be translated like Enoch and Elijah or like Romulus

---

[119] *The Temple of Glas.*   [120] *Op. cit.,* p. 215 n.
[121] *House of Fame,* II, 614–95.   [122] *Ibid.,* III, 2142–43.

and Ganymede.[123] The eagle assures him that he is not to be stellified, but is to visit the House of Fame as a reward for his services in the cause of love. After passing through the heavens, he is set down "in a Strete," and told to enter the palace of Fame.

This is situated on a high rock, which the poet ascends with difficulty, wondering

> What manner stoon this roche was.
> For hyt was lyk alum de glas,
> But that hyt shoon ful more clere;
> But of what congeled matere
> Hyt was, I nyste redely.
> But at the laste aspied I,
> And found that hit was every del
> A roche of yse, and not of stel.
> Thoughte I, "By seynt Thomas of Kent!
> This were a feble fundament
> To bilden on a place hye.
> He ought him lytel glorifye
> That hereon bilt, God so me save![124]

A further symbol of the uncertainty of fame appears when the poet notices the names of famous people engraved on the slope of the ice mountain. Those on the south side have been partly erased by the heat of the sun.

> But men seyn, "What may ever laste?"[125]

Those on the north side have been preserved by the shadow of Fame's castle, a building so beautiful

> That al the men that ben on lyve
> Ne han the kunnynge to descrive
> The beaute of that ylke place,
> Ne coude casten no compace
> Swich another for to make.[126]

---

[123] *Ibid.*, II, 584–92.   [124] *Ibid.*, III, 1123–35.   [125] *Ibid.*, l. 1147.
[126] *Ibid.*, ll. 1167–71.

Chaucer himself can hardly describe it, although he remembers it perfectly.

> Al was of ston of beryle,
> Bothe the castel and the tour,
> And eke the halle and every bour,
> Withouten peces or joynynges.
> But many subtil compassinges,
> Babewynnes and pynacles,
> Ymageries and tabernacles,
> I say; and ful eke of wyndowes,
> As flakes falle in grete snowes.[127]

This description certainly suggests Spenser's "bright towre all built of christall cleene." "Beryl" was often used in a derived sense for crystal or glass. The N.E.D., in fact, assumes this meaning in the *House of Fame,* while Professor Robinson thinks Chaucer intended the gem.[128] We cannot tell how Spenser interpreted the word, but he would certainly connect beryl with crystal and glass, and the picture would be the same in either case—a castle of dazzling beauty sparkling like a jewel in the sun. Spenser twice speaks of Panthea as made of crystal.[129] Only when he compares it with the angels' tower does he say definitely that it was made of glass. Perhaps he intended us to assume that St. George had previously believed its material to be some precious stone, like the jasper of the New Jerusalem. Only in comparison with this symbol of heavenly glory does Panthea appear as a tower of glass, its brightness dimmed, and its brittleness evident.[130]

Chaucer's House of Fame further resembles the Mirabilian palaces in its splendor. After examining the outside

---

[127] *Ibid.,* ll. 1184–92.

[128] *Chaucer's Complete Works* (Cambridge Edition), p. 893. But cf. Douglas, *Palice of Honour,* quoted below, p. 4°.

[129] *FQ,* I, X, lviii, 5. *Ibid.,* II, X, lxiii, 4.

[130] Cf. Augustine, quoted above, p. 34. Probably both glass and crystal suggested primarily brightness rather than transparency. Cf. *Rev.* 21:18.

of the castle, where he sees all sorts of bards and magicians,
and musing "longe while"

> Upon these walles of berile,
> That shoone ful lyghter than a glas
> And made wel more than hit was
> To semen every thing, ywis,
> As kynde thyng of Fames is,[131]

Chaucer passes through a gate adorned with gold into a
main hall, of which the walls, floor, and roof were

> plated half a foote thikke
> Of gold, and that nas nothyng wikke,
> But, for to prove in alle wyse,
> As fyn as ducat in Venyse,
>
> . . .
>
> And they were set as thik of nouchis
> Ful of the fynest stones faire,
> That men rede in the Lapidaire.[132]

The goddess herself sits

> in a see imperiall,
> That mad was of a rubee all,
> Which that a carbuncle ys ycalled.[133]

Chaucer makes it clear that fame is the gift of poets and
historians. The Muses sing before the goddess. She bears on
her shoulders the fame of Alexander and Hercules. A row
of pillars extends from the dais where she sits to the door,
and on each pillar stand the poets and historians who have
upheld the fame of a different city, god, or hero. The epic
poets stand on pillars of iron. On one of these is

> the gret Omer;
> And with him Dares and Tytus
> Before, and eke he Lollius,

[131] *House of Fame*, III, 1288–92.   [132] *Ibid.*, ll. 1345–52.
[133] *Ibid.*, ll. 1361–63.

And Guydo eke de Columpnis,
And Englyssh Gaufride eke, ywis;
And ech of these, as I have joye,
Was besy for to bere up Troye.
So hevy thereof was the fame
That for to bere hyt was no game.[134]

So far Chaucer's House of Fame might well serve as a model
for Spenser's Panthea. But Chaucer's goddess is quite different from Gloriana. Instead of rewarding virtue, Chaucer's Fame deals out her favors capriciously, giving good
fame, bad fame, or oblivion to good and bad men indiscriminately. In this she resembles her sister Fortune.[135] When
she summons her servant Aeolus to blow on his golden
trumpet, "Clere Laude" or on his black trumpet, "Sklaundre," she reminds us of St. Augustine's "windy glory," unworthy the service of virtue.

An even greater lack of connection between fame and
merit appears in Ariosto's temple of immortality in the
sphere of the moon. Where Chaucer depicts fame as capricious, Ariosto makes her mercenary. Astolfo learns from St.
John that the heroes escaped oblivion, not because of their
virtues, but because of the liberality of their descendants.

Non sì pietoso Enea, nè forte Achille
Fu, come è fama, nè sì fiero Ettore;
E ne son stati e mille e mille e mille
Che lor si puon con verità anteporre:
Ma i donati palazzi e le gran ville
Dai discendenti lor, gli ha fatto porre
In questi senza fin sublimi onori
Dall' onorate man degli scrittori.

Non fu sì santo nè benigno Augusto,
Come la tuba di Virgilio suona.
L'avere avuto in poesia buon gusto,

[134] *Ibid.*, ll. 1466-74.   [135] *Ibid.*, ll. 1544-47.

La proscrizione iniqua gli perdona.
Nessun sapria se Neron fosse ingiusto,
Nè sua fama saria forse men buona,
Avesse avuto e terra e ciel nimici,
Se gli scrittori sapea tenersi amici.[136]

This is far from the attitude of Spenser's Clio, who condemns evil deeds to oblivion, though she presumably expects her servants to be rewarded for their immortalizing of virtue.

Both Chaucer and Ariosto place their temples of fame in the heavens, and both exhibit a parallelism between events on earth and events in the country of fame which corresponds to the double symbolism of Spenser's Panthea. In Chaucer's poem the sounds which rise from earth to the House of Fame assume the form of the earthly speaker. In the *Orlando furioso* St. John explains to Astolfo that each earthly occurrence has a counterpart in the sphere of the moon. The poets are represented by swans, who carry the names of men from Lethe, where Time has thrown them, to the nymph presiding over the temple of immortality. She affixes the names to the pillar. There are hints that similar emblems of fame were to adorn Spenser's crystal temple. St. George is to leave the service of Gloriana after he has won a famous victory, and hung his shield "high among all knights." When Arthur died, we are told, the Fairy Queen brought his shield "to Faerie lond where yet it may be seene, if sought."[137] Probably the shields of these worthies were hung in Panthea as emblems of their enduring fame.

In Chaucer and Ariosto, then, Spenser may have found suggestions for his Panthea. The conception of a crystal or glass temple appears also in the works of several poets who wrote between Chaucer and Spenser, and who help to ex-

[136] *OF*, XXXV, xxv–xxvi.
[137] *FQ*, I, VII, xxxvi, 9. This is often taken as a reference to Leicester's death. But we are concerned here primarily with the "general intention," not with particular allusions.

plain Spenser's probable use of Chaucer's *House of Fame*. The tower of music in which Grandamour finds La Belle Pucelle in Hawes's *Pastyme of Pleasure* contains a crystal temple.[138] Lydgate's already mentioned temple of glass is not a temple of fame. In the *Fall of Princes,* however, Lydgate mentions a crystal palace which certainly reminds us of Spenser's Panthea, for it is connected not only with stellification and fame, but also specifically with Arthur himself. The reference occurs in the already mentioned passage describing Arthur's translation to the heavens.

> Thus of Breteyne translatid was þe sunne
> Up to the riche sterri briht dungoun
> Astronomeeres well reherse kunne—
> Callid Arthuris constellacioun,
> Wher he sit crownid in the hevenly mansioun
> Amyd the paleis of stonis cristallyne,
> Told among Cristen first of þe worthi nyne.[139]

The importance of the whole passage in which these lines occur will be discussed in a later chapter. At this point, it is sufficient to note that Lydgate's palace certainly represents one of the crystal temples of heaven, while his "stonis cristallyne" recalls Chaucer's "ston of beryle," and renders more probable the interpretation already suggested for Spenser's understanding of the *House of Fame*.

Another link between Chaucer's House of Fame and Spenser's Panthea is found in the *Palice of Honour* by the Scottish Chaucerian Gavin Douglas, a poet whose conception of honor is close to Spenser's. The poem is a long rambling allegory of the *Court of Love* type. The poet falls asleep on the usual May morning, and dreams of a desert place, where he sees various apparitions. After visions of Queen Sapience and her court which need not detain us, he meets a procession of the Muses with their poets. Under the

---

[138] Cap. xvi, stanza 2.   [139] *Fall of Princes,* Bk. VIII, ll. 3102–8.

guidance of a nymph bestowed upon him by Calliope, the poet eventually arrives at the palace of Honour. It lies near the well of the Muses, on a rock of "slid hard marbell stone," very difficult to ascend. Half way up is a pit in which idle folk are punished. Over this pit he is carried by the nymph, who seizes him by the hair, and in this undignified manner conveys him to the top. From this vantage point he looks down on the earth and sees a ship struggling with the waves. This turns out to be the State of Grace, and furnishes the occasion for a long sermon. The poet then turns to view the beauties of the palace, which is surrounded by a beautiful garden. In the outer court true lovers are engaged in a tournament for the sake of their ladies. The poet views with admiration

> That hevinlie Palice all of cristall cleir,
> Wrocht as me thocht of poleist beriall stone.
> Bosiliall nor Oliab, but weir,
> Quilk sancta sanctorum maid maist riche and deir,
> Nor he that wrocht the tempill of Salomon,
> Nor he that beildit the royall Ylion,
> Nor he that forgit Darius sepulture,
> Culd not performe sa craftelie ane cure.[140]

The poet sees Venus sitting on a throne holding a mirror, made of some unknown substance,

> Surmounting far in brichtnes to my dome,
> The coistlie subtill spectakill of Rome.[141]

In this mirror, which, as we learn later, signifies the beauty each lover sees in his lady's face, the poet sees a long procession of famous people, whose description gives in effect an epitome of universal history.

---

[140] *Poetical Works*, I, 55-56.

[141] *Ibid.*, p. 57. This may be another reference to Rome as "mirror of the world." More probably, however, it refers to the magic mirror made by Virgil, which enabled the Romans to foresee the approach of an enemy or traitor. See Spargo, *Virgil the Necromancer*, p. 134.

The palace is only for the virtuous. The poet sees the wicked falling down the hill in their vain attempts to reach it. Among them is Catiline, who tries to get in at a window, but is overthrown by a book hurled at him by Cicero. The court of King Honour, master of this palace, consists of personified virtues. For instance, "Lawtie" is "keipar of that hold," Patience is porter, Liberality, treasurer, and Conscience, the chancellor, is assisted by four assessors, Science, Prudence, Justice, and Sapience.

The poet admires the engraving on the golden gate of the palace, showing

> All naturall thingis men may in eird consave.
> Thair was the eirth environit with the sey,
> Quairon the schippes sailland micht I se,
> The air, the fire, all the four elementis,
> The spheris seven, and *primum mobile,*
> The signes twelf perfitelie everie gre,
> The Zodiak haill as buikis representis,
> The Pole Antartick that ever himself absentis,
> The Pole Artick and eik the Ursis twane,
> The sevin starnis, Phaton and the Charlewane.[142]

Besides these he sees the rape of Ganymede, "the douchteris fair" of Driada, the movements of the planets, and

> mony gudelie personages,
> Quilk semit all lustie quick images,
> The warkmanschip exceding many fold
> The precious mater, thocht it was fynest gold.[143]

The nymph tells him to hurry. Greater wonders are still to come.

> Wouldst thou se farleis, behold thame yonder lo.

Heeding this injunction, the poet finally enters the palace, where he sees "many worthie wight walking." The beauty of the place amazes him.

[142] Douglas, *Poetical Works,* I, 69.   [143] *Ibid.*

For like Phebus with fyrie bemis bricht,
The wallis schane castand sa greit ane licht,
It semit like the hevin imperiall;
And as the ceder surmountis the rammall
In perfite hicht, sa of that court a glance
Exceidis far all eirdlie vane plesance.[144]

After a further description of the beauties of the palace,
which dazzles him with its gold, crystal, and precious stones,
the poet tells how they ascended ten steps of topaz, and came
into the presence chamber, which is entirely made of precious stones, and full of people.

Baith to and fro amid the hall thay went,
Royall princes in plait and armouris quent,
Of birneist gold couchit with precious stanis.
Enthronit sat ane God omnipotent,
On quhais glorious visage as I blent
In extasie, be his brichtnes atanis
He smot me doun, and brissit all my banis.[145]

The nymph removes him from the dangerous presence, and
after reviving him answers his questions about the people
in the hall.

Ȝhone war (said scho) quha sa the richt discrives
Maist valȝeand folk and verteous in their lives,
Now in the court of Honour thay remane
Verteouslie, and in all pleasance thrives.
For thay with speir, with swordis, and with knives,
In just battell war fundin maist of mane,
In thair promittis thay stude ever firme and plane,
In thame aboundit worschip and lawtie,
Illuminat with liberalitie.[146]

She goes on to expound the nature of honor.

Honour (quod scho) to this hevinlie ring
Differrris richt far fra warldlie governing,

[144] Ibid., p. 70.   [145] Ibid., p. 72.   [146] Ibid., p. 74.

> Quhilk is bot pompe of eirdlie dignitie,
> Gevin for estait of blude, micht, or sic thing,
> And in this countrie prince, prelate, or king,
> Allanerlie sall for vertew honourit be.
> For eirdlie gloir is nocht bot vanitie,
> That as we se sa suddanelie will wend,
> Bot verteous honour never mair sall end.[147]

After further pious reflections upon the transitoriness of earthly glory, the nymph reveals the names of the people in the palace of Honor. They include Samson, Hercules, Achilles, "all the nobillis nyne," Scipio, Pompey, Semiramis, Hippolyta, Penthesilea, Medea, Zenobia, and several kings of Scotland.

The poet is then shown a garden attached to the palace where he finds magic fruits made of precious stones, signifying the colors of rhetoric. He crosses a perilous bridge, falls into the water, and wakes up with his thoughts still on the "lustie yle."

Douglas makes Honor a king instead of a queen, probably because his poem is dedicated to King James IV, and like Spenser's was presumably intended both as a lesson and a compliment to his royal patron.[148] His allegorical court of Honor is paralleled by Spenser's conception of Gloriana and her knights, and his distinction between vain earthly glory and virtuous honor recalls the similar distinction between Lucifera or Philotime and Gloriana in the *Faerie Queene*.

A similar attitude toward fame appears in the work of Jean Lemaire de Belges.[149] In several of his works Lemaire

---

[147] *Ibid.*, pp. 73–74.

[148] Saintsbury in *Cambridge History of English Literature*, II, 295. Honor is traditionally masculine, however, as fame and glory are feminine, probably because of the gender of the Latin words. Honor was worshipped as a god in Rome. Cf. Boccaccio, *Genealogia deorum* (Betussi's translation), p. 52.

[149] E.g., *Plainte du desiré, Couronne Margaritique, Concorde des deux langages, Temple d'honneur et de vertus.* See Becker, *Jean Lemaire,* pp.

mentions the god Honor and his sister Virtue, who pre-
side jointly over the temple which bears their names. This
building, described in the *Couronne Margaritique* as a
"noble palais Imperial situé sur la sainte montaigne de
Laborosité Spirituelle lequel tresexcellent ouvrier se fait
nommé Merite, estant de la famille de dame Justice,"[150]
figures most prominently in *Le Temple d'honneur et de
vertus*, composed in honor of Pierre II, duke of Bourbon.
This work, a mixture of prose and verse, opens in pastoral
vein with seven shepherds and shepherdesses dressed in the
colors of the seven virtues, and each representing a different
part of the duke's territory, singing songs in praise of Pan
and Aurora (Pierre de Bourbon and his wife, Anne of
France). The death of Pan is then related, and the shepherds
and shepherdesses mourn him. In pity for the grief-stricken
Aurora, the gods send Apollo to assist at the funeral, after
which Aurora goes to sleep and has a vision which consti-
tutes the major part of the poem.
She dreams that she is aroused by an angelic voice, sum-
moning all to learn of her husband's glory.

> Au bruyt: au bruyt de la louange excelse
> Du duc illustre accourez tous et toutes
> . . .
> Son grand renom le ciel cristallin perce,
> Esveillez vous par troupeaulx et par routes
> Au bruyt.
> Il a vaincu mortelle controverse
> Par ses vertus: n'en faictes nulles doubtes.
> Or vous dressez: et soyez aux escoutes:
> Si scaurez bien: en quel gloire il converse,
> Au bruyt.[151]

290–91 n. Similar conceptions were common in the French poetry of the 14th
and 15th centuries. Cf. Froissart, *Temple d'honneur*, Octavien de Saint-
Gelays, *Séjour d'honneur*, summarized in Guy, *L'École des rhétoriqueurs*, pp.
140 *et sqq.*, Jean Bouchet, *Temple de bonne renommée*, summarized in Guy,
op cit., p. 303.

[150] *Œuvres*, IV, 45.   [151] *Ibid.*, p. 215.

Upon hearing this voice, the princess, her daughter, and the shepherds and shepherdesses are immediately transported to a mountain whose summit is far above the clouds.

Si estoit icelluy mont semblable a celluy qu'on nomme Olympus en Macedone: tant floury tant verdoyant et tant revestu darbrisseaulx aromaticques et d'autres jolivetz de grant redolence: comme se ce feust ung second paradis terrestre. Et en la plaine spacieuse et herbue se monstroit ung edifice sumptueux a merveilles a maniere dung temple anticque en ouvraige, mais riche oultre mesure en sa facon. Lequel donnoit de prime face esbahissement a l'oeil, tant pour excellence de sa beaulté que pour la reflamboyance de lor et de pierres precieuses dont il estoit garni.[152]

At the gate of the temple are six female statues seated "sur fermes embassemens d'albastre, en sièges de porphire et couvertes de pavillons de cristal semez destoilles."[153] These statues have italic letters scattered over their garments, which, taken together, spell "Pierre." The visitors examine these marvels, the shepherds and shepherdesses admiring the beauty of the temple, which they compare to that of Solomon and to that of Diana at Ephesus, while the princess and her daughter attempt to solve the mystery of the letters. After various conjectures have been advanced, the apparent statues rise, and successively recite verses explaining that they represent *Prudence, Justice, Esperance, Raison, Religion,* and *Equité,* all virtues for which the duke was renowned.

The listeners prostrate themselves, and a female figure with wings like Mercury appears. Her name is written on her garments, "Entendement, Paranimphe et Garde des Vertus." She explains that she has called Aurora from sleep, and exhorts her not to grieve for her lord, since he has been translated to a better place. One might imagine this to be

[152] *Ibid.,* p. 216.   [153] *Ibid.,* p. 217.

heaven, but the immortality promised him is conceived in purely classical terms.

Il fault plourer ceulx desquelz les corps et lez noms ensemble par leur coulpe et ignavité sont ensevelis en oblivion perpetuelle. Mais ceulx ne sont pas plourables ne lamentables qui par la memoyre de leurs gestes vertueux revivent et refflourissent de jour en jour, et vollent in la bouche des meilleurs.[154]

Aurora is not to indulge in excessive grief, lest she seem envious of her husband's glory. Rather she is to build him a suitable monument, of which the temple before her, where his soul now dwells, is a model. Entendement now explains the nature of this temple.

Vecy le noble domicile: le final recet et la mansion esternelle des haultz hommes qui ont entre les humains merité tiltres dexellance. Cest le temple dedie a deux habitudes divines: c'est assavoir honneur et vertu. Cest ledifice construit et fabriqué par la main des corps celestes, habité et peuplé seullement des benoistes ames et frequenté des bienheureuz espritz. Et se tu demandes en quelle region est situé: sens en ton respiter adoratif le suavité du lieu beatificque, remire l'amenité presente et entens le tumulte armonieux qui la dedans resonne. Tu as assez ouy parler de paradis terrestre, du jardins des delices et des champs helisees, où il ne repaire que la fleur des ames felices. Juge donc sil y a lieu, en ce monde inferieur, equiparable a cestuy. Certes Nenny. . . .[155]

The supramundane character of the temple is further emphasized by comparison with the Roman temples of Honor and Virtue. They were great monuments,

Mais tel ouvraige transitoire est esvanouy et tombé en ruine quelque materiel qu'il fust. Tellement que ores nen reste aucun vestige la ou au contraire linstauracion de ce temple est spirituellement instituee des la creation des hommes, voire par avant, pour y recepvoir et introniser tous ceulx qui le meritent. Si n'envieillist jamais la structure de ce divin pourprix par

<hr>

[154] *Ibid.*, p. 223.   [155] *Ibid.*, p. 225.

temporelle decadence. Aincois est tousjours refreschy son noble edifice par nouvelle memoyre.[156]

Entendement then describes the entrance of Pierre de Bourbon into the temple. Greeted by the virtues, he received from Esperance a rich robe "tissue de gloire immortelle." A second reception committee consisting of six of his illustrious ancestors, "revestez destolles triumphales et accompaingez de plusieurs sublimes esperitz,"[157] preceded him into the temple, where he was enthroned "en riche siege tout estoffé dor et divoire: de longtemps appareillé pour luy par dame Predestinacion aux pieds dHonneur et de Vertu, souverains du temple."

His seat was adorned by the virtues with tapestry showing his memorable deeds. St. Louis then crowned him with "une couronne et aureole de louange immortelle," and gave him the titles, "tres bon, tres heureux, et tres pacific."

His right to these titles was debated "for pastime," at the request of various worthies who filled the temple. These include David, Joshua, Hector, Cato, Gideon, Judas Maccabeus, Augustus, Constantine, Charlemagne, René of Anjou, and others. The debate itself was carried on by the orators, poets, and historians, who were present as "ministres at secretaires dHonneur et de Vertu."[158]

After hearing this description of the apotheosis of her husband, Aurora and her daughter enter the temple. Entendement flies away, and the other virtues accompany the two mourners into the temple, closing the golden door behind them. The shepherds meanwhile occupy themselves with cutting epitaphs on the wall. These all emphasize the theme of immortal fame.

> Cy n'est pas mys soubz tumbe tenebreuse
> Comme homme attaint de mort noire et umbreuse

---

[156] *Ibid.*, p. 226.   [157] *Ibid.*, p. 227.   [158] *Ibid.*, p. 231.

Le noble duc tant cler et renommé
Mais vit et dure en memoire eternelle
En loz hautain et fame solonnelle
Comme le prince au mond plus aymé.[159]

Meanwhile Entendement visits the king and queen of
France to tell them of the glorious fate of the duke and his
"beatifique assumption aux mansion celestes."[160] She then
flies away to a mountain near Lyons, and recites from its
summit a closing exhortation to all men of high estate.

Mirez vous aux faitz vertueux
Du duc plain de resplendissance
Vous tous qui de lieu sumptueux
Prenez origine et naissance.
Car puisque Dieu vous a donné
Tiltre de noblesse aorné
En toute haulte prevalence
Aussi vous a il ordonné
Pour estre bons en excellence.
Pour estre bons en excellence
De mauvais train se fault garder,
Fuyr paresce et somnolence
Qui font les vertus retarder
Laisser medire et langarder
Nestre injuste n'impetueux,
Donques pour vous bien regarder
Mirez vous aux faitz vertueux.[161]

The general likeness in point of view between Lemaire
and Spenser is obvious. Both poets represent fame as the
divinely appointed reward of virtue, prolonger of days for
those "gentlemen or noble persons" whose deeds are regis-
tered in the "eternal book" of the Muses by their representatives, the poets. But Lemaire, like Douglas, fails to make
explicit the difference between the pagan immortality con-
ferred through fame and the Christian immortality secured

[159] *Ibid.*, p. 236.   [160] *Ibid.*, p. 237.   [161] *Ibid.*, pp. 239–40.

by heavenly grace. The tendency to fuse the two conceptions looks forward to their final synthesis in Milton's Christianization of the classical thirst for fame.

> *Fame* is the spur that the clear spirit doth raise
> (That last infirmity of Noble mind)
> To scorn delights, and live laborious dayes;
> But the fair Guerdon when we hope to find,
> And think to burst out into sudden blaze,
> Comes the blind *Fury* with th' abhorred shears,
> And slits the thin-spun life. But not the praise,
> Phoebus repli'd, and touch'd my trembling ears;
> *Fame* is no plant that grows on mortal soil,
> Nor in the glistering foil
> Set off to th' world, nor in broad rumour lies,
> But lives and spreds aloft by those pure eyes,
> And perfect witness of all judging *Jove;*
> As he pronounces lastly on each deed,
> Of so much fame in Heav'n expect thy meed.[162]

These lines are frequently quoted in connection with the *Faerie Queene,* and it is generally assumed that they express the same conception of fame as that symbolized by Gloriana.[163] This assumption seems to me only partly true. Milton's lines on fame mark the culmination, and indeed the abandonment, of that long struggle to reconcile pagan and Christian ideas of glory which so largely occupied the mind of the Renaissance. For to seek fame only in heaven is to echo the words of St. Augustine:

There shall be true glory, where no man shall be praised for error or flattery. True honour, which shall be denied unto none which is worthy, shall be given unto none unworthy. He himself shall be the reward of virtue which has given virtue.[164]

That Spenser agreed with Milton and Augustine in placing the highest glory in heaven goes without saying. He has

---

[162] *Lycidas,* ll. 70–84.   [163] For example, Bennett, *JEGP,* XXXI, 218.
[164] *De civ. Dei,* Lib. XXII, cap. xxx, C; Healey, Vol. II, p. 374.

said as much in the *Hymne of Heavenly Beautie*,[165] and in
the comparison between Cleopolis and the New Jerusalem
in the *Faerie Queene*. But the earthly fame that St. George
renounces is not the "golden foil" of the House of Pride,
nor the "glistering glory" of Philotime, still less the "broad
rumour" of Chaucer's Lady Fame, but a glory higher and
purer than these, the "fair Guerdon" of Gloriana, to be
renounced only after it has been won. This is the good fame
of virtuous men, founders and preservers of just empires,
expressed concretely in the honor and power they command
during their lives on earth, and prolonged ideally in the
memory of men by the enduring monuments of history and
epic poetry. This fame, unlike Milton's, is a "plant that
grows on mortal soil," albeit of heavenly seed.

For Spenser's Gloriana, as I have tried to show, is not the
supernal glory that illuminates the highest heaven, nor the
undying fame that dwells in the memory of God.[166] That
glory and that fame she indeed resembles, for she is made
in their image, and the man who seeks her may find them
through her, passing up the Platonic ladder from earthly to
heavenly things. Compared to the fleeting rewards of pleasure or ambition, the fame bestowed by the poets may well
seem eternal.[167] In the true light of eternity it is revealed as
mortal, subject to Time.

For the glory of this world, "fairest of all earthly things,"
is, like all earthly things, transitory. The kingdom of Gloriana is the land of illusion, the land of "faerie" in one of the
oldest senses of the word.[168] Spenser had many reasons, as we

[165] Especially *HHB*, ll. 260–81.
[166] Mrs. Bennett, *JEGP*, XXXI, 218, suggests this identification, arguing
that the muse of history is a symbol of the Divine Memory. But she fails
to take account of the distinction between Cleopolis and the New Jerusalem.
[167] As in the often quoted lines in *RT*, ll. 400–404. But cf. *FQ*, IV, II,
xxxii, 5–xxxiii, 9.
[168] Cf. Gower's reference to "this worldes faierie" at the head of this chapter. Strictly speaking, perhaps, the transitory is not necessarily the illusory.

shall see presently, for laying his action in Fairyland, and for celebrating Elizabeth as Fairy Queen. But perhaps not the least is to be found in the feeling, which he shared with some of his greatest contemporaries,[169] that the glory of this world, so glittering, so desirable, so praiseworthy, was after all an insubstantial pageant, a mirage whose fragile beauty owed its being to the wand of the enchanter, to the airy dreams of the poets, and was doomed at last to vanish into air, into thin air. At least, we know that Spenser thought of these things. He returns again and again, with that note of musical melancholy which is so peculiarly his own, to the theme of the world's vanity.

Nothing is sure, that growes on earthly ground.[170]

And that faire flowre of beautie fades away,
As doth the lilly fresh before the sunny ray.[171]

All things decay in time, and to their end do draw.[172]

Which makes me loath this state of life so tickle,
And love of things so vaine to cast away;
Whose flowring pride, so fading and so fickle,
Short *Time* shall soon cut down with his consuming sickle.[173]

Yet there is a strong tendency to identify them, perhaps because they are contemplated with such similar emotions—regret, pity, resignation. The importance of this somewhat sentimental melancholy in Spenser's thought is a matter upon which readers will naturally differ. I personally feel that it goes pretty deep.

[169] A. Thaler in *SAB*, X, 199–200 agrees with Greenlaw, "Shakespeare's Pastorals," *SP*, XIII, 154, that Spenser and Shakespeare were alike in perceiving the "illusion ... the specious unreality of this world's seeming substance." Cf. also E. Thompson, *Sir Walter Ralegh*, pp. 72–73. "Every writer points out that Ralegh lived in an age greedy for power and money (as if any age were not greedy for these things.) What is seldom remembered is that he was marked apart by his habit of reminding himself that all this strife in which he and his fellows were engaged was *māyā*, illusion. The world was passing away and the fashion thereof. . . ."

[170] *FQ*, I, IX, xi, 5.   [171] *Ibid*., III, VI, xxxviii, 8–9.
[172] *Ibid*., xl, 9.   [173] *Ibid*., VII, VIII, i, 6–9.

Perhaps this note of gentle sadness, of pensive regret for the evanescent beauty and glory of this world, was in Keats's mind when he wrote of "faerie lands forlorn." Certainly it is one of the most romantic qualities of Spenser's great poem. The dreamlike atmosphere, the bright dissolving views, the soft sigh in the verse like the horns of Elfland faintly blowing—these are the qualities that have made Spenser "preëminently dear" to romantic critics. But romantic critics have generally failed to realize that these qualities bear an organic relation to the main thought of the *Faerie Queene*. They express all that is implied in the statement with which Spenser partly summarized his general intention, "In that Faery Queene, I meane glory."

II

GODS AND HEROES

Vogliono le più volte i Cieli, che le persone chiare vivano, & sien note al mondo avanti che vi scendano, mentre vi sono, & doppo morte. Là ove all'incontro i vili, & oscuri, appena si può dir che vivano quel poco spatio di tempo, che qui stanno, solamente à far ombra & numero. —RUSCELLI, prefatory note to Canto III of *Orlando furioso*, Venice (1572).

Thus maye ye se
That welshmen be
Of the blood imperiall
Of nature fre
Cosyns in degre
To the goddes immortall.
—KELTON, *A Commenda-
cion of Welshmen.*

More ample spirit, then hitherto was wount,
Here needes me, whiles the famous auncestries
Of my most dreaded Soveraigne I recount,
By which all earthly Princes she doth farre surmount.

Ne under Sunne, that shines so wide and faire,
Whence all that lives, does borrow life and light,
Lives ought, that to her linage may compaire,
Which though from earth it be derived right,
Yet doth it selfe stretch forth to heavens hight,
And all the world with wonder overspred.
—*Faerie Queene.*

WHEN Arthur and Guyon come to the House of
Alma, they are shown into a room sacred to memory,
full of "old records from auncient times deriv'd." As model
Renaissance gentlemen, "the famous Briton prince and
Faery knight" are naturally interested in history. Conse-
quently when Arthur finds a book called *Briton Moniments*
and Guyon another called *Antiquitie of Faerie lond,* into
which he looks "greedily," they burn "with fervent fire"

Their countries auncestry to understond,

and crave permission, which is readily given, "to read those
bookes," the contents of which are related in the tenth canto.
Guyon's book contains the fullest and most systematic
account in Spenser's poem of the name and nature of his
Fairyland. Its importance in the general scheme of the
poem is further indicated by the reference in the Proem
to Book II:

Right well I wote most mighty Soveraine,
    That all this famous antique history,
    Of some th' aboundance of an idle braine
    Will iudged be, and painted forgery,
    Rather then matter of iust memory,
    Sith none, that breatheth living aire, does know,
    Where is that happy land of Faery,
    Which I so much do vaunt, yet no where show,
But vouch antiquities, which no body can know.

But let that man with better sence advize,
    That of the world least part to us is red:
    And dayly how through hardy enterprize,
    Many great Regions are discovered,
    Which to late age were never mentioned.
    Who ever heard of th' Indian *Peru?*
    Or who in venturous vessell measured
    The *Amazons* huge river now found trew?
Or fruitfullest *Virginia* who did ever vew?

> Yet all these were, when no man did them know;
> Yet have from wisest ages hidden beene:
> And later times things more unknowne shall show.
> Why then should witlesse man so much misweene
> That nothing is, but that which he hath seene?
> What if within the Moones faire shining spheare?
> What if in every other starre unseene
> Of other worldes he happily should heare?
> He wonder would much more: yet such to some appeare.[1]

The application of these stanzas to the fairy chronicle in canto ten may perhaps be questioned. "*All* this famous antique history" may mean "all this famous story I am telling about Arthur's visit to Fairyland," and the "antiquities" vouched to support it may be the "antique rolles" mentioned in the Proem to Book I (ii, 4), which are not necessarily identical with the *Antiquitie of Faery lond* read by Guyon. The following stanzas, however, certainly contain a reference to the "Roll of Elfin Emperors."

> Of Faerie lond yet if he more inquire,
> By certaine signes here set in sundry place
> He may it find; ne let him then admire,
> But yield his sence to be too blunt and bace,
> That no'te without an hound fine footing trace.
> And thou, O fairest Princesse under sky,
> In this faire mirrhour maist behold thy face,
> And thine owne realmes in lond of Faery,
> And in this antique Image thy great auncestry.

> The which O pardon me thus to enfold
> In covert vele, and wrap in shadowes light,
> That feeble eyes your glory may behold,
> Which else could not endure those beames bright,
> But would be dazled with exceeding light.[2]

These lines certainly state that Elizabeth's ancestry is in some way concealed in the poem, as she herself is thinly

---

[1] *FQ*, II, Proem, i–iii.   [2] *Ibid.*, iv–v, 5.

veiled under the name of Gloriana, and her kingdom under the name of Fairyland. The "antique Image" mentioned in the foregoing lines cannot refer, therefore, to the praise of Elizabeth's ancestry in the Chronicle of British kings, or in the person of Arthur, for her descent from these worthies is in no sense veiled, since they are introduced under their own names as her ancestors. It seems natural to infer, therefore that Spenser intended in these lines to direct his readers' attention to the fairy chronicle, and to insure their reading it as veiled history, not as mere fancy.

Oddly enough, however, the majority of Spenser's modern critics have persisted in ignoring his hint. The new Variorum Edition of Spenser's *Works* records only one attempt to identify any of the Elfin Emperors (Warton's) and this is very incomplete.[3] Warton recognized Elficleos, Elferon, and Oberon as Henry VII, his son Arthur, and Henry VIII, and suggested that the story of Elfinell, who overcame the Gobbelines might refer either "to the fiction of the Guelfes and Gibbelines in Italy; or to another race of fairies, called Goblins, and commonly joined with Elfes." He suggested also that Elfinan, builder of Cleopolis, might be King Lud, who founded London, and tried to identify Panthea with Windsor castle, and the bridge of brass with London Bridge, qualifying these statements, however, with the remark, "But these images of the golden wall, the crystal tower, &c. seem to be all adopted from romance. At least, they all flow from a mind strongly tinctured with romantic ideas."[4] One of Warton's suggestions, however, deserves to be followed up. "As to Spenser's original and genealogy of the fairy nation, I am inclined to conjecture, that part of it was supplied by his own inexhaustible imagination, and part from some fabulous history."[5]

[3] *Op. cit.*, II, 334 *et sqq.*   [4] *Ibid.*, p. 335.
[5] *Ibid.*, p. 334.

Later critics have adopted Warton's identification of the Tudors with the last Elfin Emperors, but have generally ignored the earlier ones as creatures of pure fancy. Greenlaw explained their introduction into the chronicle as a device to bridge the gap between the British kings celebrated in Arthur's book, and the Tudors reflected in the closing lines of the Elfin Chronicle, without mentioning the Saxon and Norman usurpers.[6] This suggestion, however, fails to account for the specific features of the Elfin Chronicle, which deserves closer examination in view both of its important position in Book II and of Spenser's own hint that it contains a veiled account of Elizabeth's "great auncestry." This last goes back much farther than Brutus, with whom the British Chronicle begins. Medieval chroniclers and genealogists habitually traced the ancestry of their noble and royal patrons from Adam or from some Biblical worthy whose descent from Adam could readily be supplied from *Genesis*. For example, Godfrey of Viterbo traces the ancestry of the Frankish kings from Adam,[7] and Hardyng precedes his account of the Trojan conquest of Britain with a similar genealogy of Brutus.[8] This rhymed genealogy with its brief account of the great deeds associated with the early rulers of Troy bears a certain likeness to Spenser's "Roll of Elfin Emperors," and may well have been one of its models.[9] A few stanzas from Hardyng's genealogy will serve to illustrate the likeness:

> Matusale gatte Lameke, who Noe gatte,
> And Noe Iaphet, who gatte Cichym than,
> That Cipre gatte, after whom Cipres hatte,
> Cipre gatte Crete, that the ysle of Crete began

[6] *Ibid.*, p. 453.   [7] *Pantheon*, p. 649.
[8] *Chronicle*, chap. vii, pp. 31 *et sqq.*
[9] Not, however, its source. See below, pp. 76 *et sqq.* For Spenser's probable use of Hardyng see Harper, *Sources of British Chronicle History in Spenser's Faerie Queene, passim.*

A famous and a ryght notable man.
And Crete gatte a sonne hight Cely,
Who gatte Saturne a wyse man and a wittye.

Of whom came then Iubiter of Frigy,
Whiche is Turky, wherein Troyes citee
In honoure stode, and in great victorye;
And Iubiter gate Dardanus no lee
That of Frigy, in great felicitee,
So reyned kyng greatly magnifyed,
And as a god amonge theim glorifyed.

Of whom came so his sonne, Eritonus,
Who gatte a sonne that first Troye edifyed,
That Troilus hight, of whom came kyng Ilis,
That Ilyon made a paleys of great pryde.[10]

This tracing of royal genealogies from the earliest times was one of the habits which Renaissance historians inherited from the Middle Ages. In his *Illustrations de Gaule et Singularitez de Troye,* Jean Lemaire traces the ancestry of Charlemagne from Noah, and Arthur Kelton, one of the Welsh opponents of Polydore Vergil, attached to his *Chronycle with a Genealogie . . . Newly Compyled in Metre* (1547) a genealogical table showing the descent of Edward VI from Osiris, who is identified with the Biblical Mizraim, son of Ham.[11]

Besides these printed works there are a number of manuscript genealogies, some of which Spenser may have seen, which trace the descent of Elizabeth, or of her immediate ancestors, from the creation of the world.[12] In view of these

---

[10] *Chronicle,* pp. 32–33.
[11] For accounts of this work see R. H. Fletcher, *Arthurian Material in the Chronicles,* p. 262 and Millican, *Spenser and the Table Round,* pp. 31–32. I have not seen the work itself, but I have used a transcript of the genealogy from the British Museum copy, furnished by Mrs. Champneys.
[12] See Gatfield, *Guide to Printed Books and MSS relating to English and Foreign Heraldry and Genealogy,* pp. 75–77.

precedents, we should naturally expect Spenser to fulfil his promise of celebrating "the famous auncestries" of his royal mistress,[13] by tracing her descent, not simply from Brutus, but from Adam and Eve. And we find in fact that the Elfin Chronicle begins by describing the creation of Gloriana's first ancestor, "the author of all Elfin kind," who must surely stand for the first father of the human race.

> It told, how first *Prometheus* did create
> A man, of many partes from beasts derived,
> And then stole fire from heaven, to animate
> His worke, for which he was by *Iove* deprived
> Of life him selfe, and hart-strings of an Ægle rived.

> That man so made, he called *Elfe*, to weet
> Quick, the first authour of all Elfin kind:
> Who wandring through the world with wearie feet,
> Did in the gardins of *Adonis* find
> A goodly creature, whom he deemd in mind
> To be no earthly wight, but either Spright,
> Or Angell, th' authour of all woman kind;
> Therefore a *Fay* he her according hight,
> Of whom all *Faeryes* spring, and fetch their lignage right.[14]

If the Elfin Chronicle is veiled history, Elf and Fay must stand for Adam and Eve. The belief that some pagan myths were garbled versions of sacred history would justify Spenser's use of the Prometheus myth as a substitute for the Biblical story of Man's creation which formed the first chapter of human history.[15] As creator of Man, Prometheus stands for God. The composite nature of Man, sharing passion with the animals and intellect with the angels,[16] may be symbolized in the description of Elf, made from parts of

---

[13] *FQ*, II, X, i, 7–8.
[14] *Ibid.*, lxx, 5–lxxi, 9.
[15] Cf. Raleigh, "History of the World," *Works*, II, 165–84.
[16] This is part of the usual discussion of man as a microcosm. Cf. Higden, *Polychron.*, II, 183; Raleigh, *Works*, II, 58.

animals, and animated with heavenly fire.[17] The theft of the fire and consequent punishment of Prometheus, however, probably refers to the Fall. Prometheus would thus stand for God as creator and for Adam as rebel against God, and the heavenly fire would have the dual significance of the human soul and the forbidden knowledge of good and evil. This may seem like very bad allegory, but it is quite in line with Boccaccio's interpretation of this myth. He tells us that the creation of Man by Prometheus has two meanings. First it stands for the real creation of Adam, the Natural Man, "huomo perfetto circa tutti gli atti terreni." In this first interpretation of the myth, Prometheus stands for God and the fire for the rational soul. In the second, Prometheus is a learned man, who brought civilization to his fellows, and thus created "l'huomo civile." The fire here stands for knowledge.[18] Boccaccio does not connect the punishment of Prometheus with the Fall of Man, but Spenser might easily have done so. Both Boccaccio and Natalis Comes identify the heavenly fire with knowledge, and recall the fact that the theft of Prometheus was the cause of all the woes which subsequently afflicted mankind. Spenser makes the punishment of Prometheus include his death, a departure from classical tradition which is comprehensible if the sin of Prometheus is meant to symbolize the sin of Adam. This interpretation is strengthened by Spenser's treatment of Prometheus in the *Mutabilitie Cantos,* where he is mentioned with other Titans as a type of human pride and a rebel against the legitimate power of Jove.[19]

Whatever the exact significance of the death of Prometheus in the Elfin Chronicle may be, his creation, Elf, is

---

[17] Lotspeich, p. 103, points out that Spenser is probably following Natalis Comes, *Mythologiae,* Lib. IV, cap. vi. N.C.'s account explains the parts of beasts as symbolizing the qualities of beasts (courage, fear, etc.). *Op. cit.,* p. 311.

[18] *Gen. de gli dei,* pp. 76 et sqq.   [19] *FQ,* VII, VI, xxix.

surely Adam, or Man in his original excellence, the paragon
of animals, in apprehension like a god. His "wandring
through the world with wearie feet" may symbolize the loneliness of man before the creation of woman, for in all probability Spenser, like Calvin[20] and Milton, reckoned the
pleasures of married love among the joys of Eden. This
seems to be the meaning of Elf's finding Fay in the Garden
of Adonis.[21] In this lover's paradise, the first man finds the
first woman, who is so beautiful that he anachronistically
names her "Fay," after the beautiful supernatural beings of
later folklore and romance. Possibly Spenser intended to
suggest an etymological connection between "fay" or "fairy"
and "fair."

In Spenser's account of Elf and Fay, then, we may recognize a reflection of that discussion of the creation and nature
of Man which formed the first chapter of the universal
histories current in his day. There are other indications
that Spenser intended to represent such a history in his
Antiquitie of Faerie lond. It was a much longer book than
the British History "from Brute to Uther's rayne," which
is summarized in the greater part of the canto. When Arthur
had finished *Briton Moniments,* Guyon was still reading.

> But *Guyon* all this while his booke did read,
> Ne yet has ended: for it was a great
> And ample volume, that doth far excead
> My leasure, so long leaves here to repeat.[22]

Spenser accordingly gives a brief summary of the contents
of this voluminous work, beginning, as we have seen, with
a veiled account of the Creation of Man, and following that

[20] *Commentary on I Cor.* 7:1. Pringle's translation, I, 223–24.
[21] For discussions of the Garden of Adonis, see *Variorum Spenser,* III,
340–52.
[22] *FQ,* II, X, lxx, 1–4.

with an account of the Elfin Emperors, descendants of Elf and Fay.

> Of these a mighty people shortly grew,
> And puissaunt kings, which all the world warrayd,
> And to themselves all nations did subdew:[23]

The capital of this empire was Cleopolis, which we recognized in the preceding chapter as a humanistic modification of St. Augustine's Earthly City, standing midway between the wicked Babylon and the most glorious City of God. Obviously the history of the world might be written from the point of view of any one of these three cities. I suggest that the *Antiquitie of Faerie lond,* which is summarized in the "Roll of Elfin Emperors," was a "speculum" of world history told from the point of view of Cleopolis, the city of justice and earthly fame. Since the early rulers of this city were ancestors of Gloriana, and since they established their empire "shortly" after the Creation, we should expect to find their originals among the ancestors of Elizabeth who were celebrated in the history of the Ancient World.

Now ancient history in Spenser's day was still largely a combination of Biblical tradition and euhemerized classical mythology. Into the scriptural framework of the five ages of the world preceding the Incarnation, Christian writers following Eusebius and St. Augustine had fitted the early traditions of pagan antiquity as recorded by Herodotus, Diodorus, and others. This method of writing history, by which the deities of Greece and Egypt and the heroes of classical epic appear as contemporaries of the Biblical patriarchs, judges, and kings, was inherited by the Middle Ages, and continued into the Renaissance, whose increased knowledge of the history and literature of classical Greece and

[23] *Ibid.,* lxxii, 1–3.

Rome was not paralleled by a more accurate understanding of remoter antiquity. Hence there is no essential difference in method and arrangement between the early sections of medieval works like the *Flores historiarum*[24] or Higden's *Polychronicon* and Raleigh's *History of the World.*

All three works adopt St. Augustine's division of history into six ages: the first from Adam to Noah, the second from Noah to Abraham, the third from Abraham to David, the fourth from David to the Captivity, the fifth from the Captivity to the Incarnation, and the sixth from the Incarnation to the Day of Judgment.[25] Of the first age secular history preserved only scanty and uncertain traditions. Pagan civilization began with Cain, builder of the first earthly city, but pagan historians were generally ignorant of this fact.[26] The second age, which closed with the choosing of Abraham as spiritual father of the Church, saw also the foundation of the Egyptian and Babylonian Empires by Ham and his son Nimrod. Abraham himself was born in the reign of Ninus,[27] legendary founder of Nineveh, whose wars with Zoroaster were well known to Spenser's old man "of infinite remembrance."[28] Inachus, first king of Argos, the father of Io or Isis, who civilized the Egyptians, was by Eusebius and the medieval historians who followed him said to be a contemporary of Jacob and Esau,[29] but later writers,[30] following Herodotus and Diodorus in allowing the Egyptian claim to a very early civilization, placed Isis and Osiris in the second age of the world. Raleigh, for instance, thought it probable that Osiris began his reign the year of Abraham's birth, and

[24] Formerly attributed to Matthew of Westminster.
[25] Based on the genealogy of Christ in *Matthew* 1: 2–17.
[26] Pagan history generally began with Ninus. Cf. Higden, II, 246: "Ab Adam usque ad Abraham nulla penitus Graeca nec barbara invenitur historia. *Methodius*."
[27] Eusebius, *Chron. can.*, p. 2.   [28] *FQ*, II, IX, lvi, 8.
[29] Eusebius, *op. cit.*, p. 15.
[30] Notably Annius Viterbiensis. See below, p. 88 *et sqq*.

that Orus, last of the gods, was the Pharaoh under whom Joseph rose to power.[31] The mythical golden age of Egypt thus furnished a striking parallel with the patriarchal period of Hebrew history, and the foundation of the first good empire among the Gentiles coincided almost exactly with the foundation of the Church. This parallel, unmentioned by St. Augustine,[32] for whom all pagan civilization was evil, may well have been important to Spenser, as we shall see later.

The third age, extending from Abraham to David, was subdivided by the all-important figure of Moses. Parallel with his institution of the Law was the beginning of European civilization in the foundation of the Arcadian kingship by Pelasgus,[33] and of Dardania (later Troy) by Dardanus,[34] progenitor of the Roman kings and emperors. Troy fell in the time of Jephthah, and three years later Aeneas arrived in Italy.[35] The subsequent foundation of the Latin kingdom was paralleled by the beginning of the Hebrew monarchy under Saul and David, whose reigns generally close the third age of the world.[36] At about the same time according to "Matthew of Westminster," Brutus inaugurated the Trojan line of kings in England.[37]

In legendary history of this type Spenser must have found the materials for his fairy chronicle, which sets forth under "covert veil" the history of Cleopolis, the glorious city of earthly fame, standing, as we saw in the previous chapter, midway between the earthly Babylon and the most glorious City of God.[38] The parallel records of these last two cities

[31] "History of the World," *Works*, III, 44, 46.
[32] Raleigh attributes Augustine's failure to mention the early kings of Egypt to the uncertainty of their chronology. *Works*, III, 37.
[33] *Ibid.*, p. 187.   [34] *Ibid.*, p. 199; Eusebius, p. 32.
[35] Raleigh, *Works*, IV, 440.
[36] Sometimes the next age begins with the building of the Temple.
[37] *Flores historiarum* (tr. C. D. Yonge), I, 32.
[38] See chart on p. 77, below.

in their earthly manifestations, had been written by St.
Augustine, for whom their double story constituted the final
meaning of all history. But history bore witness also to the
existence of a third ideal city, manifested on earth in the
record of the good empires which at least since the Flood
had always existed as foils to the wicked Babylon, and
images of the City of God. The Egyptian Empire of the just
Osiris, ruling all the world except for the Babylonian kingdom, the Trojan realm from which came the pious Aeneas,
the British kingdom founded by Brutus, whose descent from
Dardanus and Aeneas made him a worthy progenitor of the
mighty Arthur—these kingdoms, as we have seen, were contemporary in foundation and parallel in development with
the Jewish state, prototype of the Christian Church, and
could hardly have been regarded as evil by a poet for whom
Church and State were united under a single head, whose
ancestry he celebrates in his fairy genealogy.

The historical basis of this genealogy must be sought in
legendary ancient history of the type we have been considering. The founder of the Elfin race, we have seen, was Adam.
From Adam to Noah the line of descent for all humanity
was fixed by Scripture. From Dardanus on there was likewise a fixed tradition based on Virgil, Ovid, and Geoffrey
of Monmouth. For the intervening period there was a conflict of authorities, out of which emerge two main traditions, one emphasizing the Cretan, the other the Egyptian
descent of the Trojan line. According to the first of these
traditions, Dardanus is the son of Electra, daughter of
Atlas, and of the Cretan Jupiter, son of Saturn, whose descent may be traced either from Japhet or from Nimrod.
According to the second, Dardanus is a descendant of the
Egyptian Jupiter, Osiris, who is identified with Mizraim,
son of Ham. In tracing the ancestry of Elizabeth from Noah
to Dardanus, therefore, Spenser must have followed one or

GENEALOGY OF THE ELFIN EMPERORS[a]

AGES OF THE WORLD	HEAVENLY CITY	EARTHLY CITY	
	JERUSALEM CITY OF GOD	CLEOPOLIS CITY OF FAME	BABYLON CITY OF PRIDE
I Adam to Noah	Adam and Eve (Elf and Fay)		
	Abel Seth		Cain
	Noah		
II Noah to Abraham	Shem	Japhet	Ham
			Cush
			Nimrod
	Abraham	Osiris (Elfin)	Ninus
III Abraham to David		Hercules (Elfinan)	
		Tuscus	
		Atlas	
		Electra=Jupiter	
	Moses	Dardanus	Ascatades
		Erichthonius	
		Tros (Elfiline)	
		Assaracus (Elfinell)	
		Capys	
		Anchises	
		Aeneas (Elfant)	
		Postumus (Elfar?)	
	David	Brutus (Elfinor)	Alban kings
Tudor Period	Church of England	Henry VII (Elficleos)	The Papacy
		Henry VIII (Oberon)	
		Elizabeth (Tanaquil)	

a This chart shows the parallel development of the three cities during the first three ages of the world and the Tudor period in the sixth age. The names of the Elfin emperors are in parentheses next to those of their historical counterparts in the third column. Evidence for these identifications is discussed in the following pages.

the other of these two traditions, both of which were represented in historical writings which he must have known.

The older Cretan genealogy is most common in the form which derives Saturn and Jupiter from Japhet. This line of descent is probably referred to by Shakespeare's Prince Hal, when he says of those who boast of their royal blood,

> Nay, they will be kin to us, or they will fetch it from Japhet.[39]

The same genealogical tradition is found in Hardyng's *Chronicle*,[40] and Warner's *Albion's England*.[41] Hardyng gives the genealogy of Saturn in some detail; Warner simply states that Saturn was a descendant of Japhet, and goes on to relate the mythical quarrels between Saturn and his son Jupiter. Apparently following Caxton's *Troy Book*,[42] Warner also gives considerable space to the labors of Hercules, who comes into the genealogy of the British kings through his illicit love affair with the wife of King Faunus. According to this story, mentioned also by Higden,[43] Hercules on his way home from Spain stops in Italy to kill Cacus, and is secretly loved by the Latin queen, by whom he becomes the father of Latinus, whose daughter Aeneas marries. From this union spring the Roman and British kings. Brutus is thus doubly descended from the greatest of the Greek gods, through Dardanus and Hercules, both famous sons of the Cretan Jupiter.

The Cretan ancestry of Dardanus is also apparently accepted by Dante[44] and Higden,[45] and certainly by Godfrey of Viterbo, a twelfth century writer, whose universal history, the *Pantheon*, was printed in the sixteenth century.[46] God-

---

[39] *II Henry IV*, II, ii, 127-28.   [40] See above, p. 68.
[41] Bk I, chap. i.   [42] *Recuyell of the Historyes of Troy*, I, 241 *et sqq.*
[43] *Polychron.*, II, 356.
[44] *Inferno*, XIV, 95-105. Cf. *Convivio*, IV, xiv, 14-15, *De mon.*, II, iii.
[45] *Op. cit.*, II, 248.   [46] At Basle in 1559.

frey, however, derives the father of Dardanus not from
Japhet but from Nimrod,[47] perhaps from a desire to connect
the wicked but famous Jupiter, father of Greek and Trojan
kings, with the earliest type of kingly pride and power,
"that first the world with sword and fire warrayd."[48] As
builder of the Tower of Babel, Nimrod was generally regarded as founder of Babylon. In making him the direct
ancestor of the Trojan and Roman kings, therefore, Godfrey
was furnishing a genealogical basis for the spiritual kinship
between Babylon and Rome already stressed by St. Augustine. What Spenser needed was a similar connection between the rulers of the good empires which successively
represented the ideal city of earthly fame symbolized by his
fairy kingdom. For this purpose the Cretan genealogy as
given in the *Pantheon* was clearly useless, since it made
Troy the successor of wicked Babylon. The other form of
the Cretan genealogy was more complimentary to the Trojan kings, but it furnished no great ruler before Saturn as a
foil to Nimrod, and it contained the thoroughly unsavory
character of the Cretan Jupiter, whose unfilial conduct and
scandalous love affairs were generally censured by Christian
writers.[49] It is not surprising, therefore, to find that the
Cretan genealogy contains no one corresponding to Spenser's Elfin, "first and greatest" of the Elfin Emperors, who
ruled over India and America. We may find him, however,
in the second tradition, which traces the ancestry of Dardanus from Ham through Osiris, Jupiter of the Egyptians,
who first extended the benefits of civilization to India, and
whose empire divided the world with the Babylonian.

The genealogy in which Osiris appears as ancestor of
Dardanus derives from the spurious chronicle of "Berosus
the Chaldean," published at the end of the fifteenth century

[47] *Pantheon*, p. 649.   [48] *FQ*, I, V, xlviii, 2.
[49] Cf. Raleigh, *Works*, II, 172, and Higden, II, 342.

by its putative discoverer, the learned Annius Viterbiensis. Annius, whose real name was Giovanni Nanni, was a Dominican monk whose learning and eloquence won him favor at the papal court under Sixtus IV and Alexander VI. His reputation was increased by his fortunate discovery of supposedly ancient writings by Berosus, Manetho, Metasthenes, Archilochus, Fabius Pictor, and others, which he published with a commentary at Rome, in 1498, under the title *Commentaria super opera diversorum auctorum de antiquitatibus loquentium.*[50] Of this work under varying titles there were numerous editions, some with, some without the commentary, between 1497 and 1612.[51] There were two Italian translations in the sixteenth century, one by Lauro, the other by Sansovino.[52] There does not seem to have been any French translation, but several editions of the original Latin were published in Paris,[53] and the substance of the Annian Berosus and Manetho in so far as they dealt with the Trojan genealogy and with the early history of Europe was available to readers of French in Jean Lemaire's *Illustrations de Gaule et singularitez de Troye,* the last sixteenth-century edition of which was published in 1549.[54]

That Spenser was acquainted with the work of Annius we know from the reference to Berosus in the *View.* Ire-

[50] So Brunet, I, 299. The account of Annius in the *Enciclopedia italiana* cites an earlier edition without commentary at Venice, 1489.

[51] Brunet, *loc. cit.*

[52] P. Lauro's translation of Berosus and Dictys Cretensis was published in 1543, his translation of Berosus with the other Annian authors and the commentary at Venice, 1550. *B.M.Cat.* F. Sansovino's translation, Venice, 1583, includes all the Annian authors. The commentary, however, is not by Annius.

[53] In 1509, 1510, 1511, 1512, 1515. Also Lyons, 1544, 1560. *B.M. Cat.*

[54] There was no English translation during Spenser's lifetime, but in 1601 appeared *An Historical Treatise of the Travels of Noah into Europe . . . Done into English [out of Berosus,* etc.], by R. Lynche.

naeus is defending his account of Irish origins, and inciden-
tally explaining his method of historical research. It is true,
he says, that he has followed the Irish chronicles:

> But unto them besydes, I add my owne readinge and out of
> them both togeather with comparison of tymes, lykenes of man-
> ners and customes, affinitie of wordes, & names, properties of
> Natures and uses resemblances of rightes and ceremonies monu-
> mentes of Churches and Tombes, and manye other lyke Cir-
> cumstances I doe gather a likeliehoode of truth not certenlie
> affirminge anythinge but by conferringe of tymes, languages
> monumentes and suchlike, I doe hunte out a probabillities of
> thinges which I leave unto your iudgment to beleave or refuise,
> Neverthelesse there bee some verie aunciente Authors, which
> make mencion of those thinges, and some moderne, which by
> comparinge of them with the presente tymes experience and there
> owne reason, doe open a windowe of great light unto the rest
> that is yett unseene, as namelie of the oulder: *Cesar Strabo Taci-
> tus Ptolomie Plinnie,* [Solinus] *Pompeus Mela & Berosus. . . .*[55]

The account of Irish origins in the *View* apparently owes
nothing to "Berosus," who, indeed, never mentions Ireland
at all.[56] Spenser's reference to the "comparison of tymes"
suggests the possibility that he approved the chronology of
Annius, which differed in certain respects from that of
Eusebius.[57] At any rate, Spenser obviously considered Berosus an important ancient writer whose authority would lend
weight to any historical treatise.

Nor can we doubt that Spenser is referring, not to the
genuine fragments of Berosus which have come down to us,

---

[55] Renwick's ed., pp. 51–52.
[56] Renwick suggests that the historical material in the *View* has been
abridged. *Ibid.,* p. 264. The proposed *Antiquities of Ireland* might have used
Berosus for the Scythian and Spanish background of Irish history, as Holinshed uses him for the background of early British history. See next page
et sqq.
[57] Cf. Raleigh, quoted below, p. 84.

but to the writings published by Annius, which are constantly cited by sixteenth-century historians.[58] I have already mentioned Jean Lemaire's large debt to "Berosus" and "Manetho." Jean Bouchet makes a more cautious use of Annius in the *Annales d'Aquitaine*,[59] and Charles Estienne cites Berosus and other Annian authors frequently in his *Dictionarium historicum*. Another work of reference, Bodin's *Methodus ad facilem historiarum cognitionem* lists Berosus second only to Moses among the authorities on universal history,[60] and cites the other Annian authors in their appropriate sections. Harrison draws largely on the Annian Berosus in the *Description of Britain*,[61] and Caius confutes the Oxonians who denied that England was settled by civilized people before the coming of Brutus by appealing to the authority of Berosus, "antiquae memoriae scriptor," and his commentator, Annius Viterbiensis.[62] The great reputation of Annius in the sixteenth and seventeenth centuries is well summed up by Tiraboschi in the eighteenth:

> Non v'ha forse Autore. che più spesso e con maggior venerazione si vegga citato singolarmente dagli Storici de' due secoli precedenti; e non v'ha insieme Autore, che dalla moderna Critica sia più disprezzato a deriso; ne manca ancora, chi lo ha in conto di solenne impostore.[63]

The last phrase might refer equally well to the sixteenth and seventeenth centuries, for, in spite of their popularity, the authenticity of the Annian documents was early questioned, and authors who cited Berosus sometimes found it necessary to warn their readers that his authority was ques-

---

[58] Renwick's note, *View*, p. 266, fails to make this clear. "Berosus," unqualified, in the sixteenth century always implies "Annius."
[59] Pp. ai verso, aiiii recto. Also *Genealogies des roys de France*, p. cii verso.
[60] Page 332.
[61] Holinshed, I, pp. ix, 6–8, 15, 297.
[62] *De antiquitate Cantabrigiensis Academiae*, p. 14.
[63] *Storia della letteratura italiana*, VI, Pt. 2, 16.

tioned by the learned. Holinshed, for instance, after taking from Berosus the account of Celtic kings preceding Brutus, admits that their existence rests on conjecture, which he has been content to relate

. . . till time that some sufficient learned man shall take upon him to decipher the doubts of all these matters. Neverthelesse, I think good to advertise the reader that these stories of Samothes, Magus, Sarron, Druis, and Bardus, doo relie onelie upon the authoritie of Berosus, whom most diligent antiquaries doo reiect as a fabulous and counterfet author, and Vacerius [sic] hath laboured to proove the same by a speciall treatise late-lie published at Rome.[64]

Camden is more emphatic:

Neither let any man marvell, wherefore I call not Berosus heere to take my part, out of whom writers in these daies furnish themselves with so great meanes. Certes, to speake my mind at once, the edge of that Berosus his authoritie, who commonly goeth under that name, is in my account so blunt and dull, that I together with the best learned of our age, [as namely Volater-ran, Vives, Antonius Augustinus, Melchior Canus,] and espe-cially Gaspar Varrerius, think it to be nothing else, but a ridiculous figment of some craftie foister and jugling deceiver; which Varrerius in his Censure of Berosus Printed at Rome, is soone able to remoove out of the Readers mindes that errour of theires so deepely setled, concerning this writer.[65]

Raleigh, who often testifies to the respect of his contem-poraries for "that Berosus, which wandereth up and down in these days, set out by Annius," is himself convinced that the work is not genuine, "seeing so many learned men have

[64] Chronicles, I, 436.

[65] Britannia (Holland's translation), p. 10. The words in brackets do not appear in the Latin edition of 1590. The Censure of Berosus mentioned by Harrison and Camden is the Censura in quendam auctorem qui sub falsa inscriptione Berosi Chaldaei circumfertur by Gaspar Varrerius. This is a Latin translation of a Portuguese work by the same author. The dedicatory letter is dated Rome, 1563. The Latin text will be found in La Bigne, Bib-liotheca maxima veterum patrum, II, 529–44.

so demonstratively proved that fragment to be counter-feit."[66] He laments the confusion of Egyptian chronology, which he attributes to the exaggeration of the Egyptian priests, the credulity of Greek historians, and the work of Annius:

A third and general cause of more than Egyptian darkness in all ancient histories is the edition of many authors by John Annius, of whom (if to the censures of sundry very learned I may add mine) I think thus; that Annius having seen some frag-ments of those writers, and added unto them what he would, may be credited as an avoucher of true histories, where approved writers confirm him, but otherwise to be deemed fabulous. Here-upon it cometh to pass, that the account of authors, either in the chronology or genealogy of the Egyptian kings, runs three altogether different ways. The Christian writers, such as are an-cient, for the most part follow Eusebius; many late writers fol-low the edition of Annius's authors; the profane histories follow Herodotus, Diodorus, and such others.[67]

Nevertheless Raleigh does not reject Annius altogether. In another passage he censures Joseph Scaliger's denial of any value to certain historians who make use of "Annius's au-thors."

For mine own part, howsoever I believe nothing that Annius's Berosus, Metasthenes, and others of that stamp affirm, in respect of their bare authority; yet am I not so squeamish, but that I can well enough digest a good book, though I find the names of one or two of these good fellows alleged in it: I have (somewhat per-adventure too often) already spoken my mind of Annius's au-thors; nevertheless, I may say here again, that where other histories are silent, or speak not enough, there may we without shame borrow of these, as much as agrees with that little which elsewhere we find, and serveth to explain or enlarge it without improbabilities.[68]

It is evident from the foregoing discussion that the An-

[66] *Works*, II, 268.   [67] *Ibid.*, III, 38.   [68] *Ibid.*, IV, 676.

nian Berosus occupied among historians in Spenser's day a position somewhat similar to that of the British history of Geoffrey of Monmouth. Scholarly critics might reject it, and conservative chroniclers regard its authenticity as an open question, but no historian could ignore it, and defenders were not lacking. The resulting "battle of books," like that over the authenticity of Geoffrey's history,[69] was largely a conflict between scholarship and patriotism. But while the Trojan descent of Welsh kings and the size of Arthur's empire were of importance principally to natives of the British Isles, the history of Berosus was flattering to the local pride of all the principal European nations. Italians were eager to accept a work which asserted the antiquity of their civilization as against the claims of Greece, and which ascribed the foundation of many of their cities to Noah, Osiris, and Hercules.[70] A similar interest in the local antiquities of France and Spain, though it aroused the doubts of Varrerius,[71] could not but recommend the work of Annius to patriotic historians like Jean Lemaire. The belief that Britain had been anciently joined to the Celtic mainland made it possible for Harrison to gain from Berosus the assurance that England had enjoyed a high civilization and the religion of Noah a short time after the Flood.[72] And Arthur Kelton, the patriotic Welshman, could confute Polydore Vergil out of Berosus as well as Geoffrey by tracing the genealogy of Edward VI, not only from Brutus and Arthur, but also from "gods immortal" beginning with Osiris.

The second genealogical tradition, which traces the ancestry of the Trojan, and hence of the British kings, from

[69] For an account of this discussion in relation to Spenser see Greenlaw, *Studies in Spenser's Historical Allegory*, chap. I, and Millican, *Spenser and the Table Round, passim*.

[70] Tiraboschi, VI, Pt. 2, 16. [71] La Bigne, II, 540 C.
[72] Holinshed, I, 33 *et sqq*.

Osiris, founder of the first good empire among the Gentiles, was thus available to Spenser's readers in the Latin and Italian versions of the Annian Berosus, in the French of Jean Lemaire, and in the English of Arthur Kelton. To the more learned and courtly of his readers, it must certainly have been as familiar as the Cretan genealogy of the earlier tradition, which as we have seen, was far less adapted to express the patriotic imperialism which lies at the root of Spenser's political allegory. For these reasons there is a strong antecedent probability that Spenser's *Antiquitie of Faerie lond,* like Jean Lemaire's *Illustrations de Gaule* and Arthur Kelton's *Chronycle with a Genealogie,* follows the genealogical tradition sponsored by the *Defloratio* of "Berosus the Chaldean." This antecedent probability is greatly strengthened when we compare Spenser's account of the first Elfin emperors with that of the ancestors of Dardanus in "Berosus."

The *Defloratio* is divided into five books, of which the first four purport to summarize the traditions of the Chaldeans and Scythians about the times before the Flood and the genealogies of the earliest rulers of the world beginning with Noah. The fifth and longest book epitomizes the history of the world from the time of Nimrod, first king of Babylon, to Ascatades, the Assyrian ruler who was contemporary with Dardanus. The chronicle of Berosus, therefore, deals with just the period of Ancient History for which records were particularly scanty, namely, the period between the Flood and the foundation of Troy. After describing the evil life of the giants who ruled the world from their capital city of Enos, where Noah lived before the Flood, the chronicler relates how Noah, a pious giant, was enabled to predict the coming of the Flood through his skill in astrological calculation, and with his wife Tytea, his three sons, Shem, Cham, and Japhet, and their wives, Pandora, Noela, and Noegla was preserved in the ark. After landing in Armenia, where a piece of the ark still remains, Noah and his sons set about the repopulation of the world, a task which was facilitated by the fact that all their children were twins. Noah also introduced the cultivation of the vine, which occasioned the misfortune described in Scripture.[73] In the version of Berosus, however, the unfilial conduct of Cham was motivated by his jealousy of the sons of Noah born after the Flood, and consisted in the laying of a spell upon Noah, which prevented him from having any more children. Cham, as inventor of magic, is also identified by Berosus with Zoroaster, and Noah has the surnames Ogyges, Uranus, Janus, Seed of the World, and Father of the Gods. His wife Tytea, also deified after her death, was called Cybele, Vesta, Terra, and Aretia. These two ruled as universal emperor and empress during the Golden Age.

Noah divided the earth among his progeny, and established them in tributary kingdoms. First of these was the Babylonian Empire, ruled by Nimrod the giant, who with his son Belus began the Tower of Babel. Next came four kingdoms in Europe, the heritage of Japhet. Tuscany was the domain of his son Comerus Gallus; Spain was allotted to Tubal, Gaul (and according to Harrison, Britain as well) to Dis or Samothes, fourth son of Japhet; and the rule of Germany was seized by Tuyson the giant, a son of Noah born after the Flood.

Under these rulers Europe progressed rapidly in civilization until the peace was disturbed by Cham, the universal enemy of God and man, the very type of tyranny and usurpation. Not content with his own heritage of Africa, Cham invaded Italy, and set up a kingdom into which he introduced all the unnatural crimes which had flourished before the Flood. Noah and his wife therefore left Armenia, drove

---

[73] *Gen.* 9:20-27.

Cham into Sicily, and themselves ruled over Italy, where
they were later joined by Saturn, whose peaceful regency in
Armenia had been disturbed by the warlike propensities of
Ninus and Belus, whose imperialistic wars are said to constitute the first break in the Golden Age.

Cham was joined in Sicily by his sister Rhea, who had left
her husband, Hammon, king of Libya, in a fit of jealousy
at discovering that he was secretly rearing an illegitimate
son, Dionysus, in the isle of Nysa. With the aid of their
brothers, the seventeen Titans who were born to Noah after
the Flood, Cham and Rhea drove Hammon from the throne
of Libya, from which they were themselves deposed by
Dionysus, who however, adopted their son, Osiris, and gave
him the surnames Jupiter and Hammon, in memory of his
own father. Cham and Rhea meanwhile returned to Egypt,
where they had a daughter, Isis, the most virtuous and beautiful lady in the world, who later married Osiris. After their
parents' death, this noble pair ascended the throne of Egypt,
and later extended their empire over the whole world, with
the exception of the Babylonian kingdom, thus succeeding
to the greater part of the domain of their grandfather Noah,
whose life had been prolonged by divine dispensation until
the very year of their coronation.

Osiris, who is identified with Bacchus and Libyan Jove,
was the very type of a just emperor. After ruling over Egypt
for a number of years, he set out with his son Hercules and
a great army of his famous descendants and followers to
conquer the world, over which he spread the benefits of civilization. He was the first to triumph over India. After
spreading civilization in the East, he went through the continent of Europe, driving out giants and tyrants, and establishing just laws. After his triumphal return to Egypt,
however, these tyrants formed a conspiracy headed by his
brother Typhon, inheritor of the sins of Cham, and man-

aged to kill Osiris, whose death was avenged by Hercules and Isis in a great victory over the giants in Arabia.

Hercules then declared war on the giants in Europe, most of whom were sons of his brother Neptune, and went through the West destroying tyranny and establishing justice as his father had done.[74] It was at this time that he overcame the three Geriones in Spain. On his way back to Italy he married Galatea, daughter of Celte, king of Gaul, and became the father of Galateus. Hercules himself founded a city, Alexia, in Gaul, and ruled that country as part of his vast dominions, having the chief seat of his government in Aquitaine. By another lady, Araxa the Younger, who was half woman and half serpent ("like Melusine la Faee," remarks Jean Lemaire in his adaptation of this passage)[75] Hercules had a son Tuscus, who became king of Italy, and progenitor of Dardanus, founder of the Trojan line. Athos, son of Hercules and Omphale, was established on the throne of Phrygia. After dividing his kingdom between these three sons, Hercules himself ended his days in Spain, and is buried under the pillars that bear his name. This was the Libyan Hercules, not to be confused with the son of Alcmena, a mere sea robber falsely praised by the Greek poets. After a time the line of Hercules became extinct in Gaul, and Jupiter Camboblascom, a descendant of Tuscus, was called to the two thrones of Gaul and Italy. He was the father of Dardanus, who killed his elder brother, Jasius Janigena, in the baths of Viterbo, and was forced to flee the country. Landing in Phrygia, he made a bargain with Tyrrenus, a descendant of Athos, by which the latter was to succeed to the throne of Italy, while Dardanus was to be allowed to found a kingdom in the Troad. He established his capital at Dardania, later changed to Troy by Tros.

[74] The death of Albion, tyrant of Britain, is made part of this war by Holinshed, I, 432–33.
[75] "Illustrations de Gaule," Œuvres, I, 74.

Such in outline is the history of "Berosus."[76] In its general method it resembles the medieval accounts of antiquity which must indeed have been among its sources. It exhibits the same tendency to identify the characters of classical mythology with the personages of Biblical story, and the same concern with moral edification. In fact this moral purpose may have been responsible for some of the principal differences between the two traditions. The characters in Berosus are more sharply divided into types of good and evil. Although the Trojans are made to descend from the accursed Cham instead of the blessed Japhet, the Egyptian Jove, Osiris, is a more uniformly admirable character than the Cretan Jove of Greek mythology, whose quarrels with his father and his wife are far from edifying. The Libyan Hercules is as truly the first Worthy as the son of Alcmena, and his connection with the Latin kings is relieved of the stigma of adultery. The "forged Berosus" as Milton calls him,[77] reflects the humanistic desire to see the founders of pagan civilization as benefactors of mankind, while the historians of the older tradition were still influenced by the denigration of pagan history accomplished by Orosius and St. Augustine.

As Raleigh recognized,[78] Annius got most of his information about Osiris and Hercules from Diodorus Siculus, who like Augustine had aspired to write the history of the world "as though it were the history of one city." To Diodorus, historians were the servants of Divine Providence:

For as Providence having marshalled the stars (visible to us) in a most beautiful frame and order, and likewise conjoined the natures of men in a common analogy and likeness one to another, incessantly wheels about every age, as in a circle, impart-

[76] The *Defloratio* occupies pp. 35–209 of the edition of "Annius's authors" printed at Antwerp, 1552. (Cited hereafter as "Berosus.")
[77] "History of England," *Prose Works*, V, 166.   [78] *Works*, II, 229.

ing to each what is before by fate shared out and allotted for them; so these historians, by committing to writing the common actions of men through the whole world, as if they were the affairs only of one city, represent their labours as one entire account, and common repertory and treasury of human transactions.[79]

The history of Diodorus was a product of the internationalism fostered by the Roman Empire. His aim was to tell the story of the great empires of the world, beginning with the Egyptian, and culminating in the greatest of all, the Roman. Thus he declares that Caesar was greater than Bacchus or Hercules, since he had conquered Britain, a land to which no god or hero had ever penetrated.[80] Similarly in the sixth book of the *Aeneid,* Anchises prophesies that the empire of his descendants shall extend beyond the lands traversed by Hercules or those conquered by Bacchus:

> nec vero Alcides tantum telluris obivit,
> fixerit aeripedem cervam licet, aut Erymanthi
> pacarit nemora, et Lernam tremefecerit arcu;
> nec qui pampineis victor iuga flectit habenis
> Liber, agens celso Nysae de vertice tigris.[81]

Both these passages celebrate the Roman Empire as last and greatest of history, and extol Caesar as the greatest ruler of that "one city" of earthly fame which appeared to St. Augustine as the spiritual Babylon and to Spenser under the opposed aspects of Lucifera's House of Pride and Gloriana's Cleopolis. The two pagan writers make no such clear distinction between the two sides of the earthly city, but their emphasis is clearly on the good side, on the city of justice and eternal fame, rather than on the city of pride and transitory power. This is clear from the passages cited above

[79] *Historical Library,* Preface, Booth's translation, Vol. I, pp. vii–viii.
[80] *Ibid.,* v. ii; Booth, I, 310.   [81] *Aen.* vi. 801–5.

in which Caesar is coupled with Bacchus and Hercules, both famous not only as conquerors but as civilizing heroes, champions of justice and earliest exemplars of the imperial ideal.[82] This ideal, we have suggested, finds expression in the history of Spenser's Elfin Empire. We might therefore expect to find Bacchus and Hercules among the Elfin emperors, predecessors of Gloriana. And this expectation leads us again to the Annian Berosus, whose genealogy of the Trojan kings includes Osiris, generally identified with Bacchus, and Hercules, son of Osiris, inheritor of his father's power and virtue. If this genealogy is the basis for Spenser's fairy chronicle, the Bacchus-Hercules-Caesar combination of Diodorus and Virgil may be paralleled by a Bacchus-Hercules-Gloriana combination in the Roll of Elfin Emperors.

That such a combination would occur naturally to Spenser is further indicated by his own references to Bacchus and Hercules. In the *Teares of the Muses*, Calliope says,

> *Bacchus* and *Hercules* I raisd to heaven,
> And *Charlemaine*, among the Starris seaven.[83]

The points to note here are the stellification of Bacchus and Hercules and their association with Charlemagne. If the identification of Panthea with the starry heaven be accepted, the stellification of Bacchus and Hercules may mean their exaltation to the throne of Spenser's fairy empire in the same "paleis of stonis cristallyne" in which Lydgate had placed King Arthur. The same conception is suggested by Calliope's linking of the two pagan deities with the other great Christian Worthy of romance. For the coupling of Charlemagne with Bacchus and Hercules suggests both their connection with Caesar in Diodorus and Virgil, and the relation

---

[82] Cf. Horace *Carm.* iii. iii. This passage is mentioned as source of *FQ*, V, I, ii, by Lotspeich, p. 69, from Gough, p. 167.
[83] Lines 461–62.

to Queen Elizabeth postulated for Spenser's fairy chronicle. The parallel between Charlemagne, Arthur, and Elizabeth becomes even closer in the light of the Annian Berosus, who gives authority for deriving all three rulers from Osiris-Bacchus. And the traditional character of Charlemagne as the great Christian Emperor, champion of justice and spreader of civilization, makes probable the assumption that Spenser was thinking of similar qualities as responsible for the fame of Bacchus and Hercules.

This assumption is strengthened by Spenser's second reference to Bacchus and Hercules at the beginning of Book V of the *Faerie Queene*. Here they are celebrated as champions of justice and predecessors of Artegall:

> Though vertue then were held in highest price,
>   In those old times, of which I doe intreat,
>   Yet then likewise the wicked seede of vice
>   Began to spring which shortly grew full great,
>   And with their boughes the gentle plants did beat.
>   But evermore some of the vertuous race
>   Rose up, inspired with heroicke heat,
>   That cropt the branches of the sient base,
> And with strong hand their fruitfull rancknes did deface.
>
> Such first was *Bacchus,* that with furious might
>   All th' East before untam'd did overronne,
>   And wrong repressed, and establisht right,
>   Which lawlesse men had formerly fordonne.
>   There Iustice first her princely rule begonne.
>   Next *Hercules* his like ensample shewed,
>   Who all the West with equall conquest wonne,
>   And monstrous tyrants with his club subdewed;
> The club of Iustice dread, with kingly powre endewed.
>
> And such was he, of whom I have to tell,
>   The Champion of true Iustice *Artegall.*[84]

---

[84] *FQ,* V, I, i–ii, 2.

Since Artegall is not only the representative of Elizabeth's justice in the moral allegory, but also her ancestor in the historical fiction, this passage furnishes still another link with the Annian genealogy, by virtue of which Elizabeth could trace her ancestry to Osiris-Bacchus and Hercules. In another passage, Spenser compares Artegall most pointedly to Osiris, justest of ancient kings, defied as the god of justice.[85] It is possible, therefore, that this Osiris is the Bacchus of the passage quoted above, and that the Hercules who succeeds him is the Libyan hero, who is not only the prototype but the ancestor of Artegall. "The vertuous race" would then mean not simply "the race of virtuous men," but specifically the race of Osiris and Hercules, the Trojan line from which came Brutus, Arthur, Charlemagne, and Queen Elizabeth.

But is it not likely that Spenser is here referring to the more familiar Greek Hercules, the "Alcides" of Virgil? There is no final answer to this question. Spenser would know of course that there were many men named Hercules. Herodotus had distinguished two, an Egyptian god, and a Greek hero.[86] Diodorus mentions three Hercules, the Libyan, who conquered the world, the Cretan, who instituted the Olympic Games, and the Theban, credited with the twelve labors, and notes that the latter undoubtedly got credit for many exploits performed by his earlier namesakes.[87] Cicero found six Hercules,[88] and Varro forty-three, a number which was reduced by Servius to four.[89]

This ancient tradition of the multiplicity of Hercules is continued in the classical dictionaries of the Renaissance. Boccaccio discusses four principal Hercules, and mentions an even larger number, noting that all the exploits reported

[85] *Ibid.*, V, VII, ii. See below, p. 109 *et sqq.*   [86] Herodotus ii. 42–44.
[87] iii. iv; Booth, Vol. I, pp. 214–15.   [88] *De natura deorum* iii. 16.
[89] *Ad Aen.* viii. 564.

of this hero cannot have been performed by one man, and explaining his incredible career by Varro's theory of the forty-three men of the same name whose deeds were indiscriminately ascribed to the latest and best known.[90] Similarly Natalis Comes, after relating the well-known legends about Hercules, son of Alcmena, recorded by classical poets and mythographers, explains that not all authorities are agreed as to the hero's date and nationality.[91] Among the varying opinions on this subject, Comes discusses the Egyptian tradition, which would give authority for arming the earlier Libyan hero with "the club of Iustice dread, with kingly powre endewed." The Egyptians, says Comes, refuse to believe that the hero who fought giants and overcame monsters with his club was a Greek who lived shortly before the Trojan War:

> Nam Giganti nati sunt ante Troiana tempora, vel potius, ut aiunt Graeci, cum prima generatione hominum, quod tempus continet quaedam millia annorum.[92]

The characteristic accouterments of Hercules, the club and lion skin, belong also, they say, to the primitive hero:

> Clava enim & pellis leonina convenit antiquissimo Herculi, quod illis temporibus arma nondum essent inventa, atque pugnaretur lignis, & corpora protegerentur pellibus ferarum.[93]

Furthermore, the achievements of Hercules in overthrowing robbers and freeing the world from monsters agree better with an early period of history than with the times of the Trojans, when the greater part of the world was civilized.[94]

[90] *Gen. de gli dei.*, p. 228.
[91] *Mythologiae*, Lib. VII, cap. i, pp. 695-96.
[92] *Ibid.*, p. 700.   [93] *Ibid.*
[94] The same arguments are used by Annius in his long note on the subject of the many Hercules. "Berosus," pp. 168-73.

Comes himself admits the cogency of these arguments, but explains that his main purpose has been to summarize the generally diffused tradition about Hercules as he appears in classical writers. The same desire to follow the main tradition which ascribed the principal exploits of Hercules to the son of Alcmena, while admitting that they might really belong to an earlier hero of the same name, appears in the *Vita Herculis* of Lilius Giraldus (1514), a work summarizing almost all the available material on the subject, which is cited by Camden and Holinshed, and which may well have been known to Spenser.

Certainly in most of Spenser's own references to the Hercules myth, he is content, like Comes and Giraldus, to follow the common tradition of classical poetry. Thus he twice speaks of Hercules as son of Alcmena, once in the *Epithalamium*,[95] and again in the *Ruines of Time,* where Hercules appears with the Dioscuri as an example of a hero immortalized by the Muses.[96]

In several other passages Spenser refers to Hercules by his Greek name "Alcides,"[97] or as "the Amphitryonid,"[98] the Oetaean knight,"[99] and the "strong Tirynthian swain";[100] and mentions his twelve labors in a simile which contains an allusion to the Greek myth of his death.[101] Certain passages in which Hercules appears without surname are probably to be referred likewise to the general classical tradition. These include the references to the golden apples of the Hesperides,[102] to the love of Hercules for Hylas,[103] and to his servitude to Iole.[104]

---

[95] Lines 328–29.   [96] Lines 370 *et sqq.*

[97] *FQ,* I, VII, xvii, 2; II, V, xxxi, 4; III, XII, vii, 6; III, VII, lxi, 4; IV, I, xxiii, 5; V, VIII, xxxi, 4; V, X, xi, 3; VI, XII, xxxii, 2; *Mui.,* l. 71, *Daph.,* l. 166.

[98] *FQ,* VII, VII, xxxvi, 6.   [99] *Ibid.,* V, VIII, ii, 4.

[100] *Ibid.* VI, XII, xxxv, 1.   [101] *Ibid.,* I, XI, xxvii, 1–7.

[102] *Ibid.,* II, VII, liv, 5–6; *Am.,* LXXVII, 7.

[103] *FQ,* IV, X, xxvii, 1.

[104] *Ibid.,* V, V, xxiv.

In these passages, Spenser uses the well-known stories about the Greek Hercules to expand an epic simile, or to amplify a rhetorical commonplace. Like the mythographers, Boccaccio and Comes, Spenser seems to have regarded these stories as inventions of classical poets,[105] and he uses them for their decorative or moral value. For these purposes, it was not important to ask whether the stories were true, or whether they were connected with the proper Hercules. In the two passages which refer to the battle between Hercules and Albion,[106] however, Spenser seems to have been following the British chronicles rather than the mythographers,[107] and if Holinshed was his principal authority, as seems likely,[108] these passages must refer to the Libyan Hercules.

It is this Hercules, "by Moses called Laabin," to whom Harrison attributes the slaying of Bergion and Albion as part of the vengeance for the murder of Osiris. This Hercules, says Harrison, in a passage which reminds us strongly of Spenser's introduction to the legend of Artegall, was a divinely appointed deliverer, who

as one appointed by God's providence to subdue the cruell and unmercifull tyrants, spent his time to the benefit of mankind, delivering the oppressed from the heavie yoke of miserable thraldome, in everie place where he came.[109]

The likeness between Hercules Libicus, slayer of Albion, and Artegall, slayer of Grantorto, lends further weight to the suggestion that the Hercules who appears with Bacchus as a predecessor of Artegall is the Libyan hero. I do not wish, however, to press this point unduly. The Bacchus-Hercules combination, as we have seen, occurs in several places where the Greek and not the Libyan hero is unmistakably

[105] Lotspeich, p. 5.   [106] *FQ*, II, X, xi, 6–7; IV, XI, xv, 8–xvi, 8.
[107] Lotspeich, p. 35; Harper, pp. 50–51.   [108] *Ibid.*
[109] Holinshed, I, 433.

referred to. These passages may have been in Spenser's mind
when he wrote the Proem to Book V. Nevertheless, its opening stanzas take on a richer meaning if they refer to the
Libyan Hercules. First, as we said, they contain a clear compliment to the ancestry of Elizabeth. For they represent
Bacchus, Hercules, and Artegall as successive representatives
of "the vertuous race" of tyrant-killers. If the Greek Hercules is meant, the kinship between the three champions of
justice is spiritual only; if the Libyan, it is both spiritual
and biological, for the Libyan Hercules was the son of Bacchus (Osiris) and the ancestor of Artegall. Again, Spenser
calls the traditional weapon of Hercules "The club of Iustice dread with kingly powre endewed." Gough refers this
to the mace, symbol of royal authority,[110] but may it not perhaps represent the scepter itself, "Wherein doth sit the
dread and fear of kings?"[111] The son of Alcmena was a slayer
of monsters, but the Libyan Hercules was above all else a
king and the father of kings. The giants whom he slew were
not simply wicked men whom he happened to encounter
in his travels, but genuine usurpers, abusing the power dele-
gated to them by his father Osiris, whose murder was the immediate cause of their destruction. Hercules restored the rule
of "the vertuous race" when he assumed in person the crowns
of Italy, Gaul, and Spain. From him descended the future
kings of the West, and it was the "sang Herculien," which
Jean Lemaire celebrated as the true royal blood of Europe,
the guarantee of legitimacy and just rule,[112] the tie which was
to unite the ruling houses of France, England, and Austria
in a crusade against the Turks for the possession not merely
of their spiritual fatherland, Jerusalem, but of their earthly
and cultural fatherland, Troy.[113]

[110] *Faerie Queene, Book V*, p. 167.
[111] The same suggestion was made by Miss Tuve, in "Spenser's Reading:
The De claris mulieribus," SP, XXXIII (1936), 155.
[112] *Œuvres*, II, 261, 266, 268, 302, 469.
[113] *Ibid.*, I, 139; II, 251–52, 257, 314, 473.

A similar enthusiasm for the Libyan Hercules as founder of the Trojan line appears in Tudor England. The "gene-logie of the Brutes" attached to Arthur Kelton's *Chronycle with a Genealogie* begins with Osiris and ends with Edward VI. Second in line is the "great Hercules Kyng of Egipte, Italie, Almayne, Phenice, Phrigie, Libie, Argis, Affricke, Gall Seltike and Tuscan." Kelton adds in the margin, "Sainct Jherom in the x of Genesis, Diodorus Birosus affirmeth this Hercules to do the xii notable labores. And not Hercules Alcides whiche the Grekes affirmeth to be their Champion."

Spenser, as we have seen, makes no such exclusive claims for the Libyan hero. Yet one might exalt the Libyan Hercules without denying the fame of the Greek. For the name "Hercules" had a general symbolic value apart from its attribution to any particular historical character. In fact, this general symbolism of the Hercules myth may have contributed equally with the genealogical connection of the Libyan Hercules with the Trojan line to justify his position in the fairy chrónicle among the earliest rulers of Cleopolis.

According to Boccaccio, "Hercules" was the generic name for a famous hero, for Varro had said that "tutti quelli, che si diportarono valorosamente forono nominati Hercoli. Di qui adunque aviene, che leggiamo Hercole Tirintheo, Argivo, Thebano, Libico, & altri simile."[114] The idea that "Hercules" was a title rather than a proper name is apparently related to the common etymological explanations of its meaning. The ordinary classical view was that the name meant "glory of Hera." This is explained by Diodorus on the ground that the enmity of Hera was the cause of the twelve labors, and hence of the glory which Hercules de-

---

[114] *Gen. de gli dei*, p. 228. Cf. Servius *Ad Aen*. viii. 564. A somewhat similar explanation of the multiplicity of Hercules on the ground that the name was a title is adopted by Harrison, Holinshed, I, 38, probably from the Annian Xenophon, according to whom the first king of a country was called Saturn, the second Jupiter, the third Hercules. "Berosus," p. 8.

rived from them.[115] This etymology is mentioned by both Giraldus[116] and Comes.[117] A fuller discussion of the derivation of the name "Hercules" is given by Boccaccio:

Diceva Leontio Hercole haver havuto il nome da Hera; che è la terra; & Cleos, che è gloria & cosi Hercole è l'istesso, che glorioso in terra; overo da Heros, & Cleos, & cosi si dira glorioso Heroe.[118] Ma Paolo voleva Hercole essere detto da Erix, che significa Lite, & Cleos, gloria, & cosi verrebbe à chiamarsi glorioso delle Liti. Ma Rabano nel libro dell' origine delle cose dice, che credendo quegli antichi Hercole esser il Dio della virtù; istima egli cosi essere chiamato quasi Heruncleos, che latinamente diciamo fama d'huomini forti.[119]

The same idea is carried out in Boccaccio's allegorical interpretation of the marriage of Hercules and Hebe:

E stato poi finto, che togliesse la gioventù per moglie; percioche il corpo del famoso huomo, il valore, la fama, e il nome sempre piu si rinfresca, et dura giovine.[120]

These ideas about the meaning of the name "Hercules" and the significance of his apotheosis are obviously close to the central theme of the *Faerie Queene* and to the interpretation already suggested for the history of Cleopolis. A similar connection between Hercules, glory, and virtue appears in the *Vita Herculis* of Giraldus and in the *Mythologiae* of Comes. Giraldus tells us that all brave men who slew monsters were called "Hercules," and lists various interpretations of the Hercules myth collected from ancient writers. Some of these denied the historical existence of Hercules, declaring that he symbolized the power of human wisdom overcoming the monsters of pride, lust, envy, avarice, and other vices, "and they say that he is called the son of Jove because all

---

[115] *Historical Library*, iv. i.   [116] *Opera*, I, 574 A.
[117] *Mythologiae*, p. 701.   [118] Cf. Higden, II, 362.
[119] *Gen. de gli dei*, p. 228; cf. Fulgentius *Myth*. ii. v.
[120] *Op. cit.*, p. 230.

virtue proceeds from the mind, for the ancients call Jove the mind, and Hercules virtue." Others taught that Hercules was a philosopher, and that his club represented philosophy and his lion's skin prudence, by which he overcame vain imaginings. Others thought that he represented the intellect or prudence and fortitude.[121]

The association of these philosophical and moral ideals with Hercules is probably based on the story of Hercules' Choice, which is also summarized by Giraldus.[122] The story comes from Xenophon's *Memorabilia,* where it is related by Socrates as part of an argument in favor of a strenuous or ascetic life. After quoting several passages from Hesiod and Epicharmus in favor of this point of view, Socrates says:

> Prodicus the sophist, also, in his narrative concerning Hercules, . . . expresses a similar notion respecting virtue, speaking . . . to the following effect: For he says that Hercules, when he was advancing from boyhood to manhood, a period at which the young . . . begin to give intimations whether they will enter on life by the path of virtue or that of vice, went forth into a solitary place, and sat down, perplexed as to which of these two paths he should pursue; and that two female figures, of lofty stature, seemed to advance toward him, the one of engaging and graceful mien, gifted by nature with elegance of form, modesty of look, and sobriety of demeanour, and clad in a white robe; and the other fed to plumpness and softness, but made up both in her complexion, so as to seem fairer and rosier than she really was, and in her gesture, so as to seem more upright than she naturally was. . . .[123]

This synthetic lady pushes ahead of her companion, and offers to conduct Hercules along an easy path to a life of effortless pleasure. On his enquiring her name, she replies:

> My friends . . . call me Happiness, but those who hate me, give me, to my disparagement, the name of Vice.[124]

---

[121] *Opera,* p. 571.   [122] *Ibid.,* I, 574 D.
[123] *Mem.* i. vii. 21–22 (Watson's translation).   [124] *Ibid.,* i. vii. 26.

Her companion next presents her case:

I also am come to address you, Hercules, because I know your parents, and have observed your disposition in the training of your childhood, from which I entertain hopes that you will direct your steps along the path that leads to my dwelling, you will become an excellent performer of whatever is honourable and noble, and that I shall appear more honourable and distinguished in goodness. I will not deceive you, however, with promises of pleasure, but will set before you things as they really are, and as the gods have appointed them; for of what is valuable and excellent, the gods grant nothing to mankind without labour and care: and if you wish the gods, therefore, to be propitious to you, you must worship the gods; if you seek to be beloved by your friends, you must serve your friends; if you wish to be honoured by any city, you must benefit that city; if you claim to be admired by all Greece for your merit, you must endeavour to be of advantage to all Greece . . . or if you wish to be vigorous in body, you must accustom your body to obey your mind, and exercise it with toil and exertion.[125]

At this point Vice breaks in:

Do you see, Hercules, how difficult and tedious a road to gratification this woman describes to you, while I shall lead you, by an easy and short path, to perfect happiness.[126]

Virtue then denies that Vice can produce true happiness, and contrasts the sad end of those who follow her with the blessings in store for those who give themselves to the pursuit of Virtue:

Though you are one of the immortals [she tells Vice], you are cast out from the society of the gods, and despised by the good among mankind. . . . But I am the companion of the gods; I associate with virtuous men; no honourable deed, divine or human, is done without me. . . . My friends have a sweet and untroubled enjoyment of meat and drink. . . . They have also sweeter sleep than the idle. . . . The young are pleased with

[125] *Ibid.*, i. vii. 27–28.   [126] *Ibid.*, i. vii. 29.

praises from the old; the old are delighted with honours from the young. They remember their former acts with pleasure, and rejoice to perform their present occupations with success; being, through my influence, dear to the gods, beloved of their friends, and honoured by their country. And when the destined end of life comes, they do not lie in oblivion and dishonour, but, celebrated with songs of praise, flourish forever in the memory of mankind. By such a course of conduct, O Hercules, son of noble parents, you may secure the most exalted happiness.[127]

Needless to say, Hercules rejects the broad and easy road of Vice, and chooses the laborious path of Virtue.

This story shows Hercules as the typical "Worthy," winning fame by virtue. The same idea of his character is strikingly exhibited in the *Mythologiae* of Natalis Comes. He places Hercules first in the seventh book, the subject of which is "Quam iuste & utiliter viri illustres gloriam sint consecuti."[128] The Preface to this book celebrates the desire for glory, in true Renaissance fashion, as the prime necessity for the maintenance of great and honorable states. It was this desire for fame, according to Comes, which inspired all the labors of Hercules, and his whole career was nothing else but an illustration of "the glory of virtue."[129]

This passage from one of Spenser's favorite classical dictionaries is significant in pointing to a possible connection of Hercules with Cleopolis, capital of the Elfin Empire, and goal of Arthur's quest. For the mythographers of the Renaissance, Hercules had come to possess the same typical value as Spenser's Prince Arthur, representing the ideal of a gentleman, perfected in all the virtues by a life dedicated to "long labors" in pursuit of fame. This general significance of the name "Hercules" belonged to all the various heroes who had claimed it, two of whom, the son of Alcmena and the son of Osiris, were particularly celebrated by poets and

---

[127] *Ibid.*, i. vii. 31–33.   [128] Page 668.   [129] *Mythologiae*, p. 669.

historians known to Spenser. But it was the great Libyan
Hercules who most resembled Arthur, and who was best
fitted to rule in Cleopolis. For Spenser's Fairyland is not
only the land of fame. It is also the empire of justice, whose
earthly seat passed from Egypt to Troy, and from Troy to
Rome and London. Troy is central. And the Libyan Hercules is especially famous as founder of the Trojan line.

The significance of Troy in Spenser's thought can hardly
be exaggerated. Not only was it important in his historical
fiction as the original fatherland of his hero's race; it had
a deeper meaning also in relation to his general allegorical
message. More even than Rome, which for Dante and Du
Bellay was a mirror of the world, Troy was for Spenser the
symbol of earthly glory, at once transient and immortal.
For Rome was the second Troy, as London was the third.

The conception of the three Troys is developed in the
third book of the *Faerie Queene,* in a conversation between
Paridell and Britomart, descendants, respectively, of Paris,
bringer of destruction to the first Troy, and Aeneas,
founder of the second. When Britomart hears the story of
the fall of Troy, she is moved to lament the passage of earthly
glory in terms that remind us of Du Bellay's elegiac celebration of the vanished Roman splendor:

> Then sighing soft awhile, at last she thus:
>   O lamentable fall of famous towne,
>   Which raignd so many yeares victorious,
>   And of all *Asie* bore the soveraigne crowne,
>   In one sad night consumd, and throwen downe:
>   What stony hart, that heares thy haplesse fate,
>   Is not empierst with deepe compassiowne,
>   And makes ensample of mans wretched state,
> That floures so fresh at morne, and fades at evening late?[130]

[130] *FQ,* III, IX, xxxix.

She is consoled, however, when Paridell relates the story of
the founding of Rome, and in stanza xliv she hails the third
Troy:

> There there (said *Britomart*) a fresh appeard
>   The glory of the later world to spring,
>   And *Troy* againe out of her dust was reard,
>   To sit in second seat of soveraigne king,
>   Of all the world under her governing.
>   But a third kingdome yet is to arise,
>   Out of the *Troians* scattered of-spring,
>   That in all glory and great enterprise,
> Both first and second *Troy* shall dare to equalise.

Paridell then remembers that he has heard of the foundation of Troynovant by Brutus, and of his victory over the
giants,

>   A famous history to be enrold
>   In everlasting moniments of brasse,
>   That all the antique Worthies merits far did passe.

>   His worke great *Troynovant,* his worke is eke
>   Faire *Lincolne,* both renowmed far away,
>   That who from East to West will endlong seeke,
>   Cannot two fairer Cities find this day,
>   Except *Cleopolis.* . . .[131]

This last statement is inexplicable if we accept the ordinary identification of Cleopolis with London in Spenser's
political allegory.[132] To be sure the two cities are distinct in
the historical fiction. Troynovant is in Britain, Cleopolis
in Fairyland, and fairy cities are notoriously fairer than the
cities of earth. In the general moral allegory, too, we may

---

[131] *Ibid.,* l, 7–li, 5.
[132] Cf. Bennett, *JEGP,* XXXI, 213 *et sqq.* With Mrs. Bennett's interpretation of Cleopolis in the moral allegory I am in general agreement. I should,
however, modify her statement, p. 214, that "for the historical allegory the
distinction [between Cleopolis and Troynovant] does not exist." This is true
if by "historical allegory" we mean the allegory of Tudor times. But the
"veiled history" of the Elfin Chronicle is not exclusively Tudor history.

recognize a distinction between Cleopolis and Troynovant. If Cleopolis in Spenser's general intention represents the ideal city of earthly glory, counterpart of the New Jerusalem, a sort of heavenly Troy of which the earthly Troy, Rome, and London were successively the earthly counterparts, Cleopolis would be fairer than Troynovant as the ideal is fairer than the mere reflection of it which appears on earth. But if this were all, Cleopolis could have no history. It would remain a static ideal, eternal in the heavens. Actually, however, we see in the Elfin Chronicle that Cleopolis has a history. It was founded not by the first, but by the second Elfin Emperor, and walled by a third. One of its rulers fought a war with the Gobbelines; another built the crystal tower, Panthea. Furthermore, as we noted at the beginning of this chapter, Spenser has carefully indicated that this history of the Elfin Empire is not a mere fanciful elaboration of fairy mythology, but reflects under "covert veil" the actual achievements of Elizabeth's remote ancestors, who, we have suggested, are to be sought in the genealogical tradition originating with the Annian Berosus. We have seen, furthermore, that the tradition of Ancient History to which Spenser was heir furnished a succession of good empires, whose history ran parallel to that of the Church, and might therefore be considered by a "poet historicall" who had read Diodorus and St. Augustine as the history of "one city." These considerations suggest that Cleopolis represents both the Platonic idea of an imperial city and the temporal manifestations of that idea in the history of several famous cities, of which London is the last. In Spenser's day, of course, Cleopolis existed on earth only as London. Hence the traditional identification of Cleopolis with London in the political allegory of Tudor times is legitimate. But this identification does not hold for the historical allegory of the Elfin Chronicle, which relates the history of the earthly Cleopolis from its earliest beginnings. Only in the last chapter of this history can we identify London with Cleopolis, which may thus be called fairer than Troynovant, not only because the ideal pattern is fairer than its earthly reflection, but because the whole is fairer than the part.

The successive good empires which constituted the city of earthly fame in its historical manifestations were connected, as we have seen, not only by their spiritual kinship, but also by the physical relationship between their founders. To a follower of "Berosus," Dardanus, Aeneas, and Brutus were descended in direct line from Osiris and Hercules. The hereditary basis thus furnished for the spiritual unity of the first good empire with the three Troys was, we have suggested, the chief advantage of the Egyptian over the Cretan genealogy of Dardanus. It is now time to apply these ideas specifically to the interpretation of Spenser's fairy chronicle. Here is the "Roll of Elfin Emperors":

> The first and eldest, which that scepter swayd,
> Was *Elfin;* him all *India* obayd,
> And all that now *America* men call:
> Next him was noble *Elfinan,* who layd
> *Cleopolis* foundation first of all:
> But *Elfiline* enclosd it with a golden wall.
>
> His sonne was *Elfinell,* who overcame
> The wicked *Gobbelines* in bloudy field:
> But *Elfant* was of most renowmed fame,
> Who all of Christall did *Panthea* build:
> Then *Elfar,* who two brethren gyants kild,
> The one of which had two heads, th' other three:
> Then *Elfinor,* who was in Magick skild;
> He built by art upon the glassy See
> A bridge of bras, whose sound heavens thunder seem'd to bee.
>
> He left three sonnes, the which in order raynd,
> And all their Ofspring, in their dew descents,
> Even seven hundred Princes, which maintayned

With mightie deedes their sundry governments:
That were too long their infinite contents
Here to record, ne much materiall:
Yet should they be most famous moniments,
And brave ensample, both of martiall,
And civill rule to kings and states imperiall.

After all these *Elficleos* did rayne,
  The wise *Elficleos* in great Maiestie,
Who mightily that scepter did sustayne,
And with rich spoiles and famous victorie,
Did high advaunce the crowne of *Faery:*
He left two sonnes, of which faire *Elferon*
The eldest brother did untimely dy;
  Whose emptie place the mightie *Oberon*
Doubly supplide, in spousall, and dominion.

Great was his power and glorie over all,
  Which him before, that sacred seate did fill,
That yet remaines his wide memoriall:
He dying left the fairest *Tanaquill,*
Him to succeede therein, by his last will:
Fairer and nobler liveth none this howre,
Ne like in grace, ne like in learned skill;
  Therefore they *Glorian* call that glorious flowre,
Long mayst thou *Glorian* live, in glory and great powre.[133]

The first emperor, Elfin, is surely Osiris-Bacchus. He is
identified by his rule over India, first conquered by him,
and never conquered again except by Semiramis and Alexander the Great, both of whom appear as horrible examples
in the House of Pride. I have already suggested that Osiris
may be the Bacchus mentioned at the beginning of Book V
as the earliest champion of justice, head of the "vertuous
race" of whom Artegall is a later representative. A less de-
batable connection between Artegall and Osiris is indicated in the seventh canto of the same book, which describes
Britomart's visit to "Isis Church."

[133] *FQ,* II, X, lxxii, 4–lxxvi, 9.

The canto begins with a passage which makes Osiris the personification of justice:

Nought is on earth more sacred or divine,
  That Gods and men doe equally adore,
  Then this same vertue, that doth right define:
  For th' hevens themselves, whence mortal men implore
  Right in their wrongs, are rul'd by righteous lore
  Of highest Iove, who doth true iustice deale
  To his inferiour Gods, and evermore
  Therewith containes his heavenly Common-weale:
The skill wherof to Princes hearts he doth reveale.

Well therefore did the antique world invent,
  That Iustice was a God of soveraine grace,
  And altars unto him, and temples lent,
  And heavenly honours in the highest place;
  Calling him great *Osyris*, of the race
  Of th' old Ægyptian Kings, that whylome were;
  With fayned colours shading a true case:
  For that *Osyris,* whilest he lived here,
The iustest man alive, and truest did appeare.

His wife was *Isis,* whom they likewise made
  A Goddesse of great powre and soverainty,
  And in her person cunningly did shade
  That part of Iustice, which is Equity.[134]

In the temple of Isis Britomart has a dream, in which she seems to become identified with the goddess, and bears a lion to the crocodile, Osiris. In the morning the priest explains that the dream is prophetic:

  For that same Crocodile doth represent
  The righteous Knight, that is thy faithfull lover,
  Like to *Osyris* in all iust endever.
  For that same Crocodile *Osyris* is,
  That under *Isis* feete doth sleepe for ever:
  To shew that clemence oft in things amis,
Restraines those sterne behests, and cruell doomes of his.

[134] *Ibid.,* V, VII, i–iii, 4.

That Knight shall all the troublous stormes asswage,
 And raging flames, that many foes shall reare,
 To hinder thee from the iust heritage
 Of thy sires Crowne, and from thy countrey deare.
 Then shalt thou take him to thy loved fere,
 And ioyne in equall portion of thy realme.
 And afterwards a sonne to him shalt beare,
That Lion-like shall shew his powre extreame.[135]

This prophecy indicates that Britomart and Artegall are in a sense reincarnations of Isis and Osiris. The priest does not say that the British exemplars of justice and equity are literally descended from the Egyptian, but the similarity in character and destiny between the two pairs of rulers fits in well with such a connection. Artegall's shield bears the emblem of Osiris, "the Sunne brode blazed on a golden field,"[136] and Britomart's cognizance is the lion, emblem not only of Britain but also of the Libyan Hercules, from whom, according to Jean Lemaire, it passed to his Trojan descendants.[137]

The close connection of Osiris with Isis, earliest of the female worthies like Britomart and Queen Elizabeth, was probably one reason for Spenser's choosing him to head the Roll of Elfin emperors. Another reason, which probably also influenced Kelton, whose genealogy of Edward VI likewise begins with Osiris, was that he had inaugurated the reign of justice after the Flood by founding the first good empire among the Gentiles. The influence of this conception upon Spenser's Elfin Empire has already been pointed out. Furthermore, since Osiris had conquered India, it was easy to

[135] *Ibid.*, xxii, 3–xxiii, 8.
[136] *Ibid.*, V, III, xiv, 9. Spenser identifies Osiris with the sun, *Ibid.*, V, VII, iv, 8. The arms of Osiris in Jean Lemaire are a royal scepter and an eye. *Œuvres*, I, 48.
[137] *Ibid.*, I, 48. Hardyng also mentions the lion as a Trojan device. He says Brutus's shield bore two golden lions "which kynges of Troie in bataill bare ful bolde." *Chron.*, p. 31.

imagine that he had also ruled over America. Jean Lemaire
may have believed this, for he says that Osiris was the first
to triumph over "les Indes."[138] Although India and America were no longer believed to be identical in Spenser's day,
they were still closely associated in the popular mind. The
name "India" was sometimes used for America.[139] Explorers
searched for the Northwest Passage, and tales of "golden
cities" in the New World recalled the marvels related by
earlier travelers in the East. It was commonly believed that
the American aborigines had come from India. Raleigh attempts to discredit this belief in 1614.[140] Spenser might make
use of it in the 1580's to indicate that in spreading her rule
to "fruitfullest Virginia,"[141] Elizabeth was only entering
upon her rightful heritage.

If Elfin is Osiris, his successor, Elfinan, must be Hercules
Libicus. We are told that he "laid Cleopolis foundation first
of all." Like other famous heroes, Hercules was given to
founding cities or to bestowing his name upon them. Besides the numerous Heraclea's, Charles Estienne mentions
three cities named Heracleopolis, the most famous of which,
in Egypt, was the center of worship for the Egyptian god
identified with Hercules.[142] I do not know that this city was
founded by Hercules, but its name certainly suggests Spenser's fairy capital. Another famous Egyptian city, whose
foundation is associated with both Osiris and Hercules, was
Thebes of the hundred gates,[143] which Achilles coupled with
Troy as a symbol of wealth and power.[144] This city might
well stand for Cleopolis as first capital of the just empire

[138] Œuvres, I, 55.
[139] Raleigh, "The Fight about the Azores," Hakluyt's Voyages, V, 13, 42,
43; "History of the World," Works, II, 214.
[140] Ibid., pp. 333–34.   [141] FQ, II, Proem, ii, 9.
[142] Dict. hist., p. 1003.
[143] Diodorus i. i; Booth, Vol. I, p. 22, says Osiris built Thebes. Later (p.
234) he says that Hercules built a city in Africa called Hecatompylon.
[144] Iliad ix. 381–84.

whose seat passed from Egypt to Troy. The city most often mentioned as founded by the Libyan Hercules, however, was Alexia in Gaul. Jean Lemaire says that the name means "coniunctive ou copulative: pource que le tresnoble sang de deux diverses nations y fut conioint."[145] The noble blood in question was the Trojan, from Osiris, and the Gallic, from Samothes, son of Japhet, original ruler of Gaul and Britain. Since Hercules founded Alexia before the division of his kingdom, it was for a time the capital not only of Gaul, which at that time included Britain, but of his whole empire.[146] It is possible, therefore, that this city was in Spenser's mind when he said that Hercules had "laid Cleopolis foundations first of all." A city in France which was capital of an empire embracing the whole world was a suitable prototype for the London of Elizabeth, who styled herself "Queen of England, France, and Ireland, and of Virginia."[147]

In spite of the aptness of these historical parallels, however, the foundation of Cleopolis by Hercules involves a certain inconsistency in the general moral allegory. For surely Spenser cannot mean to exclude Osiris from the city of fame. We may perhaps explain the inconsistency by the analogy of Spenser's presumptive model in the *City of God*. Since Augustine's Earthly City contains the wicked angels as well as wicked men, its true founder is the devil. Its earthly founder, however, is Cain, who built the first city in the world. But the continuous history of the Earthly City begins with Babylon, whose immediate heir is Rome. Hence the

[145] *Œuvres*, I, 61.

[146] Giraldus repeats from Diodorus the statement that Alexia was the metropolis of Gaul, *Opera*, p. 583 C. There was also a tradition which connected Hercules with the foundation of Paris. Cf. *Le Cathalogue des villes et citez assises ez troys Gaulles* . . . (1539) quoted by Le Roux de Lincy, *Livre des légendes*, p. 84. These connections of Hercules with French cities are particularly significant if Spenser took the name Cleopolis from Stoa's encomium on Paris.

[147] Dedication to *FQ*.

foundation of the Earthly City might be represented by the fall of Lucifer, the founding of Henoch, or the building of the tower of Babel. Corresponding to Babylon in Spenser's scheme was Troy, and Hercules, as we have seen, was regarded more specifically than Osiris as founder of the Trojan line, possibly because his most famous conquests were in the West, destined ultimately to be ruled by princes of Trojan blood.

Furthermore, the previously mentioned allegorical interpretation of the Hercules myth made him an appropriate founder for the city of Gloriana, the goal of Arthur's quest. If Osiris was the personification of justice, the "most sacred virtue" expressed concretely in the good empire over which Elizabeth was the last and greatest ruler, Hercules was the type of all heroic virtue whose reward is immortal fame. Champion of good against evil, bearer of a name which, however interpreted, contained the element *kleos*, "glory," leader and associate of the Muses,[148] he was the prototype, as well as the ancestor, of Spenser's Prince Arthur, representative of that virtue which "is the perfection of all the rest, and conteineth in it them all."[149] In making Hercules the founder of Cleopolis, the ideal Troy, Spenser reflects an attitude similar to that expressed in the rude rhymes of Kelton:

> Who wer more worthy, then wer these three
> Hercules, Hector, and Arthur the kyng
> For their princely Magnanimitee
> Wer never none, to them resemblyng
> In bodely strength, all other surmountyng
> Lions, Dragons, monsterous and wild
> By manly constraint, made them tame & milde.[150]

We have seen cogent reasons for believing that the first two Elfin emperors are Osiris and Hercules. The last three

[148] Giraldus, *Opera*, p. 594 D.   [149] *Letter to Raleigh.*
[150] *Chronycle with a Genealogie,* quoted by Millican, p. 32.

are by general consent Henry VII, Henry VIII, and Elizabeth. The intervening rulers are less easy to identify. Obviously Spenser's list is not a complete genealogy. It passes over
"seven hundred princes" between Elfinor and Elficleos
(Henry VII), and it probably contains additional gaps in
the preceding portion. We should expect Spenser to include
only the most famous of Elizabeth's remote ancestors in such
a short list. The following identifications of the later emperors seem to me plausible, and in harmony with Spenser's
general point of view. I do not claim for all of them the
same degree of certainty as for the identification of the first
two emperors with Osiris and Hercules.

The next two emperors, Elfiline, who built the wall of
Cleopolis, and Elfinell, who overcame the Gobbelines, are
father and son. We are not told, however, that Elfiline is
the son or the immediate successor of Elfinan (Hercules),
and the possibility of a gap in the genealogy at this point
is strengthened by the comparative obscurity of the kings
between Hercules and Dardanus. I suggest, therefore, that
the pair of Elfin emperors following the two great Egyptians
belong to the history of the first Troy, "that of all Asie bore
the soveraigne crowne," and that Elfiline and Elfinell are
Tros and Assaracus.

Tros was the grandson of Dardanus, and eponymous hero
of Troy. Besides giving his own name to the city and kingdom of Dardania, he extended its territory by his military
prowess, making war on Tantalus, king of Phrygia and Jupiter, king of Crete, each of whom is credited in certain accounts with the rape of Ganymede.[151] As effectual founder
of the Trojan Empire, Tros had an important part in building the ideal Troy, which might well be symbolized by making him enclose it with a wall. Hercules had laid the
foundation of Cleopolis in that he was father of its later

[151] Boccaccio, *Gen. de gli dei*, pp. 107–8; also Caxton, *Recuyell*, I, 136, *et
sqq.*

rulers and patron of the virtues on which its fame was ultimately to rest. Tros might be said to have "enclosed it with
a golden wall" when he gave to its earthly counterpart the
name which was to be immortalized in Homer's verse, and
to haunt the imagination of Europe with the vision of "another Troy." This interpretation may seem fanciful. Yet
there was historical precedent for making the eponymous
"founder" of a city the builder of its wall. According to the
Mirabilia, buildings had been erected on the future site
of Rome by Noah, Saturn (Nimrod), Hercules, Roma the
daughter of Aeneas, and others, before Romulus enclosed
all previous settlements with a single wall, and gave his name
to the newly "founded" city.[152] A similar account of the
founding of Rome is given by Higden,[153] and Jean d'Outremeuse with characteristic precision tells us that the wall of
Romulus enclosed thirty-six cities, the largest of which was
Eneoch, founded by Aeneas.[154] Similarly King Lud, eponymous hero of London, is credited by Spenser with rebuild-
ing the "ruin'd wals" of Troynovant.[155] Thus the second and
third of Spenser's three Troys owed their names to the
heroes who had built or rebuilt their walls. If the history of
Cleopolis reflects the history of the three successive Troys,
the builder of its golden wall may well be the man who
gave his name to the first Troy, and thus "founded" the
typical city of earthly glory, mother and model of those that
followed.

The traditional connection between naming a city and

---

[152] Pages 2–5.   [153] *Polychron.,* I, 208–10.

[154] *Ly Myreur des histors,* I, 56. R. H. Fletcher, *Arthurian Material in the
Chronicles,* p. 222, says that this work is the same as the *Mer des histoires,*
"frequently referred to by the later English chroniclers." If this is true, Spenser may well have known *Ly Myreur,* but I have found no other authority
for Fletcher's identification of *Ly Myreur* with the *Mer des histoires.* According to Brunet, III, 1640, the latter work is a translation of the *Rudi-
mentum novitiorum,* a history of the world to 1473, published at Lübeck,
1475. Brunet, IV, 1449–50.

[155] *FQ,* II, X, xlvi, 4–5.

building its wall[156] also suggests the possibility that the golden wall of Cleopolis stands for the wall of Troy, considered as a symbol of earthly fame. The wall of Troy was built by Apollo and Poseidon for Laomedon, and rebuilt by Priam, but as neither of these kings could appear in a genealogy of Queen Elizabeth,[157] their building of the wall would have to be transferred in the Elfin Chronicle to some earlier Trojan king, most appropriately to Tros, who had given the city its name and its supremacy in Phrygia. The possibility that the wall of Cleopolis symbolizes not only the name but also the wall of Troy is strengthened by the connection of the other "wonders" of Cleopolis, its tower and magic bridge, with actual monuments which constituted the special glories of the second and third Troys, respectively. The likeness between Panthea and various Mirabilian Roman monuments I have already pointed out. I shall presently attempt to show that Warton was right in identifying Elfinor's bridge of brass with London Bridge.

This identification of the monuments of Cleopolis with the principal monuments of the three Troys is further supported by the use of the "wonders of the world" as symbols of earthly glory in Stoa's *Cleopolis* and in Spenser's *Ruines*

[156] Cf. also Virgil *Aen.* x. 200.
[157] The line of Trojan kings:

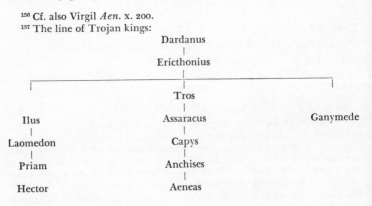

of Time. Stoa stresses the continued memory of these ancient monuments as an illustration of the power of literature to overcome the ravages of time.[158] Spenser, on the other
hand, emphasizes the destruction of ancient "wonders" in
a series of visions of this world's vanity.[159] This twofold symbolism of the "wonders of the world," signifying at once the
transience and the abiding fame of earthly cities, was ready
to Spenser's hand when he came to build up his picture of
the ideal city of earthly fame. Stoa's list of ancient "wonders"
begins with the walls of Babylon.[160] The first "wonder" of
Cleopolis may well be the wall of Troy, first built by
Apollo's lyre, and preserved in Homer's verse.

If the builder of the wall in the Elfin Chronicle is Tros,
his son Elfinell must be Assaracus. His victory over the Gobbelines I take to mean the termination of the war with
Tantalus, which established the Trojan power in Asia
Minor, and in which the sons of Tros took a leading part.
According to Diodorus, it was Ilus who drove Tantalus into
exile;[161] according to Caxton it was "Ilion and Ganymede.'"[162]
It would be simple enough for Spenser to have given the
leading part in this battle to the third brother, Assaracus,
who as founder of the Roman and British lines of the Trojan
family should certainly appear in the fairy genealogy.[163] Boccaccio says that history relates nothing of Assaracus, though
as progenitor of the Caesars he deserves great fame.[164] Spen-

[158] *Op. cit.*, p. bii.
[159] *RT*, ll. 491 *et sqq.* Cf. Renwick's edition of *Complaints*, p. 200.
[160] There are two lists of the traditional seven wonders of the world. But
the term was applied to other famous monuments. Cf. Spargo, *Virgil the
Necromancer*, p. 22, *RR*, l. 2, and *FQ*, III, IX, xlv, 7.
[161] *Historical Library* iv. iv; Booth, Vol. I, p. 138.
[162] *Recuyell*, I, 138.
[163] Assaracus was the ancestor of Aeneas and Brutus. See genealogy on p.
116 n above.
[164] *Gen. de gli dei*, p. 117. Cf. the mention of Assaracus by Dante, *De mon.*,
II, iii, quoted below, p. 127, and *FQ*, II, X, ix, 7.

ser's old man "of infinite remembrance," however, can recall the wars "of old Assaracus" along with those of Ninus
and Inachus.[165]

A second gap in the genealogy is possible between Elfinell
and the next emperor mentioned, who is introduced in the
lines:

> But *Elfant* was of most renowmed fame,
> Who all of Christall did *Panthea* build.

Surely this is Aeneas. His fame, eternized in the glory of
Roman history, and celebrated by the supreme poet Virgil,
was certainly "most renowmed." The building of Panthea
may symbolize the foundation of the Roman Empire, "glory
of the later world." In the preceding chapter, we saw reason
to connect Panthea, the temple of earthly glory, with Rome,
"mirror to all nations," itself a sort of universal Pantheon,
an image of the starry heavens, and like them a symbolic
House of Fame. The wealth of analogues makes it difficult
to identify Panthea with any particular "wonder" of Rome,
but perhaps the Mirabilian Capitol is most probable, since
this appears, as we have seen, in the *Visions of Bellay* as a
symbol of earthly fame.[166]

If Elfant is Aeneas, the succeeding emperor, Elfar, must
be either Ascanius or Postumus Silvius, depending upon
which account of the ancestry of Brutus Spenser was following. According to one version Brutus was the son of Silvius,
son of Ascanius; according to another the son of Postumus
Silvius, son of Aeneas and Lavinia.[167] The latter version,
which is given by Boccaccio,[168] and adopted in Kelton's genealogy, would make Elfar Postumus Silvius, and Elfinor
Brutus. As I shall presently show there are additional reasons for identifying Elfinor with Brutus. But this identifica-

---

[165] *Ibid.*, II, IX, lvi, 9.   [166] See above, p. 27.
[167] The divergent accounts are discussed by Higden, II, 442.
[168] *Gen. de gli dei*, p. 121.

tion is still possible if Elfar is Ascanius, for Spenser might easily omit from his list of emperors the obscure "Silvius," who according to this tradition is the father of Brutus, for this Silvius never reigned, losing his life at the hands of his son while Ascanius was still on the throne of Alba Longa. I have found no source for Elfar's slaying of the two multiple-headed giants, and can only guess at its meaning. I suspect that it refers in some way to the wars between Latins and Trojans which followed the death of Aeneas and preceded the settlement of Alba Longa.[169] According to the account of these wars given by Boccaccio, the principal opponent of Ascanius was Mezentius, who was both a giant and a tyrant, and therefore, like Tantalus, a natural enemy of the "vertuous race" of Elfin emperors descended from Hercules. I know of no authority, however, for supplying Mezentius with more than one head, or for giving him a similarly multiple-headed brother. Spenser may have found these details or the incidents symbolized by them in some "fabulous history" which I have not seen.

The last unidentified Elfin emperor to be mentioned by name is

> Elfinor, who was in Magick skild;
> He built by art upon the glassy See
> A bridge of bras, whose sound heavens thunder seem'd to bee.

I believe that Elfinor is Brutus, founder of the third Troy, and that the magic bridge stands for London Bridge, which might be connected with Brutus in the same way as the Trojan wall with Tros and the Roman Capitol with Aeneas. In each case the founder of the city's fame would be given credit in the Elfin Chronicle for constructing the particular "wonder of the world" in which that fame was concretely symbolized. Thus the Trojan wall may stand for the eter-

[169] *Ibid.*, p. 120. Cf. *FQ*, III, IX, xliii.

nal name of Troy, the Roman Capitol for the power over
"all the world" which made Rome the consummation of ancient glory, and London Bridge for the commercial and
maritime supremacy which was to make London the "glory
of the later world."[170]

But Elfinor's bridge is built, not over a river, but on "the
glassy See," and it is made, not of stone, but of brass, which
gives out a sound like "heavens thunder." Panthea bears
an obvious likeness to the Mirabilian Capitol; but where
is the likeness between London Bridge and its fairy counterpart? To answer this question, we must consider the hitherto unnoticed sources for Spencer's description of the fairy
bridge, which combines features of two famous mythical
bridges, one belonging to medieval, and one to classical
mythology. The first of these is the magic bridge of the Virgilian legend. This is built in the air, sometimes across the
sea, sometimes across a river.[171] In the English *Virgilius,* Virgil uses this bridge to connect Rome and Babylon, thus fa-
cilitating the progress of his love affair with the Sowdan's
daughter.[172] Jean d'Outremeuse omits the love affair, but
gives a more detailed description of the magic bridge, which
suggests Spenser's description in the Elfin Chronicle:

... fist Virgile l pont parmy une aighe [i.e., eau or lac] tout pendant en aire par nigromanche, qui fut li plus grans de monde
et li plus beal: mains ilh n'avoit et n'at ovriers ne jometriens
en monde qui saroit aviseir par queile manere ilh astoit fais
li commenchemens en aighe ne en terre. Et pendoit tot en aere,
et ne savoit nuls dire comment ilh soy sortenoit; si passoit ons
tout parmi à grans gens, et mult de pessans faus [fardeaux] enssi
bien et mies que sur l altre pont.[173]

[170] Cf. Dunbar, *In Honour of the City of London,* iv–v, 2.
[171] Spargo, *Virgil the Necromancer,* pp. 61, 63, 64, 65, 67.
[172] Thoms, *Early English Prose Romances,* II, 45–49.
[173] *Myreur,* I, 255.

Surely this is the bridge which Spenser introduces into the *Ruines of Time* as an emblem of this world's vanity:[174]

> Then did I see a Bridge, made all of golde,
> Over the Sea from one to other side,
> Withouten prop or pillour it t' upholde,
> But like the coulored Rainbowe arched wide:
> Not that great Arche, which *Traian* edifide,
> To be a wonder to all age ensuing,
> Was matchable to this in equall vewing.
> But (ah) what bootes it to see earthlie thing
> In glorie, or in greatnes to excell,
> Sith time doth greatest things to ruine bring?
> This goodlie bridge, one foote not fastend well,
> Gan faile, and all the rest downe shortlie fell,
> Ne of so brave a building ought remained,
> That griefe thereof my spirite greatly pained.[175]

In this passage Spenser places the magic bridge of Virgil among the "wonders of the world" as a symbol of earthly glory. The same symbolic meaning belongs to the principal monuments of Cleopolis. The use which Spenser makes of the Virgilian bridge in the *Ruines of Time* explains, therefore, why Elfinor's bridge should be "built by art upon the glassy See,"[176] for these details are obviously drawn from the Virgilian legend. But Elfinor's bridge is also made of brass, which makes a sound like thunder. These elements in Spenser's description of the fairy bridge come from the story of Salmoneus, who appears among the famous sinners in Virgil's Tartarus.[177] According to Boccaccio, the crime of Salmo-

---

[174] I do not wish to imply that the passage in the *Myreur* is necessarily the source of Spenser's description, but to emphasize that they both refer to the same bridge.

[175] *RT*, ll. 547–60.

[176] "Glassy" may simply be an epithet like "beryl" or "crystal," meaning "shining" or "bright" rather than "smooth." Cf. the "vitrea unda" of Virgil *Aen.* vii. 759, and the "vitreo ponto" of Horace *Carm.* iv. ii. 4–5.

[177] *Aen.* vi. 585.

neus consisted in his having spanned the city of Elis with a brazen bridge, over which he rode up and down in his chariot, imitating the sound of a thunderstorm. For this impiety he was smitten with a genuine thunderbolt by Jove.[178] Salmoneus was a well-known type of pride, which in Christian thought is closely connected with the notion of earthly glory, and this connection may explain the fusion of the brazen bridge of Salmoneus with the magic bridge of Virgil in Spenser's picture of the fairy bridge.

The contamination of the two legends may have been suggested to Spenser by some lines on the Parisian bridge in Stoa's *Cleopolis*. Stoa is comparing the bridges of Paris with famous bridges of antiquity:

> Quid Traiane tuum pontem memorabis: in imo
> Flumine constructum: cuius miranda per aevum
> Phama fuit: pateat fluvii quum tanta vorago.
> Dic mihi tam tumidi quae tanta audacia fastus
> Mantua te exagitat: stimuloque impingit acuto
> Ob proprium proferre caput super aera pontem.[179]

The reference here to the fame of Trajan's bridge as "miranda per aevum" recalls Spenser's comparison of the bridge in the *Ruines of Time* to

> that great Arche, which *Traian* edifide
> To be a wonder to all age ensuing.[180]

Mantua's pride in her famous bridge may have suggested both the magic bridge of the Mantuan poet,[181] and the

---

[178] *Gen. de gli dei*, p. 237.   [179] Page ciii.

[180] Possibly Spenser is referring to Trajan's arch and not to his bridge over the Danube, but the context indicates that the bridge was at least in his mind, and may have suggested the reference to the arch. Renwick assumes that the bridge is meant. See his edition of *Complaints*, p. 201. Neither the arch nor the bridge of Trajan appear in the usual lists of the seven wonders of the world.

[181] Could Spenser have taken "super aera" with "pontem" instead of with "caput"?

brazen bridge of proud Salmoneus, and Stoa's mention of these famous bridges in his encomium on Paris may have influenced Spenser's description of the Elfin counterpart to London Bridge.

Whether or not this passage from Stoa's *Cleopolis* had a direct influence on Spenser, it certainly exhibits a fairly striking combination of the same elements which we have seen underlying Spenser's description of Elfinor's bridge. The same ideas can be detected in Britomart's reference to London Bridge in her description of Troynovant as last and greatest of the three Troys:

> It *Troynovant* is hight, that with the waves
>   Of wealthy *Thamis* washed is along,
>   Upon whose stubborne neck, whereat he raves
>   With roring rage, and sore him selfe does throng,
>   That all men feare to tempt his billowes strong,
>   She fastned hath her foot, which stands so hy,
>   That it a wonder of the world is song
>   In forreine landes, and all which passen by,
> Beholding it from far, do thinke it threates the skye.

> The *Troian Brute* did first that Citie found,
>   And Hygate made the meare thereof by West,
>   And *Overt* gate by North: that is the bound
>   Toward the land; two rivers bound the rest,
>   So huge a scope at first him seemed best,
>   To be the compasse of his kingdomes seate:
>   So huge a mind could not in lesser rest,
>   Ne in small meares containe his glory great,
> That *Albion* had conquered first by warlike feat.[182]

London Bridge is here a symbol of the pride and power of Britain. It is the "foot" of the imperial city planted in triumph upon the neck of the proud river, which brings the wealth of the Indies to the royal seat of Gloriana. The

[182] *FQ*, III, IX, xlv–xlvi.

"roring rage" of the Thames recalls the fury of the Danube near Trajan's bridge.[183] The emphasis on the height of London Bridge, which makes it a "wonder of the world," is likewise reminiscent both of Trajan's "great Arche" and of the ill-fated golden bridge of the *Ruines of Time,* while the phrase "threates the skye" suggests the *hybris* exemplified in the action of Salmoneus. Last of all, this praise of London Bridge as a symbol of British power is closely linked with the praise of Brutus, in whose "huge mind" the future glories of the British Empire were first conceived.

These same ideas, I believe, are expressed "under covert veil" in the account of Elfinor and his magic bridge. The identification of Elfinor with Brutus is further indicated by the other details which Spenser relates of this Elfin emperor:

> He left three sonnes, the which in order rayned,
> And all their Ofspring in their dew descents,
> Even seven hundred Princes, which maintaynd
> With mightie deedes their sundry governments;
> That were too long their infinite contents
> Here to record. . . .

This fits Brutus, as it fits no one else in the genealogy after Hercules, for Brutus, like Hercules, divided his kingdom among his three sons. The "seven hundred princes" would on this theory be identified with the succeeding British ancestors of Henry VII. The number does not correspond to any list of British kings known to me, and seems far too large, unless Spenser is including literally "all their Ofspring," that is, subordinate princes of Trojan blood as well as actual rulers of Britain.[184] Probably, however, the number

[183] Emphasized not only by Stoa but by Dio Cassius *Roman History* lxviii. xiii.

[184] Geoffrey's list from Brutus to Cadwallader has 91 kings. Kelton gives 20 princes from Cadwallader to Edmond, Earl of Richmond, father of Henry VII.

has a mystical significance, and is not intended to be taken too literally. Harrison, following the example of Bodin, had managed to show that changes in the government and in the religion of Britain had occurred in cycles, and that the number of years in each cycle was a multiple of seven or nine.[185] The first chapter of *Matthew* furnished an example of cycles arranged according to generations. The "seven hundred princes" may thus stand for "the dynasty of Brutus" or "the first cycle of Trojan rule in Britain" rather than for an actual number of rulers. In this connection we may remember that Spenser in the British Chronicle connects the number seven hundred with the line of Brutus:

> Here ended *Brutus* sacred progenie,
>   Which had seven hundred yeares this scepter borne,
>   With high renowme, and great felicitie;
>   The noble braunch from th'antique stocke was torne
> Through discord, and the royall throne forlorne:
> Thenceforth this Realme was into factions rent,
> Whilest each of *Brutus* boasted to be borne,
> That in the end was left no moniment
> Of *Brutus,* nor of Britons glory auncient.[186]

This ancient glory is, however, restored by the accession of Donwallo, "the gracious Numa of great Britanie," whose achievement in reuniting the kingdom would naturally suggest to an Elizabethan the similar achievement of Henry VII, who follows the seven hundred princes in the Elfin Chronicle. We thus have the following parallel sequences: in the British Chronicle—Brutus, seven hundred years of glorious rule under his descendants, an interregnum of civil war, and the restoration of British glory by Donwallo; in the Elfin Chronicle—Brutus (Elfinor), seven hundred princes who rule gloriously, and "after all these" a renewal of glorious victory by Henry VII (Elficleos). The inter-

185 Holinshed, I, 49–51.   186 *FQ,* II, X, xxxvi.

regnum of Saxon, Norman, and Plantagenet kings is not mentioned in the Elfin Chronicle. The number seven hundred may thus serve to indicate the portion of the Elfin Chronicle which runs parallel with the British history in the same canto.

Another hint of overlapping at this point is given in the general commendation with which the "seven hundred princes" are dismissed. They should be, says the Elfin Chronicle,

> most famous moniments,
> And brave ensample, both of martiall,
> And civill rule to kings and states imperiall.

It will be remembered that the "Chronicle of Briton Kings" from Brutus to Uther which Arthur reads is entitled *Briton Moniments*.

These slight verbal likenesses between the British and Elfin chronicles would not of themselves be sufficient to establish the identification of the seven hundred princes suggested above. If the identification of Elfinor with Brutus be accepted, however, the number seven hundred and the phrase "famous moniments" applied to his successors may perhaps be numbered among the "certain signes" by which Spenser intended Elizabeth to recognize her "own realmes in lond of Faery," and her own ancestors in the Elfin emperors. For if the foregoing interpretation of the *Antiquitie of Faerie lond* is correct, the British and Elfin chronicles in Book II, Canto X, are supplementary. Taken together, they fulfil Spenser's promise, given at the beginning of the canto, to recount "the famous auncestries" of his royal mistress. The fairy genealogy extends from Adam to Queen Elizabeth, mentions by (fairy) name only the most important rulers between Osiris and Brutus, emphasizing particularly the founders of the three Troys, and then passes over the British kings with a brief summary in order to celebrate the three great Tudors. The British Chronicle gives the British kings from Brutus to Arthur's immediate predecessor. (His successors to Cadwallader are given in Merlin's prophecy in Book III, Canto III.) The Elfin Chronicle, which contains the praise of Elizabeth herself, is of particular importance in symbolizing the history of the single just empire, beginning in Egypt, passing through Troy and Rome to England, ruled always by members of the "vertuous race" whose fame was eternized with the fame of their royal cities in the truly "eternal city" of Cleopolis, capital of Fairyland.

Spenser's Elfin Empire, in the political allegory, represents the future British Empire regarded as the legitimate successor of the famous empires that had preceded it. The political ideal expressed in Spenser's *Faerie Queene* is thus a nationalistic modification of that great medieval dream of the Holy Roman Empire which inspired Dante's greater poem. Dante had justified the Roman claim to universal dominion partly on the score of heredity, by proving that Aeneas was allied by birth and marriage with the noblest blood of all three parts of the world:

Nam Asia propinquioribus avis, ut Assaracus et aliis qui Frigiam regnaverunt, Asie regionem . . . Europa vero avo antiquissimo, scilicet Dardano: Affrica quoque avia vetustissima, Electra scilicet nata magni nominis regis Athlantis.[187]

Similarly, the wives of Aeneas, Creusa, Dido, and Lavinia, belonged to ruling families of Asia, Africa, and Europe, respectively.[188]

A similar claim on the part of the British royal house is justified by Spenser's Elfin genealogy. The empire of Osiris had its capital in Africa, and included also America, the fourth part of the world which was unknown to Dante. Tros

[187] *De mon.,* II, iii, 10–11.   [188] *Ibid.,* II, iii, 14–17.

and Assaracus had ruled in Asia, and Brutus, through his descent from Aeneas, had claims to European sovereignty which later enabled Arthur to defy the power of Rome.

Like Dante, Spenser conceives his ideal empire as divinely instituted for the maintenance of true religion and virtue; and like Dante, he finds a model for his expression of personal patriotic feeling in the work of Virgil, to whom of all the "famous poets historicall" whom he professed to follow, he owed the profoundest, if not the most obvious debt. Spenser aspired to do for England what Virgil had done for Rome: to write an epic which should vindicate the excellency of the English tongue and celebrate the glorious destiny of the British Empire as heir of all the ages. This second purpose finds expression under "covert veil" in the fabulous genealogy of his Fairy Queen.

But why should Spenser entrust this important idea to such a brief and cryptic form of expression as the Elfin Chronicle? And why should this revelation of the history and destiny of the British Empire be made to Guyon rather than to Arthur, in whose reign that empire was first established, and by whose descendants it was to be revived? The answer to both these questions is the same. Spenser did not finish his poem. It is extremely probable that he did intend to reiterate the teaching of his Elfin Chronicle more fully and clearly in a later book, when Arthur himself should learn of his ancestry, as Merlin had promised he should[189] and should be instructed, perhaps by Gloriana herself, in the past and future glories of his race. We can even make a pretty good guess as to when this revelation was to take place. One of Spenser's favorite devices is the bringing of each subordinate hero shortly before his final adventure to an allegorical house in which he receives some important instruction as to the nature of the virtue he represents and

[189] *FQ*, I, IX, v, 9.

the rewards of its successful practice. Thus St. George visits the House of Holiness, Guyon the Castle of Alma, Scudamour the Temple of Venus, and Artegall the Palace of Mercilla.[190] It is reasonable to suppose that Spenser would use the same device in describing the adventures of Arthur. Shortly before the achievement of his final adventure, which I suspect was to be the deliverance of Gloriana from the "great Paynim King who works her teene," against whom St. George is pledged to assist her,[191] and whose great battle with Gloriana's knights was apparently designed for the principal epic action of the later books,[192] Arthur should receive some final vision or instruction which would strengthen him for the great achievement by which he was to win the favor of Gloriana. Now the logical allegorical house for Arthur to visit on this occasion is surely Panthea, the Temple of Fame. The exact nature of his experience there cannot of course be ascertained, but its general character is indicated by the fame visions discussed in the preceding chapter, all of which give several devices by which Arthur might receive a full and clear explanation of the nature of the Elfin Empire over which he was destined to rule, along the lines indicated by the veiled account already given in the *Antiquitie of Fairy lond.* Guyon's experience in the chamber of memory would thus foreshadow Arthur's

---

[190] Calidore's open air vision of the Graces might be added to these. Like them it occurs in the tenth canto. Book III alone has no such "House of Chastity" or "True Love," but Book III is in many ways apart from Spenser's usual scheme.

[191] *FQ*, I, XII, xviii, 3–9.

[192] Cf. the appeal to the Muse, I, XI, v, 6–vii, 9. This passage has sometimes been taken to refer to a later poem or to the battle with the Soldan in Book V, but the interpretation suggested in the text seems most probable. An epic action at the end of the *Faerie Queene*, uniting the heroes of the separate quests, would give an excellent opportunity for the rehearsal of antecedent material promised in the *Letter to Raleigh,* as well as being almost obligatory for a poem which was professedly modeled on the epics of Homer, Virgil, Ariosto, and Tasso.

experience in the House of Fame. The idea of the just empire, eternized because of its justice, is first revealed "under covert veil" to Guyon, then developed more clearly, but less completely, in connection with Britomart and Artegall, to be finally expressed completely and clearly in the culminating vision of Arthur himself.

As to the obscurity of the Elfin Chronicle in Spenser's day, that would vary with the reader. Everyone could see that it contained a compliment to the Queen and a celebration of her ancestry, since it made her descend from a line of great emperors who had ruled over the whole world. A reader with some knowledge of the ancient history derived from "Berosus" (and every educated reader would possess this knowledge) would recognize the first two emperors as Osiris and Hercules, and naturally assume that the succeeding emperors included the Trojan line. An educated reader with a taste for puzzles might go on to work out a more detailed identification of the Elfin emperors along the lines suggested above. The failure of modern critics to reach such an interpretation is to be explained by their lack of familiarity with the "fabulous history" of Berosus, which gives the clue to Spenser's fairy chronicle.

But why should this chronicle be read by Guyon? The other minor hero with whom these ideas are associated is Artegall, and Artegall is not only the knight of Justice, but the ancestor of Elizabeth. The fact that Guyon is singled out to receive the first expression of the ideas we have detected in the Elfin Chronicle would seem to indicate that he also occupies a position close to Arthur in the historical fiction and in the moral allegory. The position of Guyon in the historical fiction is still obscure. If he represents some historical or legendary ancestor of Elizabeth, Spenser has certainly concealed his identity, at least from us, under a "shadow," which is far from "light." Similarly if Guyon's importance derives from his representing some prominent Elizabethan, no one has so far pointed out any convincing identification. With the moral allegory, however, we are on surer ground.

At first sight this statement may seem questionable. What has the notion of the single just empire and its eternal counterpart in the city of fame to do with the virtue of temperance? And how does the reading of chronicles prepare Guyon for the overthrow of Acrasia? This last question has always puzzled Spenser critics, many of whom have felt that this canto was a somewhat dull interpolation, without organic connection with the book in which it appears.

This position receives partial support in Dr. Strathmann's recent paper on Book II,[193] which denies any structural importance to Canto X. "The structural equation," he says, "is between Canto 10 of Book I and Canto 9 of Book II."[194] In other words, it is not Guyon's reading of chronicles, but his previous tour of Alma's castle which parallels St. George's experience in the House of Holiness and on the mount of Heavenly Contemplation. Yet since Cantos IX and X form "a single narrative episode,"[195] one would think that Guyon's reading of the Elfin Chronicle would parallel St. George's vision of the New Jerusalem. Our problem, then, is to explain in what way Guyon's total experience in the House of Temperance, culminating in his reading of history, prepares him for the overthrow of Acrasia.

The solution depends not only upon our interpretation of the Elfin Chronicle, but also upon our understanding of the virtue of temperance as Spenser conceived it, and hence of its importance in the general scheme of his poem. Like justice temperance is an inclusive virtue, which consists in

---

[193] "The Structure of Book II of the *Faerie Queene*," abstracted in *Variorum Spenser*, II, 467–71.
[194] *Ibid.*, p. 467.   [195] *Ibid.*

the maintenance of a certain relationship between the different parts of the soul. A man was temperate when his passions and appetites were controlled by his reason, or in the
language of Elizabethan psychology, when his animal and
vegetative souls were controlled by his rational soul. The
importance of this psychology in the moral allegory of Book
II has often been pointed out.[196] Dr. Strathmann in particular has shown that the Castle of Alma, which summarizes
the main teaching of the book, is itself an epitome of current
psychology, and has found in the exposition there presented
of the relation between the three souls, the answer to the
question with which this enquiry began. Guyon's adventures are divided into two parts, in the first of which he
combats wrong uses of the *irascibile,* and, in the second,
wrong uses of the *concupiscibile.*[197] Now these two functions
of the animal soul, whose rational control is temperance,
correspond to the two main activities of a knight, war and
love. A true gentleman fights, "not for malice and conten-
tious crimes," but for the "praise and honour" which can
only be attained in a just quarrel.

This idea is well developed by William Blandy in *The
Castle or Picture of Pollicy* (1581), a book which Spenser
probably knew, since it was dedicated to Sidney, and contained an enthusiastic encomium on Sir John Norris, under
whom the author had presumably served in the Low Countries. In answer to the question: "Is the contempt of death
in all men equally honored?," Blandy first rules out suicides
and "those who offer themselves to daunger, not with judgement, and prudent advise, but being pricked forward with
a rage or fury of minde conceived either of hatred, envy, or
some other earnest & hoate affection," and those who go into
danger with a hope of escaping. Blandy then describes the

[196] *Ibid.,* pp. 458–71.   [197] Cf. *FQ,* II, VI, i.

true "marke whereunto . . . this contempt of death should be directed":

The marke and end which this contempt of death ought to respect and looke upon, is the glory of Christ, the honor of our Prince, the cause of our countrye, the defence of our name and honesty. They that venture theyr lives for these poyntes, are appoynted in the right course and race of true honor: for that they obtayne the true and undoubted end of vertue: wherefore all other that purpose unto themselves riches fame and glory depending on the consent of the unlettered multitude, and respect not the true soveraygne good, they are rather to be accompted men puft upp with vayne desire, and ambition, then valiant and couragious men.[198]

Blandy is discussing courage, not temperance, but his brave man has obvious affinities with Spenser's Guyon. In fact, no detailed consideration of temperance could avoid describing true courage, which is essentially the right use of the *irascibile*.

Still more important is that part of a knight's activity which involves the *concupiscibile*. A true knight desires neither wealth and the esteem that may be paid to it, nor mere sensual pleasure, but glory. He rejects Philotime and overthrows Acrasia because he loves Gloriana. Now this is the teaching not only of Book II, but also of the whole *Faerie Queene*.

"Fierce warres and faithfull loves shall moralize my song,"[199] says Spenser in his "proposition." The wars are the conflicts waged against evil by the Fairy knights, and especially by Arthur, and of the "faithfull loves" the most important is the love of Arthur for Gloriana, which kindled "glorious fire" in his heart. The virtue of temperance, or passion under the control of reason, is presented negatively in Book II, in Guyon under the control of the Palmer, over-

[198] Page 12.   [199] *FQ*, I, Proem, i, 9.

coming temptations to make a wrong use of his passions, and in Arthur defending Alma from the assaults of Maleger and his crew. The positive side of this virtue, merely hinted at in the career of Guyon, would be fully exemplified in the main adventures of Arthur. His conquest of Orgoglio and the Soldan, and probably his later defeat of that other "proud Paynim king," combining the evil qualities of the other two, and like them representing the power of Spain, would symbolize the right use of the *irascibile,* as his love for Gloriana the right use of the *concupiscibile.* This fundamental likeness between the moral significance of Guyon and Arthur, the one exhibiting the negative, the other the positive side of temperance, is illustrated in the choice each makes of a partner in Alma's parlor. Guyon chooses Shamefastness, which withholds from evil actions; Arthur chooses Prayse-Desire, which inspires to good ones.

The virtue of temperance is thus in a special sense the virtue of a gentleman, and Guyon, as truly as Arthur himself, is the "image of a brave knight," dedicated to the quest of glory, bearing the picture of the Fairy Queen upon his shield. To withdraw Guyon from this knightly pursuit is the aim of Archimago,

> For all he did, was to deceive good knights,
> And draw them from pursuit of praise and fame,
> To slug in slouth and sensuall delights,
> And end their daies with irrenowmed shame.[200]

The exact opposite of Guyon is Braggadochio, the imitation gentleman,[201] who lacks all the qualities of the true, gentle blood, knightly training, courage, indifference to

[200] *Ibid.,* II, I, xxiii, 1–4.

[201] For this reason I question the common identification of Braggadochio with Alençon, who, unpopular though he might be, was still one of the first gentlemen in Europe and a prince of the blood.

money, and the power of feeling a generous indignation or
a genuine love,

> For in base mind nor friendship dwels nor enmity.[202]

In Belphoebe's rebuke of Braggadochio Spenser expresses
the knightly ideal of a strenuous life spent in the active
pursuit of honor:

> Who so in pompe of proud estate (quoth she)
>   Does swim, and bathes himselfe in courtly blis,
>   Does waste his dayes in darke obscuritee,
>   And in oblivion ever buried is:
>   Where ease abounds, yt's eath to doe amis;
>   But who his limbs with labours, and his mind
>   Behaves with cares, cannot so easie mis.
> Abroad in armes, at home in studious kind
> Who seekes with painfull toile, shall honor soonest find.
>
> In woods, in waves, in warres she wonts to dwell,
>   And will be found with perill and with paine;
>   Ne can the man, that moulds in idle cell,
>   Unto her happie mansion attaine:
>   Before her gate high God did Sweat ordaine,
>   And wakefull watches ever to abide:
>   But easie is the way, and passage plaine
>   To pleasures pallace; it may soone be spide,
> And day and night her dores to all stand open wide.[203]

In these lines the ideal of a true gentleman, servant of
Gloriana, honor, is distinguished from the ideal of a mere
idle courtier, servant of Acrasia, pleasure. A similar spirit
with even more emphasis on the military side of the knightly
ideal is shown in Guyon's rejection of Mammon's offer:

> *Mammon* (said he) thy godheades vaunt is vaine,
>   And idle offers of thy golden fee;
>   To them, that covet such eye-glutting gaine,
> Proffer thy giftes, and fitter servaunts entertaine.

[202] *FQ*, IV, IV, xi, 9.   [203] *Ibid.*, II, III, xl–xli.

> Me ill besits, that in der-doing armes,
> And honours suit my vowed dayes do spend,
> Unto thy bounteous baytes, and pleasing charmes,
> With which weake men thou witchest, to attend:
> Regard of worldly mucke doth fowly blend,
> And low abase the high heroicke spright,
> That ioyes for crownes and kingdomes to contend;
> Faire shields, gay steedes, bright armes be my delight:
> Those be the riches fit for an advent'rous knight.[204]

The essentially aristocratic nature of temperance as Spenser conceived it gives one explanation for the likeness in moral significance between the adventures of Guyon and Arthur. Another may be found in the political theory connected with the psychological definition of temperance. In the Castle of Alma, as Dr. Strathmann and others have pointed out, Spenser portrayed the body of a temperate man as a mansion containing the three souls all in their appropriate positions, and all under the control of Alma, the rational soul. In developing this idea, Spenser makes use of an old figure which compares the body of the individual to the body politic:

> But in a body, which doth freely yeeld
> His partes to reasons rule obedient,
> And letteth her that ought the scepter weeld,
> All happy peace and goodly government
> Is setled there in sure establishment;
> There *Alma* like a virgin Queene most bright,

[204] *Ibid.*, II, VII, ix, 6–x, 9. Cf. Blandy, *op. cit.*, pp. 18–19. "The Profession . . . of the . . . Souldiar . . . resteth in the maintenaunce to death, of a good and rightfull cause: the condition no less paynefull then full of perill, the quality, cleane, diligent, duetifull, delighting rather in brave furniture and glittering armor, then in deynty dyet, womanlyke wantonnes, and vayne pleasures. . . . Finally the onely chiefe grace, that beautifieth the minde of a Souldiar, is the contempt of Spoyle and refusall of riches. For the corrupt opinion of wealth and pleasures, are the enemies of verue [*sic*. "vertue?"], the allurements not to so fond, as wicked endevors."

Doth florish in all beautie excellent:
And to her guestes doth bounteous banket dight,
Attempred goodly well for health and for delight.[205]

Probably the earliest, and certainly the most famous use of
this comparison is in Plato's *Republic,* where the different
parts of the soul are made to correspond to the different
classes in society. Thus the rational part of the soul cor-
responded to the guardians or philosophers, the "spirited"
or animal part to the auxiliaries or soldiers, and the "con-
cupiscent" part to the producing classes. Similarly the three
souls of Elizabethan psychology might be made to correspond to the traditional three estates of medieval political
theory. The rational soul would correspond to the clergy,
the animal soul to the nobility, and the vegetative soul to
the commons. Such a division, however, would hardly
please a Tudor monarch, particularly after the Reformation. Yet the notion of fixed social classes persisted in Elizabethan political thinking.[206] A typical example is William
Blandy's already mentioned *Castle or Picture of Pollicy.* In
this dialogue the ideal commonwealth is depicted under the
figure of a castle of two stories, each containing three rooms.
The three upper ones are inhabited by the prince, who
must have preëminence, the justiciar, and the soldier; the
three lower by the merchant, the artisan, and the peasant.
There is no mention of the clergy at all, though Blandy has
much to say of religion, especially in his portrait of the ideal
general who suggests both Guyon and Arthur:

A Generall ought first and chiefely behold the Maiestye of
God, and cause therefore his true Religion in his Armye to be
had in due reverence: in such sort, that his Souldiars may per-

[205] *FQ,* II, XI, ii.
[206] Cf. Shakespeare's use of the fable of Menenius Agrippa in *Coriolanus,*
I, i, and the very full discussion of this whole subject in Mohl, *The Three
Estates in Medieval and Renaissance Literature,* pp. 143–255, 276 *et sqq.*

ceave he is indeede Religious. And lett him by all meanes cause
the Priestes and Ministers of his holy will and testament, in his
Armye to retayne their dignitye, and to be esteemed and rever-
enced of his Souldiars: for if the very Paynims by due observa-
tions of their fayned Religion, did keepe their Armies in
marvelous obedience and order: how much more shall true Religion, delivered from our Lord and Saviour, prevaile a Generall, and Armye that loveth him, to the atchieving great and
miraculous victoryes. Also the Generall ought to be modest,
prudent, and temperate; geven to no ryot and excesse, neither
miserably bent to filthy lucre. It standeth greatly on him to
avoyd the name of a vaunter: which is seene in this, that he doe
not vendicate to himselfe alone the prayse of good successe: but
do impute the same first to God. Secondly to his Captaynes.
Thirdly to his Soldiars. Furthermore it behoveth a Generall to
be a noble Gentleman, trayned up in those sciences, through
the knowledge wherof, he shall sooner attayne that perfection,
which in a Generall is needefull. Lastly, . . . a Generall must be
religious, temperate, sober, wise, valiant, liberall, curteous, Elo-
quent, & of good fame and reputation.[207]

Blandy's division of society does not correspond to the
three souls, nor need we assume that his idea of the number
and relative importance of classes in society would correspond exactly to Spenser's. It is not difficult, however, to
work out the comparison suggested in the stanza quoted
above between the castle of Alma and a Spenserian "Castle
of Pollicy" to which Plato, Blandy, and a host of other
writers may have contributed directly or indirectly. Alma,
the rational soul, corresponds to the Queen, to whom absolute obedience is due. The three wise sages, Imagination,
Reason, and Memory, faculties of the rational soul, who
assist Alma in her government, may represent the learned
men of the realm. Or perhaps they symbolize her thorough
knowledge of literature, philosophy, and history, the studies
which feed the rational soul. The ladies and their para-

[207] *Castle or Picture of Pollicy*, p. 19.

mours, with whom Guyon and Arthur disport themselves in the parlor, the realm of the passions, or animal soul, would represent, together with the two knights themselves, the nobility and gentry whose principal function was war in the service of the Queen. The lower regions of Decoction, Digestion, and so forth, would correspond to the merchant and laboring classes who supply the material wants of the state, as the vegetative soul attends to the physical needs of the body.

Plato had said that a State was just if each of its various classes did their own work, without interfering with that of the others, and that it was temperate when the auxiliaries, the spirited class, were obedient to the guardians. Spenser's giant with the scales in Book V suggests a similar view of justice as dependent on fixed order. We may perhaps see in the comparison of the castle of Alma to the commonwealth ruled by a Virgin Queen, a similarly Platonic notion of temperance in the State. In a temperate State, Spenser would say, the nobility and gentry are obedient to the crown. Under the rule of a wise and virtuous prince, the aristocracy will be given over neither to fierce domestic factions, as in the old turbulent feudal days which were still remembered, nor to the enervating and immoral luxury which Englishmen saw in the courts of France and Italy. In a temperate State the nobility would be a chosen army of stainless knights, dedicated to the pursuit of glory for themselves and for their country under the wise rule of a virtuous prince.

The virtue of temperance is thus of special importance to a gentleman, not only because it is necessary for the development of his other virtues, but also because in its exercise he fulfills the end for which his class exists, and does his duty in that state of life unto which it has pleased God to call him. The experience of Arthur and Guyon in the House of Temperance is thus a preparation not only for their victories over Maleger and Acrasia, but also for Arthur's destined winning of Gloriana. As Dr. Strathmann has pointed out, the preparation consists in the exhibition of the working of the three souls in the body of a temperate man. Spenser's conception of temperance as an aristocratic virtue makes it natural that he should pay most attention to the two higher souls. Guyon and Arthur observe the workings of the vegetative soul in their tour through the hall and kitchen, and are thus presumably fortified against intemperate indulgence in the pleasures of the table, but as this type of intemperance has played no part in the previous adventures of Guyon, and is only briefly hinted at later in the Bowre of Blis, we may assume that Spenser did not regard it as a serious danger to the aristocrat. Accordingly Guyon and Arthur do not comment on what they see in Alma's hall and kitchen, nor do they perform any action there. It is otherwise in the parlor, realm of the passions, which Aristotle had said was the realm of moral choice,[208] and which was the special field for the display of temperance both in the individual and in the State. Here the knights choose two ladies, who, as we have seen, symbolize two aspects of the gentleman's ruling passion, the desire to shun dishonor and to attain glory. In the upper chamber of memory they learn the rational basis for this choice. For the glory which the gentleman seeks, not only for himself, but also for his country, is recorded in history, which shows forth the fame of our ancestors, and inspires us to deserve equally well of posterity. It is for this reason that the culminating experience of Arthur and Guyon in the House of Temperance is the reading of chronicles, and that this episode is structurally parallel to St. George's vision of the New Jerusalem. In each case the hero is instructed in the end for which his particular virtue exists. The end of holiness is

[208] *Nichomachaean Ethics* i. xi.

beatitude, heavenly glory. The end of temperance, as of all
knightly virtue, is earthly glory, or fame. Thus, while St.
George sees a vision of the heavenly city, where he is at last
to dwell, a saint with saints, Guyon reads the history of the
earthly city, Cleopolis, in whose glories he has a worthy part
as servant of Gloriana and destined conqueror of her enemy,
the evil fay, Acrasia, destroyer of knightly fame. The method
by which Guyon learns the end for which his virtue exists
and the reward of its successful operation, is certainly less
vivid and less attractive than the method by which St.
George receives a similar instruction and inspiration. As
we have seen, however, Spenser had a reason for this difference in method. To present Guyon or Arthur, whose end
is the same as Guyon's, with a vision of Cleopolis, to depict
the glory which is recorded in history as a pageant instead of
as a chronicle, would have been to anticipate prematurely
the climax of his poem. Yet his didactic scheme made it
essential that the episode of the House of Temperance
should close with some presentation of the idea that under-
lies not only the Legend of Sir Guyon but also the central
story of Arthur's quest, namely, the desire of fame. This
emotion, which is both personal and patriotic, is stimulated
by the reading of history. Hence, while Arthur's patriotism
is aroused by reading the Chronicle of British Kings, to
which he is himself to add the most glorious chapter, Guyon
reads of the earlier and later glories of Arthur's race, of
Cleopolis, the eternal city, the Troy that fears no Achilles,
of Panthea, the temple of fame, mirror of the world, of the
brazen bridge spanning the sea, and of Gloriana, last of the
Elfin emperors, whose preëminence in virtue made them
fitting rulers over Fairyland, the kingdom of earthly fame.

In the preceding chapter we discussed one line of tradition
which seems to have influenced Spenser's conception of
Fairyland. Another line is suggested by our interpretation

of the Elfin Chronicle. Both allegorical poetry and fabulous
history would furnish hints for a mythology which should
celebrate earthly fame as the end of heroic action. In his
account of the origin of the fairy nation, Spenser treats his
elves and fays as contemporary historians treated the pagan
gods, that is as famous men, whose immortality is the earnest of their fame. The first two of Spenser's Elfin emperors,
as we have seen, are to be identified with gods of classical
mythology. Others, like Aeneas, were deified. Jean Lemaire
says that gods, goddesses, and nymphs are merely old terms
for royal and noble men and women. He quotes Boccaccio
in support of the statement that the classical nymphs were
simply high-born ladies.[209] All kings in antiquity, he says,
were called "gods." The terms was like the modern "saint."
Harrison expresses the same idea in the passage where he
tells us that the greatest of these "gods" were honored with
"a place in heaven, among the shining starres."[210] But not all
great worthies could have such an honor, he goes on to say,
for there are not stars enough in the heavens. For this reason, "another place was in time imagined, where they
reigned that were of a second calling, as the Semones who
were gods by grace and favour of the people." For the third
class of gods, who resemble Spenser's Elfin emperors, the
ancients imagined "also a third place that is to say an earth,
where those gods dwelled which were noble men, officers,
good governors and lawgivers to the people, and yet not
thought worthie to be of the second or first companie. . . . "[211]

May not this "earth" be Spenser's Fairyland, a mythical
land of fame where departed heroes, the ancestors of his
royal and noble patrons, enjoy an extended, if not an im-

<hr/>

[209] *Œuvres*, I, 197–98. The passage in Boccaccio is in *Gen. de gli dei*, p. 128.
He says some nymphs were personifications of rivers; others, like Circe and
Calypso, were mortals.
[210] See above, p. 142.
[211] Holinshed, I, 38.

mortal life, closely resembling their heroic lives on earth? In interpreting the symbolic meaning of Spenser's Fairyland, we have already seen cogent reasons for identifying it with the world of history, the land of earthly fame. In attempting to reconstruct the mythology by which this symbolic meaning is conveyed, we must be more cautious. In view of the fragmentary state of the *Faerie Queene,* we cannot be sure that Spenser's Fairyland is not purely symbolic, a timeless world in which Arthur, Huon, and Elizabeth Tudor are contemporaries simply in virtue of their exemplary and symbolic characters, and in which the famous dead and the famous living exist side by side with purely abstract embodiments of the virtues and vices which assure or prevent the achievement of lasting fame. Yet Spenser called his ideal country "Fairyland," and Fairyland had a mythology of its own in folklore and romance, which could hardly be ignored. Part of this mythology, the fairy mistress story, forms the basis of Spenser's "historical fiction." Furthermore, Spenser aspired to write an epic, and no epic poet had ever dispensed with mythology. Spenser himself was preëminently a myth maker, and, as Dr. Lotspeich's study has shown, his way with myths was conservative. He combined and adapted existing myths; he seldom invented an entirely new one. It seems likely, therefore, that the general conception of Fairyland as a land of fame has a mythological basis, an amalgam of already existing myths, among which the fairy mythology of romance or folklore must certainly be included. In the classical notions about the homes of gods and heroes, who euhemeristically considered are different only in the degree of their fame, we find suggestions for such a mythology. It utilizes conceptions familiar to Spenser and to his readers, is easily combined with the notions of Fairyland known to them from folklore and still more from romance, and is already associated with the symbolic meaning which was Spenser's general intention. We may thus imagine Osiris, Hercules, Aeneas, and Brutus, with their distinguished followers, withdrawing after their deaths to a blessed island in the western seas, perhaps to Britain itself, where, as Harrison proudly reminds us, Plutarch had located a portion of the Elysian Fields.[212] Here we may imagine them building a city in which is immortalized the glory of the three Troys, whose foundations they laid on earth, and raising the crystal tower which symbolizes not only the eternal part of Rome but the crystal heaven of the stars, home of Harrison's "gods of the first rank." From this royal seat we may imagine the heroes as reigning successively for long years, and dying perhaps at last, as the daemons and heroes die in "The Ceasing of Oracles."[213] In this land as on earth, we are perhaps to imagine the inhabitants as loving, marrying, and having children, the race of "Elfin born" who inherit the long lives and antique virtues of their parents,[214] and like them wage continual warfare against the giants and monsters who represent the forces of tyranny, injustice, and all evil.

The presence of these evil creatures in a heroes' paradise might seem to call for explanation. Spenser does not call

[212] Holinshed, I, 183, 216. For the ancient identification of Britain with the Land of the Dead, see Comes, Lib. III, cap. xix, p. 274, Le Roux de Lincy, *Livre des légendes*, pp. 92–93, Plutarch, *Moralia*, King's translation, pp. 93–94, 245 *et sqq.*, Drayton, *Poly-Olbion*, Song I, ll. 27–30, and Selden's note. Harvey's commendatory verses to the *Faerie Queene* probably contain a punning reference to this belief. ("Elyzas blessed field" = "Elysian field.") For Celtic legends of happy isles near Britain, see L. Whitney, "Spenser's Use of the Literature of Travel in the *Faerie Queene*," *MP*, XIX (1921), 143–62.

[213] Cf. Harrison, in Holinshed, I, 216. He doubts that "infernall spirits can die and give up their ghosts like mortall men, though Saxo seems to consent unto him [Plutarch] in this behalfe."

[214] The idea that the earlier generations of men were very long-lived is common in the Renaissance. The long lives of the heroes link them with the fairies of romance, who are generally represented as living "until the day of Judgment." Oberon, who was half a mortal, lived several hundred years.

Archimago, Orgoglio, and Busirane fairies, and we cannot
be sure that he conceived of them as belonging to the same
race as the denizens of Cleopolis. If they are subjects of
Gloriana at all, they are certainly rebellious ones. Yet their
presence within her domain is not really inconsistent with
the idea that Fairyland is a land of fame whose inhabitants
partake of the nature of gods and demigods. There is good
fame and ill fame. Sinon and Thersites are just as immortal
in story as Hector and Odysseus. History preserves the ill
fame of Geryon, Busiris, and Tantalus, along with the good
fame of Hercules and Tros. The types of evil which history
preserves as warnings generally appear in classical pictures
of the other world, like the sixth book of the *Aeneid*, as inhabiting a country near the abode of the blessed. Spenser
allows them to roam about and exhibit their natures in action, instead of confining them to a single place of punishment.

As we have seen, Lucifera is really a goddess of false glory,
typifying the sinful pride which inspired those whose lives
are remembered as warnings, while Gloriana stands for the
true glory, inspiration of the heroes whose lives are remembered as examples. The two queens thus typify the two main
teachings of history—and of "historical poetry." This symbolic meaning is borne out by their mythological ancestry.
While Gloriana is descended from Osiris-Jupiter, progenitor of the just generation of gods and heroes, Lucifera is
the daughter of Pluto and "sad Proserpina, the Queen of
Hell." Similarly Duessa, the three sons of Aveugle, and
Pyrochles and Cymochles are connected with the deities of
the lower world. Their ancestry goes back to the earlier pre-
Olympian dynasty of gods "begot in Demogorgon's hall."

These infernal deities, rationalized like the gods of
Olympus, appear in the ancient histories of Spenser's day.
In *Albion's England,* for instance, Pluto is a pirate king who

carries off Proserpina, daughter of Ceres, queen of Sicily. Hercules "harrows" the city of Dis, whose capital is so wicked that it is "a figure" of Hell.[215] The giants also figure prominently in these histories, particularly in those derived from "Berosus," in which Biblical legend and classical myth combined to present them as types of evil. Harrison, who devoted a chapter to the subject of giants,[216] tells us that those before the Flood were descended from Cain:

> Berosus also the Chalde writeth, that neere unto Libanus there was a citie called Oenon (which I take to be Hanoch, builded sometime by Cham) [*sic.* It should be Cain.] wherein giants did inhabit, who trusting to the strength and hugeness of their bodies, did verie great oppression and mischeefe in the world. The Hebrues called them generallie Enach, of Hanach the Chebronite, . . . although their first originall was derived from Henoch the sonne of Caine, of whom that pestilent race descended, as I read.[217]

This first generation of giants was destroyed by the Flood, but a new brood soon arose, most of whom were sons of Cham, who had learned all his bad habits from the earlier giants among whom he had lived before the Flood.[218]

The Bible is of course the original authority for the notion that Cham was the father of the giants. Tyndale mentions it in a passage which is significant for the understanding of Spenser's Orgoglio. After speaking of the edifying moral to be drawn from the literal sense of the story of Noah and his sons, Tyndale goes on to say:

> Notwithstanding, this text offers us an apt and an handsome allegory or similitude to describe our wicked Ham, antichrist the pope, which many hundred years hath done all the shame that heart can think unto the word of promise . . . wherewith we are begotten. . . . And as the cursed children of Ham grew into

---

[215] Bk I, chap. vi, *Chalmer's English Poets*, IV, 519.
[216] Holinshed, I, 14 *et sqq.*   [217] *Ibid.*, pp. 15–16.
[218] Lemaire, *Œuvres*, I, 18–19.

giants, so mighty and great that the children of Israel seemed but grasshoppers in respect of them; so the cursed sons of our Ham, the pope, his cardinals, bishops, abbots, monks and friars, are become mighty giants above all power and authority; so that the children of faith, in respect of them, are much less than grasshoppers. They heap mountain upon mountain, and will to heaven by their own strength, by a way of their own making, and not by the way Christ. Neverthelater, those giants, for the wickedness and abominations which they had wrought, did God utterly destroy, part of them by the children of Lot, . . . and seven nations of them by the children of Israel. So no doubt shall he destroy these for like abominations, and that shortly. For their kingdom is but the kingdom of lies and falsehood; which must needs perish at the coming of the truth of God's word.[219]

Tyndale's reference to the giants "heaping mountain upon mountain" suggests the point of likeness between these Biblical giants and the classical Titans with whom they are confused by "Berosus" and other historians. I have already mentioned the part played by these Titans in the war between Cham and Hammon. The same giants later tyrannized over Italy, until they were defeated by Osiris and Hercules in three great battles.[220] Neptune, son of Osiris, was the father of a number of giants, who inherited the evil propensities of their great grandfather, Cham. Among these were Lestrigo, tyrant of Italy, and Albion, both of whom were killed by Hercules.[221] Speaking of the evil customs and "superstitious rites" introduced into Britain by "Albion and his Chemminites,"[222] Harrison says:

From Cham and his successours proceeded at the first all sorcerie, witchcraft, and the execution of unlawful lust, without respect of sex, age, consanguinitie, or kind: as branches from an

[219] "Obedience of a Christian Man," *Doctrinal Treatises,* pp. 311–12.
[220] Lemaire, *Œuvres,* I, 55 *et sqq.*
[221] *Ibid.,* Holinshed, I, 433.
[222] *Ibid.,* pp. 33–34.

odious and abhominable root, or streemes derived from a most filthie and horrible stinking puddle.[223]

It will be remembered that the last remnants of Albion's giant race were destroyed by Trojan Brutus of the line of Hercules.

The existence of giants had been denied by Goropius, whose *Gigantomachia* is mentioned both by Jean Lemaire and by Harrison. The latter offers a significant summary of the various arguments advanced in the controversy over giants:

I do not meane herein to dispute whether this name Gigas or Nephilim was given unto them, rather for their tyrannie and oppression of the people, than for their greatnesse of bodie, or large steps as Goropius would have it (for he denieth that ever men were greater than at this present) or bicause their parents were not knowne, for such in old times were called Terrae filii; or whether the word Gigas dooth onlie signifie Indigenes, or homelings . . . neither whether all men were of like quantitie in stature, and farre more greater in old time, than now they be: and yet absolutelie I denie neither of these, sith verie probable reasons may be brought for ech of them, but especiallie the last rehersed, whose confirmation dependeth upon the authorities of sundrie ancient writers, who make divers of noble race [e.g. Hercules] equall to the giants in strength and manhood, and yet doo not give the same name unto them, bicause their quarels were just, and commonlie taken in hand for defense of the oppressed.[224]

It is obvious that Spenser's giants, types of pride, lust, and tyranny, owe a great deal to this tradition, and their presence in Fairyland as a foil to the fairy knights is another link between Spenser's poem and the euhemerized mythology that passed for ancient history in his day.

The world of the *Faerie Queene* is very largely the world of this history, and the life of Fairyland, kingdom of earthly

[223] *Ibid.,* p. 37.   [224] *Ibid.,* p. 15; cf. *FQ,* III, III, xxxii.

glory, is still the life of that heroic age which succeeded the age of gold and still partook of its splendors. It is not a peaceful world, nor a world without evil, but it is a happy world, for in it virtue is always triumphant, and its heroes are rewarded by the favor of Gloriana, descendant of Osiris, who reigns in the city of Hercules.

This city I have suggested is symbolically the eternal city of earthly fame, of which the three Troys were successively the earthly counterparts, and mythologically the city of departed heroes located in the Elysian Fields. For this latter conception Spenser might have taken some hints from Lucian's *Vera historia,* a popular work which Miss Whitney has suggested as a partial source for the final adventure of Guyon.[225]

Lucian finds the dead inhabiting a group of islands in the western sea. Some of these islands are inhabited by giants, some by the wicked, and one by the blest. Landing on this latter island, Lucian and his companions are questioned by Rhadamanthus, and, after being censured for their rash curiosity in invading the sacred precincts, are given permission to remain seven months with the heroes. They are then taken to the city of the blest, which, in several respects, resembles Spenser's Cleopolis:

The city itself is all of gold, but the wall around it is of emerald. There were seven gates, each a single piece of cinnamon. But the streets of the city and the ground within the walls were ivory. The temples of all the gods were built of beryll stone, and the great altars in them, on which hecatombs are offered, are single amethysts. Around the city flows a river of the sweetest unguents, fifty yards broad and twenty-five deep, so that one may swim in it pleasantly. The baths of this country are great buildings of crystal filled with the fragrance of burning cinnamon. But instead of water there is warm dew in the pools.[226]

[225] *Variorum Spenser,* II, 449. Professor J. B. Fletcher suggests that the *Vera historia* may have influenced the story of Paridell and Hellenore.

[226] Translated by E. J. Smith, *Selections from Lucian,* pp. 171–72.

The inhabitants of this city are disembodied souls, but "unless you should lay hold of them, you would not detect that what your eye rested on was incorporeal." Outside the city is the Elysian Field proper, a beautiful meadow where the heroes hold their banquets. After describing the wonders of the Elysian feasts, Lucian tells of his conversation with the dead, and of their games in honor of the Festival of the Dead. After this comes another episode which may have influenced Spenser's fairy mythology:

Hardly were the games at an end when word was brought that the criminals who were being punished in the realm of the wicked had broken their chains and overpowered the guard, and were marching against the island. Phalaris of Agrigentum was in command, the report said, with Busiris the Egyptian, the Thracian Diomede, and Skeiron and the Pine-bender, with their followers. When Rhadamanthos heard these tidings he marshalled the heroes on the beach, the commanders being Theseus, Achilles, and Telamonian Ajax, who had by this time recovered his wits. The forces joined battle and the heroes were victorious, owing chiefly to the exploits of Achilles. Sokrates, too, distinguished himself in the right wing much more than at the battle of Delium, while he was living. For when the enemy advanced he kept his place with unflinching front. As a reward for his bravery a prize was bestowed on him later in the shape of a very large and beautiful garden in the suburbs, where he assembled his followers and conversed with them, calling the place the Academy of the Dead. The vanquished were collected, of course, and sent back again in irons to still greater punishments. Homer wrote an account of this battle, too, and presented me with a copy on my departure for me to carry to men in this land, but I lost it afterwards, with my other belongings. The first line of the poem was this:

Sing to me now, O Muse, the wars of the shades of the heroes.[227]

May not Spenser have aspired to restore this lost epic of the other world? Certainly its subject, a battle between good

[227] *Ibid.*, pp. 178–79.

and evil spirits in the land of the dead, would be admirably
adapted to convey the twofold meaning of his war between
Gloriana and the great Paynim King, whose final defeat in
a "great battle" was to be described in epic splendor,[228] and
whose conquest was probably to constitute the crowning
adventure of Arthur in his quest for Gloriana's love. For
this great battle, in Spenser's general intention, must surely
mean the final conquest of Vice, which destroys Glory, by
Virtue, which wins Glory, and in his particular intention,
it can hardly mean anything else but a repetition of the
victory over the Armada in a final defeat of Spain. An attack
by the powers of Hell upon the island of the blest is surely
an ideal symbol for both these meanings, particularly the
latter. For to the Elizabethans, the Spaniards were literally
children of Hell, and England was truly an isle of heroes,
"another Eden, demi-Paradise."

The conception of Fairyland as a mythical land of fame
inhabited largely by dead heroes may seem inconsistent with
the presence of Elizabeth Tudor as its reigning sovereign.
The appearance of a living worthy among the famous dead
in a symbolic Pantheon is, however, quite common.[229] The
Roman Emperors were deified while alive, and other classical examples must have been known to Spenser. Moreover,
from the point of view of Arthur, Elizabeth was not living,
but unborn. And a belief that souls unborn inhabited the
land of the dead had most respectable antecedents.[230] The
mythology which permitted Aeneas to see his most famous
descendants in the lower world might surely allow Arthur
to meet his most illustrious successor in Spenser's mythical
Fairyland.

[228] FQ, I, XI, vii, 1–6.
[229] Cf. the quotation from Coke above, pp. 15–16.
[230] For example, in Plutarch (The Face Appearing on the Orb of the
Moon), in Plato (Vision of Er at the end of the Republic), in Virgil (Aen. vi.
719 et sqq.) and in Cicero (Somnium Scipionis).

This Platonic-Virgilian conception of the Elysian Fields as the abode of souls awaiting rebirth may also serve to explain the anachronism of having Huon precede Arthur in Fairyland, though, since Huon is not a fairy, this falsification of chronology might better be justified by the same epic license which allowed Virgil to make Dido the contemporary of Aeneas, and Tasso to represent Rinaldo d'Este as taking part in the First Crusade. But not even the large freedom allowed to a "poet historicall" could justify the inclusion of the Tudor kings in a chronicle of events preceding the reign of Arthur.

For this license, as I have suggested, Spenser might have found a mythological justification in the work of Virgil, the poet whom above all others he aspired to imitate. The sixth book of the *Aeneid*, so important to Dante, may well have contributed largely to the mythological framework of Spenser's *Faerie Queene*. In Aeneas, as Spenser believed, Virgil had depicted the ideal of a gentleman, perfected in both the private and public virtues. Arthur was to exhibit the private virtues in Fairyland before he was king, in the twelve books of the *Faerie Queene,* and the public virtues in Britain after he was king, in Spenser's projected sequel. The subject of this poem resembles that of the last six books of the *Aeneid,* which take place in Italy, and show Aeneas actually establishing his kingdom. The previous books are preparatory to this achievement, and the final preparation is the visit to the lower world in Book VI, in which Aeneas learns of the glorious destiny that awaits his descendants, and is purified and strengthened for the final performance of his destined mission. May not Spenser have been following Virgil in preparing Arthur for his great task, the foundation of the British Empire, by sending him on a journey through Fairyland, a mythical country peopled like the lower world with examples of virtue and vice, and finally bringing him to the capital, Cleopolis, which corresponds to the Elysian Fields in being the heaven of heroes, where that fame which is the meed of virtue is set forth for his inspiration and destined reward? The last book of the *Faerie Queene* would thus correspond to the sixth book of the *Aeneid*,[231] and its model the eleventh book of the *Odyssey*, and like them would occupy a central position in the completed epic which would probably contain twenty-four books.

I do not mean to suggest that Spenser's Fairyland is in all respects identical with the classical land of the dead as it appears in Homer, Virgil, or Lucian. The inhabitants of the classical Elysium are strengthless and incorporeal, whereas Spenser's fairies, like the fays and fairy knights of romance, do not differ in appearance from living men and women. Furthermore, in most of the classical accounts we have considered, the land of the dead is a static place of rewards and punishments, whereas Spenser's Fairyland, like Lucian's Elysium, is a theater of heroic action resembling the world of history. Spenser's Fairyland is a creation of his own, born of the fusion of classical and romance mythologies in the alembic of his imagination, shaped to carry his message, which in its turn is both traditional and personal, rooted in contemporary habits of thought as well as in literature, ancient and modern. His fairies are descended from the gods and demigods of the heroic age, and their life shows to his hero, Arthur, a permanent image of the struggle between good and evil which is the eternal theme of history. Their country is the land of earthly glory, the eternal empire of justice on earth, to whose history Arthur himself is destined to contribute a glorious chapter. In preparation for this, his earthly mission, he is permitted to take part in the symbolic struggles of Fairyland, which foreshadow both

[231] In a sense, of course, the whole *Faerie Queene* would correspond to the sixth book of the *Aeneid*.

his own history and the history of his famous descendant, Elizabeth, in the mythical land of fame in which her "true glorious type," Gloriana, is the queen and the tutelary goddess.

To "this happy land of Faery," no man "that breatheth living aire" has ever penetrated, but one may imagine that, in Arthur's day, it was possible to pass from Britain to Fairy-land, and Arthur himself, who after his death was destined to reign there, might well be permitted to visit that enchanted country in his youth, as Dante was permitted to visit the Christian heaven, and Aeneas the Elysian Fields. Certainly a visit to the land of heroes, and association with its inhabitants, might fittingly represent that early training in ethics, partly through precept, but still more through the exemplary teaching of history, which was necessary "to fashion a gentleman . . . in all vertuous and gentle discipline."

III

"THE FAYERYE"

Ful ofte tyme he Pluto and his queene,
Proserpina, and al hire fayerye,
Disporten hem and maken melodye
Aboute that welle, and daunced, as men tolde.
                    —CHAUCER, *Merchant's Tale.*

Il a des lieus faés es marches de Champaigne,
Et ausi il en a il en la Roche Grifaigne,
Et si croy qu'il en a aussi en Alemaigne,
Et on bois Bersillant, par desous la Montaigne;
Et nonporquant ausi en a il en Espaigne,
Et tout cil lieu faé sont Artu de Bretaigne.
                    —*Brun de la montaigne.*

He was an Elfin borne of noble state,
And mickle worship in his native land;
Well could he tourney and in lists debate,
And knighthood tooke of good Sir *Huons* hand,
When with king *Oberon* he came to Faerie land.
                    —*Faerie Queene.*

THE TWO preceding chapters attempted to describe Spenser's "general intention" in the *Faerie Queene* as primarily an expression of the Renaissance cult of fame, regarded as the decisive stimulus to moral action both for the individual gentleman and for the national State in whose service he finds his fullest self-expression. The first chapter was devoted principally to defining this central idea as a humanistic compromise between classical and Christian conceptions of earthly glory, the second to exhibiting Spenser's expression of this idea in the mythology of his Fairyland. As the first chapter centered on the phrase in the *Letter to Raleigh,* "In that Faery Queene I meane glory," the second was focused on the Elfin Chronicle in Book II. And the interpretation of this passage suggested by "Berosus" and other chroniclers gave us reason to believe that Spenser's Fairyland was a land of fame, resembling the classical Elysium, that its earliest rulers were gods and heroes of classical mythology, and that its legendary history was a reflection of the concrete realization of justice on earth in the history of those successive good empires of which these heroes had been the founders and defenders during their lives on earth.

Assuming that this theory is correct, why should Spenser call his land of heroes "Fairyland," and change Osiris and Hercules into "Elfin Emperors"? Why should not his ideal gentleman seek Glory in the Earthly Paradise or in the Elysian Fields, or in a purely allegorical Land of Fame which borrowed features from both? No doubt the answer to these questions lies chiefly in Spenser's "historicall fiction." Arthur was destined to visit Fairyland just as Aeneas was destined to a place among the Olympian gods. But while the strong fairy element in Arthurian tradition was probably the decisive factor in Spenser's choice of Fairyland as

setting for his poem, there were other features of the fairy
mythology current in his day which may well have influenced him to symbolize the pursuit of glory through virtue
in the story of Arthur's quest for the Fairy Queen, and to
present the history of the ideal just empire under the veil
of an Elfin Chronicle. Some consideration of this fairy mythology as Spenser received it from folklore and romance is
therefore a necessary pendant to the discussion of his probable use of fabulous history and classical mythology undertaken in the preceding chapter. The following study is by
no means exhaustive, and might well be supplemented by
a more thorough examination of the romance background
of Spenser's *Faerie Queene*. Such a study is one of the principal *desiderata* of Spenser scholarship, but I am not qualified to undertake it, nor is it strictly necessary to my present
purpose of showing why the fairy mythology was an especially suitable vehicle for Spenser's general meaning.

It is customary to distinguish between the fairies of folklore and the fays of romance, and to emphasize Spenser's
larger debt to the latter tradition.[1] The distinction is somewhat misleading because the fays of romance did not spring
full grown from the heads of medieval men of letters, and
there is some likelihood that the romances in which fays
appeared seemed less artificial to Spenser's generation than
they do to us, because of the persistence of similar stories in
living oral tradition.[2] Yet, broadly speaking, the distinction
remains between "the coarse and country fairies" of Elizabethan folklore and the beautiful fairy queens and enchant-
resses of romance, and Spenser's greater debt to the latter
tradition is borne out by Miss Latham's recent study, *Eliza-*

[1] See Keightley, *Fairy Mythology*, I, 91–98, A. Jack, *Chaucer and Spenser*,
pp. 320–39, Scott, "On the Fairies of Popular Superstition," *Minstrelsy of the
Scottish Border*, II, 350 n., Delattre, *English Fairy Poetry*, p. 87 *et sqq.*,
Latham, *Elizabethan Fairies, passim.*
[2] See references to *Melusine* and *Helyas* below.

bethan Fairies. She shows indeed that the fairies of Elizabethan folklore were not "little people," who could easily
develop into the diminutive airy beings of Shakespeare's
imagination, but so far resembled Spenser's fairies in being
often indistinguishable from men and women.[3] But she also
shows that the characteristic fairies of Elizabethan folklore
were malevolent tricksy beings, given to pinching sluttish
dairy maids and stealing children, and she agrees with Scott
and Keightley that in the few cases where Spenser makes use
of this folklore,[4] he falls into inconsistency.[5] In her very thorough study of Elizabethan fairy lore, however, Miss Latham
mentions certain features of the fairy tradition which she
does not herself relate to Spenser, but which fit in with the
conception of his fairyland suggested in the previous chapter.

She reminds us, for instance, that the fairies had already
been identified both with the pagan gods and with the
spirits of the dead.[6] The underground fairyland thus becomes the classical Hades. Pluto and Proserpina appear as
king and queen of the fairies in Chaucer's *Merchant's Tale*.
In the Middle English romance of *Sir Orfeo*, the classical
story of Orpheus and Eurydice is assimilated to the type of
a Celtic fairy tale.[7] Queen Heurodys is carried off, not to
Hades, but to a fairyland under the earth. The palace of the
fairy king in this romance recalls the marvelous gold and
crystal buildings already mentioned as analogues of Spen-

[3] Pages 188 *et sqq.*
[4] For example, his use of the changeling motif in *FQ*, I, X, lxv–lxvi and
III, III, xxvi.
[5] *Elizabethan Fairies*, pp. 23–24 n.   [6] *Ibid.*, pp. 44, 48–49.
[7] On *Sir Orfeo*, see Kittredge, "Sir Orfeo," *American Journal of Philology*,
VII (1886), 176–202, and Loomis, "Sir Orfeo and Walter Map's De Nugis,"
MLN, LI (1936), 28–30. On the Celtic fairyland in general, see Nutt, *The
Happy Otherworld in the Mythico-Romantic Literature of the Irish*, A. C.
L. Brown, "The Knight of the Lion," *PMLA*, XX (1905), 673–706, H. R.
Patch, "Some Elements in Medieval Descriptions of the Otherworld," *PMLA*,
XXXIII (1918), 601–43.

ser's Panthea. Sir Orfeo, seeking his lost love, has followed
a troop of fairy ladies into a rock:

> When he was in the roche y-go
> Well three mile other or mo,
> He came into a fair countray
> As bright soonne sommers day.
> Smooth and plain and alle grene,
> Hill ne dale nas none y-seen.
> Amiddle the lond a castle he seigh,
> Rich and real and wonder high.
> All the utmoste wall
> Was clear and shine of cristal.
> An hundred towers there were about,
> Deguiselich and batailed stout.
> The buttras come out of the ditch,
> Of rede gold y-arched rich.
> The bousour was anowed all
> Of each manere diverse animal.
> Within there were wide wones
> All of precious stones.
> The worst pillar to behold
> Was all of burnished gold.
> All that lond was ever light,
> For when it should be therk and night,
> The riche stones light gonne
> Bright as doth at none the sonne,
> Ne man may tell ne think in thought,
> The riche work that there was wrought.[8]

This identification of the fairies with the gods of the lower
world, and their kingdom with the land of the dead, is perhaps connected with the tradition that the fairies were fallen
angels, related to the Platonic daemons. Miss Latham finds
only two examples of this theory of fairy origin in the litera-

---

[8] Quoted Keightley, *Fairy Mythology*, I, 85–86. I have checked this with
Zielke's edition of *Sir Orfeo*. Keightley's version differs only in spelling.

ture of the sixteenth century,[9] but it would certainly be familiar to Spenser from *Huon of Burdeux*.[10]

The folklore conception of fairies as nocturnal dancing sprites, generally in female form, who haunted certain spots by wood and fountain, made it inevitable that they should be associated with the nymphs of classical mythology. Jean Lemaire uses "nymphe" and "fée" as synonymous terms.[11] Miss Latham notes that "after the publication of Douglas' translation of the Aeneid . . . the fairies begin to appear in Elizabethan translations of Virgil and Ovid . . . as the English equivalents of nymphs and hamadryads of the Latin originals."[12]

To the identification of the fairies with nymphs was often added the identification of the Fairy Queen with Diana, a notion which obviously influenced Spenser's Gloriana and Belphoebe as well as Shakespeare's Titania. Miss Latham cites a number of references to this idea, including a quotation from King James's *Daemonologie*, in which he mentions "that fourth kind of spirits, which by the Gentiles was called Diana, and her wandering court, and amongst us was called the Phairie."[13]

Commenting on the generally unfavorable conception of the fairies in Elizabethan folklore, Miss Latham wonders that Spenser should have celebrated Elizabeth as Fairy Queen.[14] The identification of the Fairy Queen with Diana would certainly be one obvious explanation. Belphoebe and Britomart, the two characters in Spenser's poem who ex-

[9] *Elizabethan Fairies*, p. 43.   [10] Berners' translation, I, Pt. 2, 592.
[11] *Œuvres*, I, 198.   [12] *Op. cit.*, p. 15.
[13] *Ibid.*, pp. 49–52. This common identification of the Fairy Queen with Diana may perhaps help to explain the frequent appearance of the Fairy Queen in pageants presented before Elizabeth, which may have influenced Spenser. See Baskervill, "The Genesis of Spenser's Queen of Faerie," MP, XVIII (1920), 48 *et sqq.*
[14] *Elizabethan Fairies*, p. 34.

emplify the chastity of Elizabeth, are both named from Diana, and complimentary identifications of the maiden queen with the maiden goddess of the moon appear frequently in the literature of the period.[15] Besides being celebrated for her chastity, Diana or Luna was mistress of the sea. This idea appears in Chaucer's *Franklin's Tale,* where Aurelius, praying to Phoebus, describes the dependence of sun, moon, and sea upon each other in the following words:

> Youre blisful suster, Lucina the sheene,
> That of the see is chief goddesse and queene
> (Though Neptunus have deitee in the see
> Yet emperisse aboven hym is she).[16]

This character of Diana or Cynthia, which Spenser applies to Elizabeth in *Colin Clout's Come Home Againe,*[17] is also adapted to express the side of her character symbolized in Gloriana, namely, her power as "most royall Queene or Empresse."[18] The identification of Gloriana in Spenser's general intention with the goddess of fame, queen of the dead, fits in also with the common identification of Luna and Proserpina, found in Chaucer's *Franklin's Tale,*[19] and in Plutarch's *On the Face Appearing on the Orb of the Moon,* where the virtuous souls in the "Meadow of Hades," an Elysian region of the air between earth and moon, await the second death, which is to take place in the realm of the heavenly Persephone.[20]

This second death bears a certain analogy to the Christian Day of Judgment,[21] which is always represented as the term of life for the fairies of romance, and which as the end of history would also logically put an end to Spenser's Fairyland

---

[15] Raleigh, *Cynthia,* Lyly, *Endymion,* Chapman, *Shadow of Night,* Shakespeare, *MND,* II, i, 161–64.
[16] Ll. 1045–48.   [17] *CCCHA,* l. 166. Cf. Raleigh, *Cynthia.*
[18] *Letter to Raleigh.*   [19] Ll. 1074–75.
[20] *Moralia,* King's translation, p. 251 *et sqq.*
[21] In that it precedes the final entrance of the elect spirits into bliss.

considered as the symbol of earthly fame. Moreover, as we
have seen, several of the temples of fame which were probably analogues of Spenser's Panthea were situated in or near
the moon.[22] It is possible, therefore, that the belief in two
Persephones, one heavenly, dwelling in the moon, and one
earthly, or rather infernal, presiding over the lower world,[23]
may have influenced Spenser's contrasted figures of Gloriana
and Lucifera. Lucifera is the daughter of Pluto "and sad
Proserpina, the Queene of Hell,"[24] and her own kingdom
certainly resembles that of her parents. The character of
Lucifera as antitype of Gloriana suggests the relationship
between the two Persephones; and the identification of the
infernal Persephone with the Fairy Queen in Chaucer
would make natural the similar but more complimentary
identification of Gloriana with the heavenly Persephone,
which would be demanded by Spenser's scheme.[25]

Besides the identification of the Fairy Queen with Diana,
Miss Latham mentions the confusion between fairies and
nymphs as an exception to the generally unfavorable view
of the fairies which prevailed in Elizabethan literature, outside of Spenser, before Shakespeare's recreation of English
fairy mythology in *Midsummer Night's Dream.*[26] This exception, she says, is only apparent, for to Christian writers
the nymphs were "pagan and heathen spirits and to the common people fearful beings."[27] But though the "ruder clown"
might regard nymphs and fairies equally with superstitious
fear,[28] the better educated, who could read in Boccaccio[29]
that nymphs were simply high-born ladies, and who, like

[22] Cf. *FQ*, II, Proem, iii, 6–9.
[23] In Plutarch the chthonian goddess of the dead is Demeter. *Moralia*,
p. 251.
[24] *Ibid.*, I, IV, xi, 1–2.
[25] The Fairy Queen in *Arthur of Little Britain* is named Proserpine.
[26] *Elizabethan Fairies*, p. 61. Cf. also pp. 34–35.   [27] *Ibid.*, p. 61.
[28] *FQ*, VI, X, vii, 4–6.   [29] *Gen. de gli dei*, p. 128.

E. K., could see the idea that fairies were supernatural beings as a relic of the dark ages of monastic ignorance,[30] were
free to use the fairy mythology as they used the mythology
of Greece and Rome, for purposes of literary compliment
or ethical teaching. Similarly the belief that the fairies were
spirits of the dead might be used by a man who did not
seriously believe it, as the basis for a literary mythology. As
examples of this belief, Miss Latham cites Stanyhurst's
translation of the *Aeneid* and Burton's *Anatomy of Melancholy*.[31] The latter passage, which, though later than Spenser's poem, refers to a long-current belief, is of particular
interest because it connects the fairies not only with the
spirits of the dead, but also with the euhemerized conception of the pagan gods. "There is a foolish opinion, which
some hold,[32] that they [the devils, of whom the fairies are a
species,] are the souls of men departed, good and more noble
were deified, the baser grovelled on the ground, or in the
lower parts, and were devils."[33] This "foolish opinion,"
which Spenser must have known, would give him authority
for placing Osiris and Hercules among the fairies.

Another connection between Hercules and the fairy nation is suggested by Desperiers, in a legend he tells as an
example of the nonsensical tales which historians like Jean
Lemaire were gullible enough to believe:

Je vous veus donques ici ramentevoir deus histoires sur le fait
de cet Hercules, pour l'antiquité de nostre Gaule, les quelles
sont contées par Parthène grégois en ses Amouretes, et Sile
poëte latin, en son troiziesme livre et autres auteurs anciens,
dont l'une est qu' Hercules allant de Grèce en Espagne pour
pilher Gérion, et passant par la Gaule, vint herberger chez un

---

[30] *SC*, "June," Glosse.   [31] Latham, p. 45 n.
[32] Among them Augustine. *De civ. Dei*, Lib. IX, cap. xi, Welldon's ed.,
Vol. I, p. 385. Augustine traces this opinion to Plotinus. See also Blondus,
De Roma triumphante, fol. i.
[33] *Anatomy of Melancholy*, Pt. I, Sect. II, Mem. I, Subs. II.

seigneur du pais nommé Bébrix, homme puissant demourant
es montagnes qui sont entre la Gaule et l'Espagne, qui avoit
une belle fille nommée *Pyrène,* la quelle Hercules n'eust pas
si tost veue qu'il en fut amoureus, et la vous mena si beau
avecque belles promesses de mariage qu'il l'engrossa, puis reprint son chemin: et son entreprise exécutée, s'en retourna la
revoir, la quelle avoit pendant son voiage enfanté un—devinez
quoi? un beau petit joli serpenteau, et

> De cette race serpentine
> Est descendu Mélusine.[34]

The story of Pyrene, mentioned by Pliny as fabulous,[35] is
told at length in the *Punica* of Silius Italicus.[36] Commenting on this passage, Salmasius wonders whether the son of
Hercules and Pyrene might not have been the Galates mentioned by Diodorus as father of the Celts,[37] whom we have
already met in "Berosus" and Jean Lemaire as the son of
Hercules and Galathea. In making this suggestion, Salmasius apparently discarded the story of the serpent offspring
of Pyrene, which Desperiers singles out for special attention
in casting ridicule upon the mythical histories connecting
Hercules with the "antiquities of Gaul." In these stories
Hercules is apt to be connected with serpents. Celtine may

[34] Quoted by Le Roux de Lincy, *Livre des légendes: Introduction,* pp.
108-9 from B. Desperiers, *Discours non plus melancholiques que divers*
(1556). I have not been able to check this quotation. The reference to Parthenius is apparently to the story of Celtine, daughter of Bretannus, with whom
Hercules stayed on his way home from Spain. Celtine hid the kine of Geryon,
and refused to give them back unless Hercules would satisfy her love. Unable
to resist the combined persuasions of beauty and blackmail, Hercules made
her the mother of Celtus, "from whom the Celts derived their name."
Parthenius, *Amorous Tales,* translated by S. Gaselee, p. 335. Another version
of this story is referred to by Buchanan. "Those who contend, that the
Britons were a colony of the Gauls, allege that Hercules had a son by Celto,
a Gallic virgin, called Britannis, from whom the nation of the Britons
sprung." *Hist. of Scotland,* translated by Aikman, I, 14. Spenser used Buchanan's work in his *View of Ireland.* See *View, loc. cit.,* and Renwick's notes,
passim.
[35] *Nat. hist.* iii. 1. 3, Teubner Edition, Vol. I, p. 233.
[36] *Punica* iii. 420-41.   [37] *Ibid.,* pp. 163-64 n.

have been a mere mortal, and Galathea simply a giantess, but the first wife of Hercules, ancestress of the Trojan line in "Berosus," is Araxa the younger, half woman and half serpent. From her son, Tuscus, Jean Lemaire traces the ancestry of Charlemagne. Another "femme serpente" is celebrated by Jean Bouchet as mother of the earliest settlers in Aquitaine. He tells the story, which comes originally from Herodotus,[38] in the *Annales d'Aquitaine.*[39] On his way back from stealing the cattle of Geryon, Hercules landed on an island of the Scythians, where he found a serpent lady by whom he had three sons, ancestors of the three tribes of Scythians. From one of these, Agathyrsus, descended the Picts,[40] from whom Poitiers took its name.

These stories which connect Hercules as father of the Celts and Trojans with serpent ladies or serpent offspring form a link between the fabulous history of the Annian Berosus and the fairy mythology of romance. The likeness was recognized, as we have seen, by two of the sixteenth-century writers who mention these legends. Jean Lemaire describes Araxa as half woman and half serpent, "comme on dit de Melusine la Faee,"[41] and Desperiers uses the same comparison to ridicule Lemaire, dismissing Pyrene and her serpent child as founders of the "race serpentine," whose most famous descendant was the well-known fairy of Lusignan. Whether or not the passages we have just quoted from Lemaire and Desperiers were known to Spenser, we should expect him to see the same likeness as they did between the serpent wife of Hercules in "Berosus" and the serpent fairy of the well-known romance. We should expect him to rationalize the story so as to get rid of the serpent form, which he could only use as a symbol of evil in the figure of Echidna,[42] and to assimilate Araxa and Melusine to his

[38] iv. 8.   [39] Page aiii.
[40] Virgil had spoken of "picti Agathyrsi," *Aen.* iv. 146.
[41] *Œuvres,* I, 74.   [42] *FQ,* VI, VI, x; V, X, x–xi.

own conception of a fairy queen. The assimilation would be made all the more easily since Melusine, like Araxa, was celebrated principally as founder of a noble lineage.

The connection between Hercules and Melusine, therefore, leads us to another aspect of the fairy mythology which probably influenced Spenser: namely, the traditions in which the fairies, like the pagan gods of classical epic, appear as ancestors of noble families. In these stories a noble lineage springs from the union of a fairy and a mortal, which is usually terminated because the mortal violates a taboo upon the observance of which the continuance of their relationship depends. The two best-known examples of these stories, which Spenser must certainly have known, are the legends of Melusine, fairy ancestress of the Lusignan family, and of Helyas, Knight of the Swan, supernatural progenitor of Godfrey of Bouillon.

In the romance of Melusine as related in the French prose of Jean d'Arras and translated into English about 1500,[43] the fairy Pressine, sister of the lady of the lost isle, Avalon, marries King Elyas of Albany on condition that he shall never see her in childbed. When he violates this command, she leaves him, and takes her three daughters, Melusine, Melior, and Palatine, to Avalon. Learning of their father's perfidy, Melusine and her sisters shut him up in a high mountain in Northumberland. This, however, angers their mother, who condemns them to various punishments. Melusine is to be a serpent every Saturday until she finds some one who will marry her and promise never to see her on that day. "For notwithstandyng the unlawfulness of thy fader/

---

[43] Ed. A. K. Donald, *EETS*, extra series, No. 68, 1895. All my references to *Melusine* are to this version. There was also an English translation of the verse romance of Melusine by La Coudrette, *The Romans of Partenay, or of Lusignen*, ed. Skeat, *EETS*, original series, 22, 1866. Spenser may have known either of these in MS, though he is more likely to have read the French version of Jean d'Arras, printed in 1478, and several times reprinted.

bothe thou & thy sustirs he shuld have drawen to hym, and ye shuld shortly have ben out of the handes of the Nymphes and of the fairees, without to retourne any more."[44] If Melusine's husband keeps his word not to see her on Saturdays, she will be a woman all her life, and from her "shall yssue a fayre lynee, whiche shalbe gret & of highe proesse." If he disobeys her, however, she will retain her serpent shape until the Day of Judgment, and will appear three days before the castle she shall make "at every tyme whan it shall have a new lord, and lykewyse also whan a man of thy lynee shall dey."[45]

Melusine marries Raymondin, Count of Poitiers, and bears him five sons, all of whom have some deformity except the two youngest. The most famous of her sons is Geoffrey of the Great Tooth, who succeeds his father as Count of Poitiers. Another son, Guyon, who in the romance becomes king of Armenia, is identified with Guy de Lusignan, king of Jerusalem and contemporary of Richard Coeur de Lion. Melusine was famous for her building activities. Besides the castle of Lusignan, she

bigged & fownd many a fayre place thrughe the lande of Poytou unto the duchie of Guyenne. She bilded the Castel and the burgh of Partenay so strong and so fayre without comparyson after that she did doo make þe Toures of Rochelle & the Castel also, & bygan a part of the toune, and thre leghes thens was a grete toure and bigge, which Julius Cesar did doo make. . . . That toure made the lady to be walled and fortyfyed . . . and made it to be called the Castle Eglon. And afterward she edefyed Pons in Poytou and fortyfyed Xaintes that was called at that tyme Lynges/ and after she made Tallemounte and Tallemondois and many other tounes & fortres. And gate & acquyred so moche Raymondin thrugh the polycye & good governaunce of Melusyne, what in Bretayne, what in Gascoynne and in Guyenne as in Poytou, that no prynce was about hym/ but he doubted to dysplaise hym.[46]

[44] *Melusine*, p. 15.   [45] *Ibid.*   [46] *Ibid.*, pp. 103-4.

No wonder Raymondin was happy with Melusine. Even when he is persuaded by his brother to pry into the secret of her weekly disappearance, and discovers her, like Duessa,[47] bathing her transformed body, his one thought is that now he must lose the most courteous and loyal lady in the world. It is not until her son Geoffrey burns down the monastery in which his brother Fromond is a monk, that Raymondin begins to suspect that Melusine may be an evil spirit. He then remembers that most of her living children have some deformity, and that her son Horrible, who has three eyes, has already killed two of his nurses. When she tries to console her husband for the burning of the monastery by saying that Geoffrey's act was permitted by God because of the wickedness of the monks, Raymondin blames her for the actions of her sons, and reproaches her with her weekly change of form. When she tells him that he has doomed them to eternal separation, however, he is sorry, and begs her forgiveness. After a touching farewell scene, she flies off in the form of a serpent amid the lamentations of her people. Her obsequies are observed in the churches she has built. She returns occasionally in serpent form to watch over her two youngest children, with whom she uses a regime like that followed by Ceres with her mortal nursling, hardening them by roasting them before a fire. When danger threatens her descendants or any of the kings of France, Melusine returns, and howls about the castle of Lusignan.

The last of these appearances took place while Spenser was at Cambridge. In January, 1574/75, the castle of Lusignan was destroyed, as a Huguenot stronghold, by the Catholic forces under the Duc de Montpensier. The appearance of Melusine on this melancholy occasion is attested to by Mézeray and Brantôme, both of whom rationalize her story

[47] Cf. *FQ*, I, II, xl–xli.

as the mythographers and chroniclers rationalized the marvelous tales of antiquity. Mézeray, for instance, says:

The great acts of Melusine, her riches, her extraordinary knowledge, which she derived either from communication with higher intelligences, or rather perhaps from the cabala of the Rabbins who were then very numerous in France, have procured her immortal renown in the mouth of posterity; who, not knowing her real history, have invented marvellous tales concerning her. These I leave to amuse old women and children. But I am enabled to report, on the credit of many persons of honour, and who are not generally thought credulous, that it has been observed that whenever one of her descendants, or a king of France, was about to die, she appeared on the great tower in a widow's habit, and uttered long and terrible cries; and that she was thus seen before the siege of Lusignan; and that when her castle was about to be demolished, she was seen longer than ever before, shrieking aloud in so lamentable a voice that she cleft all hearts with pity, but that she has since never been seen or heard save very rarely.[48]

Theologians, he goes on to say, may decide whether these appearances are due to the illusions of demons, or to "the bounty of God, who to demonstrate to unbelievers the immortality of the soul, permits heroic spirits to appear sometimes in the places which they have loved during their lives."[49]

To Brantôme also Melusine was

une dame des plus nobles en lignée, en vertu, en esprit, en magnifficence et en tout, qui fust de son temps, voire d'autres . . . de laquelle y a tant de fables; et bien que soient fables, sy ne peut on dire autrement que tout beau et bon d'elle; et si l'on veut venir a la vraye vérité, c'estoit un vray soleil de son temps, de laquelle sont descendus ces braves seigneurs, princes, roys et capitaines portant le nom de Luzignan, dont les histoires en sont plaines.[50]

---

[48] Quoted from *Histoire de la France*, III, 359 (fol. 1685) in Introduction to *Romans de Partenay*, pp. xv–xvi.

[49] *Ibid.*, pp. xii–xiii.

[50] *Vies des hommes illustres . . . français*, Discours LXXXI, Art. Monpensier. Quoted Marchand, *Légende de Mélusine*, pp. v–vi.

The story of Melusine and the comments of Mézeray and Brantôme upon it may well throw light upon Spenser's probable attitude toward the fairy ancestors of noble families, and hence upon his own use of the fairy mythology as a vehicle for his moral and political teaching. In the romance of *Melusine* we find three different attitudes toward the original folklore material. In the first place there are traces of the belief that fairies were dangerous and even actively malignant powers. The serpent form of Melusine, the deformities of her sons, particularly of Horrible, the cruelty of Pressine's punishment of her children, the desire of Melusine to escape from Avalon "out of the hands of the nymphes and the fairees," and to resume her human heritage—all these elements in the story suggest the attitude of fear and loathing toward the fairy race of which Miss Latham has collected so many examples. Yet so far as Melusine herself is concerned, these unpleasant features of her race are completely subordinated to the charming and sympathetic portrayal of her character as ideal wife, mother, and feudal lady. Her serpent form is the result of enchantment. All her actions are motivated by love for her husband and children. She is as patient as Griselda, never reproaching Raymondin for his lack of faith in her, and she gives orders to burn her son Horrible only because she foresees that he will bring sorrows upon her people if he is allowed to live.

I do not wish to suggest that this favorable view of Melusine's character is necessarily less primitive than the unfavorable one which is implied in the view of fairies as malignant beings, or that it depends upon the fact that in the story as we have it she is only half a fairy. The tradition of a beneficent and protective fay of the fountain may well have been primitive. The fear and loathing inspired by the fairies is probably due at least in part to Christian preaching which identified them with devils, and a fairy in serpent form would be particularly suspect. Moreover in this particular case the behavior of the historical Geoffrey of the Great Tooth may have helped to preserve uncomplimentary traditions about his ancestry. People who burned monasteries were not regarded as public benefactors before the Reformation, and Raymondin's reproach of Melusine when he learns of Geoffrey's act is probably a fair reflection of contemporary opinion.[51] There were other famous characters in the Middle Ages whose behavior made it easy to believe that they were genealogically connected with the devil.[52] Later writers, wishing to praise the descendants of these men might be expected to adopt a more complimentary theory of their ancestry, and either to suppress the diabolical element altogether, or to minimize it, as in the story of Melusine.

This desire to celebrate Melusine as founder of a noble dynasty is central to the romances we possess, and we cannot doubt that it helped to preserve, if it did not create, the humane and attractive conception of her personality. It is this third element in the romance tradition which completely dominates in Brantôme and Mézeray. For them Melusine is the ancestress of a noble lineage and the foundress of famous towns. Everything else in her story is fabulous. The fairy mythology of the romances is thus treated by these Renaissance writers in the same spirit in which contemporary mythographers treated the legends of classical antiquity. The fairies, like the pagan gods, appear as ancestors of noble families, men and women of superior intelligence and virtue, who were therefore credited by the superstitious and ignorant of past ages with a supernatural origin.

It seems likely that Spenser's use of the fairy mythology reflects a similar attitude. His good fairies are thoroughly humanized and rationalized. They possess, or at least exhibit, no supernatural powers that are not also possessed

[51] *Melusine*, pp. 314–15.   [52] See below, pp. 178–79.

by the human characters. In fact the principal enchanted weapons in the poem[53] belong to Britomart and Arthur, neither of whom is a fairy. Merlin is of course an enchanter, but except for this traditional figure, enchantment and shape shifting are the mark of Gloriana's enemies. Duessa turns Fradubio and Fraelissa into trees.[54] Acrasia holds Verdant by a "horrible enchantment."[55] Other examples will readily occur to every reader of the *Faerie Queene*. Miss Latham has pointed out that English and Scottish law of the sixteenth and seventeenth centuries recognized a close relationship between fairies and witches.[56] Spenser applies the name "witch" to Duessa and Acrasia, never to Gloriana or to Belphoebe.

This tendency to reduce the marvelous element in his presentation of the fairies, though it has parallels in the romances, particularly in the blurring of the distinction between "fay" and "enchantress," perhaps reflects Spenser's desire to disassociate his good fairies from the race of supernatural beings in league with the powers of evil, and to present them as virtuous men and women of "antique times" whose deeds were immortalized in history for the instruction of later ages. The story of Melusine is significant in this connection, because it reminds us that some noble families in Spenser's own day could trace their ancestry to fairies, who, as Brantôme's comment shows, might be rationalized into historical characters of superior virtue. The identification of the fairies with the pagan gods might thus take on a new, more complimentary meaning, not only because of the more favorable attitude toward the gods which naturally attended the Renaissance worship of antiquity, but also because of the common character of gods and fairies as euhemerized supernatural ancestors of noble houses.

[53] Arthur's shield and Britomart's spear.   [54] *FQ*, I, II, xxxiv *et sqq.*
[55] *Ibid.*, II, XII, lxxx, 9.   [56] *Elizabethan Fairies*, p. 16.

Melusine, we are told, was the ancestress not only of the Lusignan and Parthenay families in France but also of the House of Pembroke in England.[57] Another famous fairy with English descendants was Helyas, Knight of the Swan, ancestor of Godfrey of Bouillon. Spenser probably knew the story of Helyas in Copland's translation of the French romance, first published by Wynkyn de Worde in 1512, and reprinted by William Copland. This work was dedicated to the Duke of Buckingham, at whose suggestion it had been undertaken, and who was lineally descended from Helyas.[58] The same illustrious ancestry belonged to Queen Elizabeth herself, for by virtue of her Plantagenet blood, she could claim descent from Godfrey of Bouillon,[59] and hence from his ancestor, the fabulous swan knight. We might therefore expect Spenser to be even more interested in Helyas than in Melusine.

The story of Helyas has undergone a more thorough Christianization than that of Melusine. None of the characters are definitely stated to be fairies, and the shape shifting and other miracles are all interpreted as marks of divine favor to the ancestor of the future deliverer of the Holy Sepulcher. Nevertheless, the fairy elements in the story are still perceptible.

Helyas is the son of King Oriant and Queen Beatrice of "Lislefort." It is clear that Beatrice was originally a fairy.[60] Oriant finds her by a fountain to which he has been led by a stag. She is extremely beautiful, her lineage is unknown, and she rebukes him haughtily for trespassing on her do-

[57] *Melusine*, pp. 355–56.

[58] "The Knight of the Swanne" in Thoms, *Early English Prose Romances*, III, 16. The whole "prologue of the translator" recalls the tone of Spenser's dedicatory sonnets to Cumberland and Oxford.

[59] Coke, *Debate between the Heralds*, p. 68. Hardyng, *Chron.*, p. 257 *et sqq.* Godfrey's niece married Fulk of Anjou, father of Geoffrey Plantagenet. This relationship gave the Angevin kings a claim to the throne of Jerusalem.

[60] May she not perhaps be the same as the Beatrice who appears among the fairies at Ogier's birth? See below, pp. 213–14.

main. Later she consents to marry him. The mystery of her ancestry, however, is left unexplained, and gains her the hatred of Matabrune, the king's mother, who objects to a daughter-in-law of unknown race and apparent poverty.

While Oriant is away at the wars, Beatrice bears seven children at one birth, each with a silver chain around the neck. This would seem to be another clear mark of fairy origin,[61] but the author states specifically that the miracle of the chains was a sign to demonstrate "the pure and singuler dignite of the noble mother and her childe and that God wolde upon them extend his divine grace."[62] Matabrune steals the children, and persuades her son that the queen has given birth to a litter of puppies. Beatrice is condemned to perpetual imprisonment, which she accepts meekly as a punishment for some unrecognized sin. Meanwhile the children are preserved by the compassion of the groom who was ordered to destroy them. He leaves them in a field where they are found by a hermit, who brings them up with the assistance of a miraculous white goat, "sent bi Goddes grace."[63] One of the children, Helyas, is absent with his godfather, the hermit, when Matabrune again attempts to kill the children, of whose existence she has accidentally learned. Her emissaries, however, remove the silver chains from the children's necks as tokens to show Matabrune that her commands have been obeyed.

As soon as the chains are removed, the children are changed into swans. Later Helyas discovers them and wonders at their friendliness. When Helyas is full grown an angel comes to reveal to the hermit the lineage of his ward and the identity of the swans, and to instruct him to send Helyas to the rescue of his mother, who is facing death on a false charge of plotting to poison her husband. Helyas ac-

---

[61] Cf. Pressine, who has triplets. Multiple births were either miraculous or a sign of adultery.
[62] Thoms, III, 41.   [63] *Ibid.*, p. 49.

cordingly reveals himself to his father, defends the honor of his mother against Matabrune's champion, and finally puts Matabrune to death. The swans are restored to their human form, except one, whose silver chain has been melted to make a cup for Matabrune.

Some years later, this swan brother appears on the river before the castle, drawing a boat. Helyas enters it, and is carried to the Emperor's court, where the widowed duchess of Bouillon is seeking a champion against her brother-in-law. Helyas defends the lady's cause, and afterward marries her daughter. Their child is Ydain, mother of Godfrey of Bouillon. One day the wife of Helyas expresses curiosity about her husband's ancestry and place of birth. Helyas tells her that she must never question him on these matters. The taunts of another lady move her to disregard this warning, and the swan appears to take Helyas away. They return to their native land, where the swan regains his human shape, and Helyas enters a monastery. His wife continues to send out messengers in search of him, and at last one of them finds him in time to reunite the pair on their death bed.

The fairy elements in this story are evident enough, but they have been thoroughly subdued to the Christian hagiographical purpose of the writer. The shape shifting of the swan children, unlike the transformation of Melusine, is not magic but miracle, the divinely appointed means of saving the children's lives.[64] Similarly Helyas restores sight to the groom whose eyes have been put out by Matabrune when she discovers that he has left the children in the field instead of putting them to death;[65] and the last swan brother regains his original form through a religious ceremony.[66] All the good characters in the story are saints, and the wicked repent with edifying frequency. Even Matabrune acquiesces

[64] *Ibid.*, p. 62.   [65] *Ibid.*, pp. 93–94.   [66] *Ibid.*, pp. 124 *et sqq.*

in the justice of her punishment, and is piously forgiven by Helyas before he burns her to death.[67]

The likeness between the termination of Helyas's marriage and that of Melusine points to a common fairy origin, and in fact this part of the story of Helyas is left without explanation. Nevertheless, his departure leads up to the final transformation of the swan brother, and since the mother of Godfrey has been born, the divinely-ordained purpose of Helyas's marriage is apparently accomplished.

In view of the predominantly Christian version in which the story of Helyas must have reached Spenser, we cannot be sure that he would have regarded the swan knight as a fairy or the son of a fairy. There was, however, another tradition which connected Helyas with an unmistakable fairy genealogy. According to Dunlop, Oriant, who in our romance appears as the father of Helyas, was himself the son of Meurvin, son of Ogier le Danois and Morgan le Fay.[68] Dunlop gives no authority for this statement, but implies that it is to be found in the romance of *Meurvin*,[69] which he mentions without giving an abstract of it, as being "totally uninteresting."[70] It was nevertheless printed three times in the sixteenth century,[71] and was translated into English at the beginning of the seventeenth.[72] There is therefore every likelihood that Spenser knew it, and that he would be interested in the relationship between Meurvin and Helyas by virtue of which Godfrey of Bouillon and the Plantagenet

[67] *Ibid.*, pp. 100–101.

[68] *History of Prose Fiction*, I, 337.

[69] *Lhistoire du preux Meuruin, filz de Oger le dannoys, lequel par sa prouesse conquist Hierusalem, Babilone et plusieurs autres royaulmes . . .* (Paris, 1531). An Italian version is summarized in Ferrario, *Storia . . . degli antichi romanzi*, III, 320–29.

[70] *History of Prose Fiction*, I, 337.

[71] In 1531, 1539, and 1580. Brunet, III, 1687.

[72] *The Most Famous and Renowned Historie of That Woorthie and Illustrious Morvine, Son to Oger the Dane*, translated by James Markham (London, 1612).

kings of England could trace their ancestry back to Arthur's sister, the fairy queen of Avalon.

The Angevin kings are connected with the fairy nation in other legends, some of which must have been known to Spenser. Scott quotes Sir David Lindsay as saying that "the first Duk of Guyenne was born of a *fée*, and, therefoir, the arms of Guyenne are a leopard."[73] I have not been able to trace this story, which would seem to imply a fairy ancestry for Eleanor of Aquitaine. Possibly, however, it is a confused reference to the well-known legend of the demon countess of Anjou, ancestress of Geoffrey Plantagenet.

This story, which has often been compared to that of Melusine,[74] is told as follows by Giraldus Cambrensis.[75] A certain countess of Anjou, "formae conspicuae sed nationis ignotae," was observed to attend church but rarely, and always to leave before the elevation of the host. At last her husband ordered four soldiers to restrain her forcibly from leaving the church; whereupon she flew out the window, carrying two of her children with her, and was never seen again. One of the two children whom she left behind was the ancestor of Geoffrey Plantagenet. Giraldus tells us that Richard Coeur de Lion often referred to this story, "dicens non esse mirandum, si de genere tali et filii parentes et sese ad invicem fratres infestare non cessent; de diabolo namque eos omnes venisse et ad diabolum dicebat ituros esse."

The same story is told by the Scottish historian Bowmaker in a chapter entitled "Quomodo reges Angliae de genere sive generatione Diaboli ex uno latere processerunt."[76] Another variant appears in the romance of *Richard Coeur de Lion*,[77]

---

[73] *Minstrelsy*, II, 311. Quoted from a MS on heraldry in Advocates Library, Edinburgh (W. 4, 13).

[74] Scott, *Minstrelsy*, II, 311 n.; L. Hibbard, *Mediaeval Romance in England*, p. 151; Giraldus Cambrensis, *Opera*, VIII, 301 n.

[75] *De. princip. instruct.*, Lib. III, cap. xxvii.

[76] Fordun, *Scotichron.*, Bk. IX, chap. vi.   [77] Printed 1509 and 1528.

where the demon lady becomes the mother of Richard and John.[78]

The uncomplimentary tone of the references to this supernatural ancestress of the Plantagenet kings forms a contrast to the Christianization of Beatrice and the humanization of Melusine. In itself, however, the story of the demon countess is capable of a different treatment, and we should expect Spenser to regard it in a more flattering light than did the monkish chroniclers by whom it has been preserved to us. The Angevin kings were extremely popular with the Elizabethans, largely because of their difficulties with the Roman Church,[79] and the fairy lady who could not abide the Mass might well appear to a Protestant poet as a worthy predecessor of his royal mistress.

It is tempting, therefore, to connect Spenser's Guyon in some way with this fairy ancestry of the Angevin line. Of the other two heroes of Spenser's first three books, St. George is Saxon, Britomart Welsh. The Tudor kings could claim descent not only from the ancient British line but from Egbert and William the Conqueror. The coronation of Henry VII represented not only the return of the Trojan dynasty but a union of all the racial elements in the nation in a ruling house whose accession marked the end of civil war. Modern Spenser scholarship has stressed the importance of the Arthurian "return motif," and has implied that Spenser had no interest in the Saxon and Norman kings, whom he regarded as usurpers. But while they were originally usurpers, and therefore justly punished by foreign conquest and civil war, their exploits were the natural object of patriotic pride, which could have free play when their position had been regularized by the mingling of their blood with that of

[78] The same story is told in Gervase of Tilbury, *Otia Imperialia*, ed. Liebrecht, p. 26, but not connected with the Angevin family.

[79] Cf. Holinshed's characterization of Richard I, *Chronicles*, II, 271 and Bale's *Kyng Johan*.

the ancient British dynasty. And this union of diverse strains
in the royal house was to mark a new unity in the nation.
So Merlin prophesies in the *Faerie Queene:*

> Thenceforth eternall union shall be made
> Betweene the nations different afore,
> And sacred Peace shall lovingly perswade
> The warlike minds, to learne her goodly lore,
> And civile armes to exercise no more.[80]

The example of Virgil as well as the facts of Tudor history
would combine to make Spenser celebrate this union of
races in the ancestry of his royal mistress. It is natural to
think, therefore, that in Guyon, a fairy with a French name,[81]
Spenser was in some way celebrating the Norman-French
element in the ancestry of Elizabeth and in the composition
of the English nation. Guyon bears the picture of the Fairy
Queen on his shield. As patron knight of temperance, we
have seen that he exemplifies, most clearly of all Spenser's
minor heroes, the aristocratic knightly ideal which was associated with the old nobility of England, the Norman and
Angevin blood. He reads the Fairy Chronicle while Arthur
reads the British; and he has been knighted by Huon, who
was Duke of Aquitaine.[82]

None of these facts constitute proof that Guyon was intended for a legendary fairy ancestor of the Plantagenet
kings. It is possible that he stands for the ancestor of some
great lord of Norman blood, the Earl of Oxford, for instance, whose ancestry we know is somewhere concealed in
the poem,[83] or that his French name, which reminds us of
Guyon, son of Melusine, and his connection with Aquitaine

---

[80] *FQ*, III, III, xlix, 1–5.

[81] Miss Winstanley thought Guyon's name came from Guyan (Guyenne),
Faerie Queene, Book II, p. lxxii. But the name is very common in French
romances. Ogier had a brother Guyon. Cf. also the son of Melusine.

[82] *FQ*, II, I, vi, 8–9.   [83] Cf. *Ded. Son.* to Oxford.

through Huon are intended as a general complimentary allusion to the French element both in the English royal family and in the English nobility. Certainly it is significant that the part of France which had belonged to the popular English kings, Richard Coeur de Lion and Henry V, and which in Spenser's own day was the stronghold of the Huguenot allies of England, should also be the part of France most frequently connected with the fairies. In Aquitaine, Hercules established the main seat of his Gallic kingdom. On the borders of Aquitaine he had the love affair with Pyrène, whose offspring was the ancestor of Melusine. And in Poitou, according to Jean d'Arras, there "have ben shewed unto many oon right famylerly many manyeres of thinges/ the whiche somme called Gobelyns/the other ffayrees, and the other 'bonnes dames' or good ladyes,"[84] some of whom married lords of that country, and became progenitors, like Melusine, of a "noble lynee . . . that shall regne forever unto thend of the world."[85]

The identification of the fairies with pagan gods, spirits of the dead, and ancestors of noble families in France and England, makes them suitable inhabitants of a land of fame resembling the classical Elysium. The identification of Fairyland in its symbolic meaning and largely in its mythology with the Elysian Fields is further strengthened by the fact that of the three traditional locations of the Elysian Fields, that in the air links them with the allegorical temples of fame considered in chapter one and with the starry heavens, home of the gods, while the other two locations, under the earth and on an island to the west, are linked with the folklore and romance locations of fairyland. Of the underground fairyland we have already spoken. The other tradition, which was most suited for Spenser's purpose in view of the Plutarchan identification of the island of the

[84] *Melusine*, p. 4.   [85] *Ibid.*, p. 6.

blest with Britain, would fuse most readily with the conception of fairyland which was enjoined by his choice of the Arthurian story. For Arthur, like other heroes of romance who followed him, and whose adventures must have entered into Spenser's conception of fairyland, ended his career on the fairy island of Avalon, "Insula pomorum quae fortunata vocatur,"[86] whose resemblance to the Islands of the Blest must have been as obvious to Spenser as it is to modern scholars.[87]

The story of Arthur's translation to Avalon was well known to Spenser and to his readers. From Geoffrey of Monmouth to Malory chroniclers and romancers had related how after the fatal battle with Modred, Arthur went to the isle of Avalon for the healing of his wounds. There according to one tradition he continued to live, waiting for the time of his return to Britain, which was mystically accomplished by the accession of Henry VII. The importance of this "return motif" in Spenser's thought has been sufficiently emphasized by the late Professor Greenlaw and the scholars who have followed him.[88] They have pointed out that the legend of Arthur's return was interpreted mystically to mean the return of the ancient British dynasty in the Tudors. Arthur was dead, as indeed all the Elizabethan historians tell us. Nevertheless, the story of his return had a certain truth. Similarly the old belief in his continued life in Avalon might be rationalized into a symbol of an Elizabethan ideal. Arthur was dead, but his fame was immortal. In virtue of it, he continued to live in Fairyland.

I do not know whether this interpretation of Arthur's continued life in Avalon was ever clearly suggested before

[86] *Vita Merlini*, quoted Paton, *Studies in the Fairy Mythology of Arthurian Romance*, p. 38.
[87] *Ibid.*, pp. 44–47, Maury, *Fées du moyen age*, pp. 41–44, Ferrario, III, 312.
[88] See especially Greenlaw, *Studies in Spenser's Historical Allegory*, and Millican, *Spenser and the Table Round*.

Spenser wrote his *Faerie Queene*, but there is a hint of it in Lydgate's version in the *Fall of Princes*, which combines an account of Arthur's fabled reign in Fairyland with the description already mentioned of his stellification and translation to a crystal palace in the heavens. I quote the whole passage:

> Afftir the bataile Arthour for a while
> To staunche his woundis & hurtis to recure
> Born in a liteer cam into an Ile
> Callid Avaloun; and ther of aventure,
> As seid Gaufrid recordeth be scripture,
> How kyng Arthour, flour of chevalrie,
> Rit with his knihtis & lyveth in Fairye.
>
> Thus of Breteyne translatid was þe sunne
> Up to the riche sterri briht dongoun—
> Astronomeeres well reherse kunne—
> Callid Arthuris constellacioun,
> Wher he sit crownid in the hevenly mancioun
> Amyd the paleis of stonis cristallyne,
> Told among Cristen first of þe worthi nyne.
>
> This errour yit abit among Bretouns,
> Which foundid is upon the prophecie
> Of olde Merlyn, lik ther opynyouns:
> He as a kyng is crownid in Fairie,
> With sceptre and suerd, and with his regalie
> Shal resorte as lord and sovereyne
> Out of Fairye & regne in Bretayne.[89]

I have already suggested that the crystal palace mentioned in this passage is an important analogue, and perhaps a principal source of Spenser's Panthea, which may also be a sym-

---

[89] Bk. VIII, ll. 3095-4015, *EETS* Ed., Vol. III, pp. 909-10. Lydgate's "Breteyne" may be Brittany, not Wales or England, but to Spenser these lines would certainly suggest the return of the British, i.e., Welsh Arthur to his island kingdom. For Breton beliefs about Arthur's return, see Tatlock, "Geoffrey and King Arthur in *Normannicus Draco*," *MP*, XXXI (1933), 1-18, 113-25.

bol of heaven.[90] Possibly Spenser was acquainted also with Celtic legends about a tower of glass, which is sometimes associated with Arthur, and which is generally recognized as an Otherworld castle. The clearest reference to this tower appears in Nennius's account of the settlement of Ireland by three sons of a Spanish soldier, who arrived with thirty ships,

and having remained there during the space of a year, there appeared to them, in the middle of the sea, a tower of glass, the summit of which seemed covered with men, to whom they often spoke, but received no answer. At length they determined to besiege the tower; and after a year's preparation, advanced towards it, with the whole number of their ships, and all the women, one ship only excepted, which had been wrecked, and in which were thirty men and as many women; but when all had disembarked on the shore which surrounded the tower, the sea opened and swallowed them up. Ireland, however, was peopled . . . from the family remaining in the vessel which was wrecked.[91]

In an obscure Welsh poem attributed to Taliessin, the fame of Arthur is connected with the "vitrea turris" of Nennius, "which was doubtless the glass fort," says Rhys, "to which Taliessin extends Arthur's fame."

Beyond the Glass Fort, Arthur's valour they had not seen;
Three score hundred stood on the wall:
It was hard to converse with their watchman.[92]

This glass house with which Arthur is connected in Welsh tradition reminds us of Spenser's Panthea, the fairy palace or temple which is the goal of Arthur's quest, and probably the place of his final abode. Though there is no evidence that Spenser knew Welsh, his introduction of Welsh words into the British Chronicle[93] shows that, like other Elizabethan

[90] See above, p. 48.
[91] *Historia Brittonum*, Gunn's translation, p. 7.
[92] *Celtic Heathendom*, p. 264.   [93] *FQ*, II, X, xxiv, 8–9.

antiquaries, he was interested in Welsh traditions, which had acquired considerable prestige with the accession of the Tudors, and which were probably discussed in the learned circles which Spenser frequented before he left England. Greenlaw reminds us that Sir Henry Sidney was for some time Lord President of Wales, and suggests that Spenser may have acquired a knowledge of Celtic folklore and legend during his association with the Sidney family.[94] Possibly Spenser was also acquainted with Camden and Harrison, both of whom were interested in ancient British history and legend.[95]

Spenser's long residence in Ireland makes it probable that he was acquainted with Irish legends of the Happy Otherworld, and certain scholars have suggested that his fairy mythology may have owed as large a debt to Irish folklore and legend as to classical mythology and Italian romance epic.[96] This thesis is in my judgment still "not proven."[97] In the nature of the case proof is difficult and perhaps impossible to establish. It is easy enough to find "Celtic faerie" in Spenser's poem. It is quite another thing to trace this fairy lore directly to Irish sources rather than to English, French, or Italian romance, or even to oral tradition current in England and Wales. The fairy mythology which Spenser inherited from his literary predecessors was already an amalgam of folklore, Celtic and classic myth, and romanticized history, and the adaptation of this composite

[94] "Spenser's Fairy Mythology," *SP*, XV (1918), 109.

[95] Renwick, *Complaints*, p. 194, suggests that Spenser may have known Camden. Harrison was acquainted with Harvey, and established near Rochester. Renwick suggests that he may be Diggon Davie of *September*. See Renwick's ed. of *SC*, p. 210.

[96] Greenlaw, *SP*, XV, 105–22, Henley, *Spenser in Ireland*, S. Michie, "Celtic Myth and Spenserian Romance," *Univ. of Virginia Abstracts of Dissertations* (1935), pp. 11–13. See also Whitney, *MP*, XIX (1921), 143–62, R. Smith, "Spenser's Irish River Stories," *PMLA*, L (1935), 1047–56, and "Una and Duessa," *ibid.*, pp. 917–19 for examples of alleged Irish influence.

[97] Miss Michie may have proved it. I have not seen her dissertation.

mythology to his own artistic purpose would tend to blur still further the distinctions between its original elements. Furthermore, it is probable that Irish literature, like Irish scenery, had more influence upon the details of the *Faerie Queene* than upon its central plan or continued allegory. Though much of the poem was written in Ireland, it was planned in England, and was intended for English readers, who knew a great deal more about Hercules, Arthur, and Melusine than they did about Fand and Mannannan. To the average Elizabethan, "Fairyland" would suggest, not the Land of the Living to which Bran and Connla voyaged, but "the lost isle" of Avalon, where Melusine was brought up, and Arthur healed of his wound.[98]

In Melusine, Avalon appears simply as the land of the fairies, a mysterious and rather terrifying place. In other romances, it is also the paradise in which specially favored heroes enjoy immortal life. The popularity of this conception of Avalon, which links it to the Elysian Fields as a land of fame, is attested by the stories about Gargantua, who was well known to Elizabethan theatergoers when Shakespeare wrote *As You Like It*.[99] Two French versions of these pre-Rabelaisian giant stories have been recently reprinted.[100] In one Gargantua is transported to Fairyland at the close of his earthly career by Melusine and Morgan the Fay.[101] In the longer version, which is thought to have existed in a lost Elizabethan translation, it is Merlin who leaves Gargantua "en Faerie, ou estoit jà allé le bon Roy Artus avec sa seur Morgain, Ogier le Dannois, et Huon de Bordeaulx, où ilz vivent encore et font grant chère au chasteau d'Avallon."[102]

---

[98] That the two places were originally the same does not affect the argument.

[99] *AYLI*, III, ii, 238-39. Cf. H. Brown, introduction to F. Girault, *The Tale of Gargantua and King Arthur*, pp. xxiv *et sqq.*

[100] *Ibid.*   [101] *Ibid.*, p. 126.   [102] *Ibid.*, p. 102.

Ogier and Huon, like Arthur in Breton tradition, do not die and go to Fairyland, but go to Fairyland instead of dying. But side by side with them we find heroes like Gawain[103] and Roland, whose deaths were famous, enjoying the hospitality of Morgan. For these heroes, as for the Arthur of the Elizabethan chronicles, the immortal life of Fairyland may well be symbolic of the fame which the poets had bestowed upon them, and the same symbolism might be extended to the equally famous heroes who had reached Avalon without tasting death.

That the fairyland of romance was in some respects a land of fame is evidenced by the fact that only the greatest knights are permitted to visit Avalon, just as only the greatest heroes had a place in the Elysian Fields. In the *Bataille Loquifer*, for instance, the hero Renoart is carried in his sleep to the magic city of Avalon by three fairies who exhibit him to Arthur as

le meilleur champion
Qui onques fust en fable n'en chancon.[104]

When Renoart awakes, the fairy people are invisible to him. He sees them only after he has fought a successful battle with the goblin Kapalu, a monster who can only be changed back into human form by the blood of Renoart. After the fight, Arthur introduces Renoart to the people in the fairy castle, in words that emphasize their past earthly fame:

Je suis Artus dont l'on a tant parlé,
Renoart frère, ce sont la gent faë
Qui sont du siècle venus et trespassé
Vez la Rollant ce vermeil coulouré
Et c'est Gauvain à ce poile roë,

---

[103] Cf. Chaucer, *Squire's Tale*, ll. 95–96. Caxton had seen Gawain's skull at Dover. *Morte d'Arthur*, Vol. I, p. 2.
[104] Le Roux de Lincy, *Livre des légendes*, p. 249.

Et puis Ivain un sien compaing privé,
Et cele bele au vis enluminé
Icele est Morgue ou tant a de biauté.[105]

It is unlikely that Spenser knew the *Bataille Loquifer*, which was never printed in his day, but he probably knew some version of the story of Ogier le Danois, whose adventures in Fairyland were similar to Renoart's. In the version given by Jean d'Outremeuse in *Ly Myreur des histors*, Ogier is shipwrecked on the island of Avalon, and fights with various enchanted beasts and later with Arthur and Gawain, both of whom he overthrows but cannot wound because they are enchanted. Their conflict is stopped by Morgan, at the request of her son Oberon, who is with her in the Castle Plaisance. Like Renoart, Ogier becomes the lover of Morgan.[106] In the prose romance of *Ogier le danois*,[107] the hero is shipwrecked on the rock of the Adamant, and after the loss of his companions, is miraculously guided to the enchanted castle of Avalon, invisible by day, but shining at night. There he fights various beasts, meets Morgan in a garden, and receives from her a crown of oblivion and a ring which conveys the gift of eternal youth. She introduces him to her brothers, Arthur and Oberon, and to Mallembrun, the friendly "beast of the sea" who plays such a large part in *Huon of Burdeux*. Oberon places a troop of spirits at Morgan's disposal for the entertainment of her guests. These sometimes take the form of Lancelot, Tristram, and other knights, who discuss the laws of the Round Table with Arthur or engage in tournaments in which Ogier takes part. Sometimes they appear as giants and monsters that the heroes

---

[105] *Ibid.*, p. 256.   [106] *Myreur*, IV, 50 *et sqq.*

[107] I have not seen this romance, which was several times printed in the sixteenth century. My account of it is based on the summaries in Paton, pp. 74–80, Keightley, I, 75–82, Ward. *Catalogue of Romances*, I, 605–9, and Dunlop, I, 329–37, and on the selections quoted in *Brun de la montaigne*, pp. xi–xiii. An Italian version is summarized by Ferrario, III, 284–320.

may have the pleasure of overcoming them. Nothing disturbs this delightful existence except a rebellion of Capalus, King of the Goblins, who, however, is reconciled to Arthur by the good offices of Ogier. Ogier remains in Fairyland for two hundred years, and then returns to deliver France from the heathen. Just as he is about to marry the French queen, he is carried off by Morgan to remain in Fairyland "until the day of Judgment."

Several elements in this story are suggestive of Spenser's poem. Like Arthur, Ogier is beloved of the Fairy Queen. Morgan's power of bestowing eternal youth and immortality upon Ogier reminds us also of Gloriana, who as goddess of fame must surely be able to grant similar favors to her chosen knight.[108] The other conditions of Ogier's life in Fairyland are also similar to those we have postulated for Spenser's Prince Arthur. Through the magic art of Oberon, Ogier is enabled in a sense to turn back the clock, and to take part in the heroic life of Arthur's day, which continues in Fairyland. Similarly, if my hypothesis be correct, the Prince Arthur of Spenser's historical fiction passes from sixth-century Britain into the world of past history, and takes part in the heroic struggles against giants and monsters which had characterized the age of Hercules. The rebellion of Capalus, King of the Goblins, reminds us of the enmity between the fairies and the "Gobbelines" in the Elfin Chronicle. And the fact that Ogier's sojourn in Fairyland is broken by a return to France recalls the necessity for Arthur's similar return to Britain at the close of the *Faerie Queene.*[109]

Another Carolingian hero who attained to immortal life in Fairyland was Huon of Bordeaux. Unlike Ogier and Renoart, he achieves this, not by marrying the fairy queen,

---

[108] For a fuller discussion of this point see the following chapter.
[109] See below, p. 223.

but by winning the friendship of the fairy king. In *Huon*, the throne of Fairyland is clearly the reward of knightly virtue. "For the great trouthe and noblesse that I fynde in you," says Oberon to Huon, "I shall make you kyng of all the fayrey."[110] The fairyland over which Oberon rules is also, in some respects at least, a place of departed heroes. Huon meets several great knights there whose earthly lives have ended. Arthur disputes with him for Oberon's crown. Carahew, the great friend of Ogier, is present at the coronation feast.[111] Ogier himself has been left behind, but Morgan is there with their son, who, it will be remembered, was an ancestor of Helyas. The child is singled out for special attention in Oberon's address of welcome:

'syr kynge Arthure ye ar welcome, and Morgan your syster, and Transelyne your nece/ and syr, I praye you shewe me what fayre chyld is that I se there before your syster Morgan'/ 'syr,' quod Arthur, 'he is called Marlyn, & is sone to Ogyer ye dane/ who hath wedded my syster Morgan, and I have lefte hym in my countre to rule it tyll I retourne'/'syr,' quod kynge Oberon/'ye chyld shall have good fortune, he shalbe in his tyme feryd and doughted/for Ogyer his father is a good and a valyant knight.'[112]

When the rival claim of Arthur has been settled, Huon is invested with Oberon's crown. It was presumably on this occasion that Spenser's Sir Guyon received his knighthood:

at good Sir *Huon's* hand,
When with king *Oberon* he came to Faerie land.[113]

By an anachronism allowable in a follower of Virgil and Tasso, Spenser represents Huon's arrival in Fairyland as antedating Arthur's reign in Britain. In the Elfin Chronicle, Oberon is the father and predecessor of Gloriana, and Huon is not mentioned as a fairy sovereign. Perhaps Spenser in-

---

[110] *Huon of Burdeux*, I, Pt. 2, 598.   [111] *Ibid.*, p. 605.
[112] *Ibid.*, p. 601.   [113] *FQ*, II, I, vi, 8–9.

tended to represent Huon's reign as a regency, and to equate
him in the political allegory with Somerset, to whom Henry
VIII (Oberon) had entrusted "his last will,"[114] and who exer-
cised the royal power during the first part of Edward's mi-
nority. Somerset had Plantagenet blood, and might thus be
fittingly represented in Spenser's allegory by Huon, the
duke of Aquitaine.

Neither in the prose romance nor in the *chanson de geste*
of *Huon roy de fayerce* do we find that Huon created new
fairy knights at his accession, but the latter poem tells us
that his coronation feast was attended by ten thousand fairy
knights and ladies.[115] On such an occasion the creation of
new knights would certainly be appropriate, and there may
possibly be a reference to this in some unexplored romance
material which Spenser may have known. Certainly it is
tempting to believe that he found Guyon in a list of fairy
knights who appeared at Huon's coronation,[116] just as he
found Artegall among the knights who were present at
Arthur's coronation feast in Geoffrey of Monmouth and
Hardyng.[117] At any rate, Guyon seems to be linked with the
Carolingian heroes who reigned in Faërie much as Artegall
is linked with the Arthur of the British chronicle tradition.

In *Huon of Burdeux,* Fairyland appears as an empire,
ruled by Oberon from his capital city of Momur, which
seems to be located in India. Other fairy kingdoms are ruled
by tributary kings, of whom Arthur is chief. This conception may be related to the folklore view of Fairyland as a
series of enchanted places situated in different parts of the

[114] Cf. *ibid.,* II, X, lxxvi, 5.

[115] "Huon, roy de fayerce," *Ausgaben und Abhandlungen aus dem Gebiete
der romanischen Philologie,* XC (1892), 85.

[116] Jean d'Outremeuse mentions a tradition that Morgan and Ogier had
other children besides Meurvin. *Myreur,* IV, 56. Perhaps one of them was
named Guyon.

[117] Harper, p. 143.

world. In *Brun de la montaigne* is a list of well-known "lieues faés," all of which are represented as under the control of Arthur.[118] In *Huon*, Arthur leaves Ogier in charge of his (fairy) kingdom of Britain, while he himself comes to Momur seeking Oberon's imperial crown. When this is awarded to Huon, Arthur is recompensed with the overlordship of the fairies of Tartary.[119]

This conception of the nature of Fairyland may well have been of importance to Spenser. For the idea that each part of the world had a fairy counterpart, and that all these fairy kingdoms were united under one ruler, Oberon, Huon, or Arthur, would naturally make Fairyland an excellent symbol for the center of an ideal world empire. We have seen that the *Antiquitie of Faerie lond*, which Guyon reads in the chamber of memory, is probably a "speculum" of universal history, in which each of the important events leading up to the final destined triumph of the Tudors has an elfin counterpart. The creation of man, the establishment of justice in east and west by Osiris and Hercules, the gradual building up of the ideal earthly city by their descendants, the founders of the three Troys, and the final revival of antique glory by the Tudors—these events, we have seen, may be reflected in the fairy chronicle, and the history of the world may be mirrored in the history of Gloriana's empire. A similar parallelism between world geography and fairy geography appears in the fairy empires of Oberon and Arthur. The center of Oberon's realm was India, the land associated particularly with Osiris, first of the Elfin emperors, and, by extension to America, with Elizabeth, Empress of Virginia. The tradition which made Arthur the supreme fairy king, however, would naturally place the capital of his empire on the fairy island corresponding to Britain. The parallelism between the fairy world and the real world,

---

[118] Quoted at head of this chapter.   [119] *Huon*, I, Pt. 2, 603.

which appears in the romances we have been considering, may thus have helped Elizabeth to recognize her "own realme in land of Faerie."

The fairy cities and palaces described in these romances are certainly among the influences which determined Spenser's conception of Gloriana's capital.[120] Their resemblance to the allegorical and Elysian cities already mentioned forms another link between the diverse elements of Spenser's fairy mythology. The Castle of the Adamant, which in *Ogier* seems to be on the island of Avalon, is described in *Huon* as built by Julius Caesar as a place to enjoy the love of his fairy mistress, Oberon's mother, "the queen of the privy isle." The castle, built "by crafte of the fayrey," was

the fayrest and most rycheste howse in ye worlde, within the whiche was so moch golde and rychesse that no man levinge coude esteme the walue therof/for the pyllers within that howse were of Cassedony/and the walles and towres of whyghte Alablaster. There was never dyscryved in scrypture nor hystory the beauty of such a castell as this was, for whenne the sonne cast his rayes on it it semyd a far of to be of fyne christal, it was so clere shynynge.[121]

The towers were "rychely coveryd with fyne gold of Arabe." The gates were also of gold, richly ornamented. One chamber was "made of Chrystall paynted rychely with gold and asure. And there was porturyed all the bataylys of Troye and all the dedys of Alexander."[122] From this castle Huon is rescued by a griffon who flies with him to a crystal rock or island containing the fountain of youth and a tree whose apples convey the gift of youth.[123]

[120] The influence of *Huon of Burdeux* on the *Faerie Queene* has been discussed by J. B. Fletcher, J. Macarthur, R. Tuve, and H. Golder. The three latter mention the likeness between Cleopolis and Momur. See *Variorum*, I, 290–91.
[121] *Huon*, I, Pt. 2, 369.   [122] *Ibid.*, p. 412.   [123] *Ibid.*, p. 439.

On their way to Momur, Huon and Esclarmonde are entertained in another fairy castle which was built in an hour. In it there is a church "paved with whyght marble powdered with flowre de lyses of golde entermedled with red roses/and the vault was checkered with Ambre and Chrystall."[124] The fallen angels who inhabit this castle lead Huon and Esclarmonde to the confines of Oberon's kingdom. They climb a mountain,

and then within a lytell season huon sawe before hym apere a great citye, and on the one syde thereof a fayre and a ryche palleys/the walles and towers of the citye & paleys were of whyghte marble polysshed, the whiche shone so bryght agaynst the sonne as though it had bene al of christall/then Huon sayde to his wyfe, 'dame, yonder before us, we may se the citye of Momure, whereas kyng Oberon is.'[125]

Besides Momur, whose likeness to Cleopolis has often been pointed out, the other royal seat of the fairy kingdom in the romances is Avalon. This is described in the *Bataille Loquifer* as *moult riche cité*. Its wall is made of a single great stone, which cures all diseases. It shines like a furnace. The door is of ivory, and the principal tower is full of precious stones. The roof is of gold, surmounted by a golden eagle.[126]

Perhaps this is the same eagle which surmounts the fairy pavilion on Mount Perilous in *Arthur of Little Britain*,[127] and which symbolizes Florence, protégée of the Fairy Queen, and destined bride of Arthur.[128] An obvious analogue to Panthea appears in Florence's castle of Clere Toure,

[124] *Ibid.*, p. 590.
[125] *Ibid.*, p. 596. Both Macarthur and Miss Tuve note the likeness to *FQ*, I, X, iv.
[126] *Livre des legendes*, pp. 249–50.
[127] Translated by Berners, Utterson's reprint, p. 44.
[128] *Arthur of Little Britain*, p. 39. Spenser's use of *Arthur of Little Britain* was suggested by Greenlaw, "Britomart at the House of Busirane." See *Variorum*, III, 362–64. See also Michie, *op. cit.*, pp. 12–13.

first seen by Arthur under circumstances which remind us of St. George's vision of the New Jerusalem and of Huon's first sight of Momur. If the *Faerie Queene* had been completed, we should probably have had a similar picture of Arthur's first sight of Panthea in Cleopolis.

Than thei rode to the botom of a grete mountayne, and there thei alighted: & Arthur alone a fote mounted up to the hiest therof, and there he saw the castell of the Clere Toure, wheron there were pynacles of bryghte cristall, and it dyde shyne so agaynst the son, that no man coude clereli loke ayenst it. . . .[129]

Similarly dazzling is Morgan's Castle Plaisant on the isle of Avalon, described in *Ly Myreur des histors*. The castle is made of precious stones, and is set in the midst of an enchanted garden. There are three moats, crossed by three bridges "tout de berilh cristal, entrelachez d'yvoir."[130] The wall paintings within the castle make it a sort of hall of fame:

. . . toutez les chambrez sont pointez à histors, l'un de Dieu, l'autre de Troie. Li grande sale fut del roy Uter et Artus et de siens toute l'estoire escript et pointe, et touz les chevaliers de leurs temps.

En l'autre sale astoit le histoir Peppins et Charle, et leurs chevaliers, pointe en une des pareux, en l'autre pareux astoit li histoir Doon de Maienche, et à la thierche li histoir Garin de Monglaive; et à casconne des trois gieste astoit Ogier poins . . . Morghe aloit touz les jours al matin veoir les chevaliers, s'ilh n'y avoit nul destruis; car parmi chu, savoit elle touz les mals des chevaliers qui n'astoient nient fuis et qui fesist violenche ou trahison, le siene ymage tournoit le dos a son signour.[131]

As chatelaine of this castle Morgan acts as register of fame, and might easily be identified with the goddess of fame her-

[129] *Arthur of Little Britain*, p. 469. The connection of this description with *FQ*, I, X, liii *et sqq.*, has been suggested by H. Golder, "Bunyan and Spenser," *PMLA*, XLV (1930), 230.

[130] *Myreur*, IV, 52.   [131] *Ibid.*, pp. 52–53.

self. Later in the story she again appears as recorder of noble deeds. When she brings Ogier into the castle, the fairy damsels ask who he is. Morgan gives them a complete genealogy, and then makes it appear painted on the wall. Later Ogier asks Arthur who in his opinion were the best knights of the Round Table. Arthur answers Tristram first, and Lancelot second, but adds that Morgan can answer the question more vividly by enchantment. Morgan then causes a picture of Tristram and Lancelot to appear on the wall at the head of other knights of the Round Table. Galahad's picture appears in a corner, and the other knights bow to him.[132] Here we have a fairy queen fulfilling the functions of a muse of history or epic poetry. A similar use of fairy power is implied in the various allegorical pantheons scattered through the *Orlando furioso* (the fountain of chaste ladies for instance).[133] It is likely that these and other similar likenesses between the "power of the fairy" and the power of the muses influenced Spenser in identifying his Fairy Queen with Glory and setting her in Cleopolis, city of fame.

The fact that the fairy paradises we have been considering, in which heroes enjoyed immortal youth, were sometimes made of air,[134] would also serve to connect their makers with the muses by whom heroic actions are immortalized in words, which though they are made of thin air, are yet the most enduring of monuments:

> Not marble nor the gilded monument
> Of princes shall outlive this powerful rhyme.

This idea, so common in the Renaissance, so dear to Spenser himself, is built into the very fabric of his vision. His

[132] *Ibid.*, p. 57.   [133] *OF*, XLII, lxxviii *et sqq.*

[134] Jean d'Outremeuse, *Myreur*, IV, 55–56, tells how Merlin taught Morgan and many other British ladies how to make "habitations pour demoreir à touz jours sens avilhier et de pure aire." Cf. Virgil's garden walled with air and his bridge of air. Spargo, pp. 60–61.

Cleopolis, like Morgan's city of Avalon, like Oberon's Momur, is a work of enchantment, of faerie, an illusion which
is yet the most enduring, as it is the fairest, of earthly
things. The walls of Troy, on which Priam set golden
crowns,[135] are no more, and Rome preserves no trace of her
gold and crystal Capitol; but Troy lives on in Homer's verse,
and the lasting monument of Roman glory is the temple
built by Virgil, on the green plain beside the waters of Min-
cius.[136] So the golden wall of Cleopolis and the crystal tower,
Panthea, shall continue to stand even after the lofty bridge
of the third Troy shall have crumbled to dust. Only the
heavenly city can outlast the city of fame. This last will
endure, like the sojourn of Huon and Ogier in Fairyland,
"until the day of judgement."

The conception of Fairyland as a magic city, often on an
island, presided over sometimes by a king, but generally by
a queen, in which heroes were welcomed at the close of their
lives on earth, was probably the most important contribu-
tion of the romances to Spenser's fairy mythology. Possibly
they furnished him with suggestions for other features of
his mythical world. In *Huon of Burdeux, Ogier le danois,*
and other romances, we find a race of monsters called *luitons* (goblins) who may be related to Spenser's "wicked Gobbelines." The best-known *luitons* are Mallembrun, Papillon, and Capalus. All these were originally men, changed
into the form of beasts because they incurred the displeasure
of a fairy. Mallembrun was doomed to be a beast of the sea
for three hundred years for unintentionally causing the
death of one of Morgan's nymphs.[137] Papillon, the enchanted
horse who welcomes Ogier to the Castle of the Adamant,
and later transports him back to France, "estoit luiton et

---

[135] Lydgate, *Troy Book*, Bk. II, ll. 589–91.
[136] *Georgics* iii. 10–39. This passage may also have contributed to Spenser's
conception of Panthea.
[137] Ferrario, III, 325.

avoit este ung grant prince; mais le roi Artus le conquist, si fust condampne a estre trois cens ans cheval sans parler ung tout seul mot; mais apres les trois cens ans, il devoit avoir la couronne de joye de laquelle ils usoient en faerie."[138]

Most formidable of the *luitons* is Capalus, who is described in the *Bataille Loquifer* as having the head of a cat, the tail of a lion, the body of a horse, and the claws of a griffon. He was born in the isle of Orion. His mother was a fay named Bruhan, who, while bathing in the fountain Albon, was surprised by Rigalez, a *muton (luiton?)*. Kapalu was born a fair child, but his mother enchanted him, and Arthur shut him up in the castle of Avalon until Renoart should come to deliver him.

The combat in which Capalus regains his mortal shape was later transferred from Renoart to Ogier.[139]

Arthur has been engaged in a long struggle with the *luitons:*

Or estoit le roy Artus en grant debat avec le roy des luytons et le vouloit getter le roy capalus roy des dis luitons hors du chastel de faerie. Si viendrent plusieurs assaillir le dit chasteau et tant que ils gaignerent la basse court. Adonc se print a crier de recief. Ou es tu roy artus ie te deffie corps a corps. Et si tost que Ogier l'ouyt si fut tout eschauffe si demanda qui se pouvoit estre qui parloit de si estrange facon car il n'a pas parolle d'homme, se dit Ogier. Et le roy artus lui dist plainement. Ogier mon amy ie vous compteray la verite. Je vous dy que le roy des lutons a grant envie sur moy. Et de fait trouveroit voluntiers le moyen et facon de me getter de ce chasteau.[140]

Arthur further explains that the previously mentioned transformation of Papillon into a horse was one of the in-

---

[138] *Ogier le danois*, quoted by Keightley, I, 77.

[139] In the version of Jean d'Outremeuse, *Myreur*, IV, 48–49, Capalus is the soul of Benoist, Ogier's squire, doing penance in the form of a monster. His penance ends when he fights with Ogier, and draws blood from him. These combats seem to reflect an earlier fight between Arthur and a cat-like monster, who is sometimes credited with Arthur's death. See J. D. Bruce's

cidents in the war with Capalus. Ogier then obtains permission to act as Arthur's champion against the king of the
goblins:

si tost quil fut dehors il trouva capalus qui se vint apparoistre
a luy en figure dung chevalier grant et fort.[141]

When Ogier reveals his identity, however, Capalus immediately surrenders. Ogier brings him to Arthur and Morgan,
and asks that the ex-goblin shall always remain in human
form. Capalus is baptized, and becomes Arthur's ally in all
his wars.[142]

These goblins, who are really men undergoing punishment, resemble the werewolves, whose country forms one
of the subdivisions of Oberon's empire. It will be remembered that Oberon threatened to turn Arthur into a "were-
wolf of the sea," if he failed to do homage to Huon.[143]
Although these monsters generally appear in the romances
as harmless and friendly servants of the fairy sovereigns and
mortal heroes, their monstrous forms, which are always in
the nature of a punishment for sin, would connect them
with the monsters of classical mythology, who were generally
regarded as types of evil, and with the damned souls of
Tartarus, and their human origin would fit them for a place
in Spenser's very human fairyland. I have already suggested
that the earthly counterpart of Elfinell's war with the Gobbelines may be the expulsion of Tantalus from Phrygia. In
the Elysian Fields this war might be reproduced as a conflict
between the blessed and the damned like that described in
the *Vera historia*. In giving his land of fame a romance
dress, Spenser might identify the good spirits with the fair-

---

edition of *Mort Artu*, pp. 304–5, and E. Freymond, "Artus' Kampf mit dem
Katzenungetüm," *Beiträge zur romanischen Philologie, Festgäbe für G.
Gröber*, pp. 311–96.
[140] Quoted *ibid.*, pp. 344–45. [141] *Ibid.*, p. 345.
[142] *Ibid.* [143] *Huon*, I, Pt. 2, 602.

ies, and the evil or damned spirits with the *luitons*. The sub-
jugation of these monsters by the Elfin rulers of Cleopolis
would form a natural part of the early history of Fairyland,
and would explain the continued enmity between the Elfin
nation and the race of monsters like Error and the Blatant
Beast, as well as preparing for their possible later revolt
against the Fairy Queen which might be expected to take
place when she was attacked by the great Paynim King, who
may perhaps be related to Capalus.

If the Paynim King is not a monster like Capalus, we
should certainly expect him to be a giant, and in fact the
giants also appear as traditional enemies of the fairies in
the romances of the Huon cycle. The enmity between the
Saracen giant Angolaffer and Oberon is an important motif
in the old French poem, *Auberon,* and in the prose romance
of *Huon of Burdeux,* and in the earlier poem, *Huon, roy de
fayerce,* Huon has to fight a long war with a tribe of giants
before he is secure on his throne.

As the Olympian deities intervene to help their descendants in the battles of classical epic, so the fairies in the romances we have been discussing come to the assistance of
their mortal friends and relations, and enchanted heroes
who have taken up their abode in Fairyland may return to
their former homes in moments of great national danger.
Thus Oberon frequently comes to the rescue of Huon, and
Huon himself leaves Fairyland with a troop of fairy knights
to aid his distressed descendants on earth. Ogier sends his
son Meurvin, born in Fairyland, back to France to fight for
Christianity under Hugh Capet, and himself returns for a
similar purpose, according to one version under Hugh
Capet, according to another under Philip the Fair, himself
a descendant of Ogier. In the latter version, that of Jean
d'Outremeuse, he is assisted by Arthur and Gawain at the
head of ten thousand fairy knights, who are invisible to the

other combatants.[144] Similarly in the *Faerie Queene,* St. George, a hero of whom legend already related similar miraculous interventions,[145] comes from Fairyland to deliver the king and queen of Eden, a country which is sometimes described as contiguous to Avalon. Similarly Artegall was destined to return from Fairyland to help save his native Britain from the invasion of "forreign Paynims."[146]

But St. George and Artegall came to Fairyland by a different route from that of the other heroes we have been considering. They were changelings, stolen in their cradles by "false fairies,"[147] who left their "base elfin brood"[148] in place of the royal infants whom they carried off to Fairyland. For this use of contemporary folklore, Spenser has been adversely criticized by both Scott and Keightley. The latter, for instance, remarks, "It was quite incongruous to style the progeny of the subjects of Gloriane a 'base elfin brood,' or themselves 'false Fairies,' especially when we recollect that such a being as Belphoebe . . . was born of a Fairie."[149] We have already seen, however, that not all the subjects of Gloriana were so virtuous as Belphoebe, and a place might easily be found for the "false fairies" of folklore among the unruly nation that included "the wicked Gobbelines" and such devotees of the black art as Archimago and Duessa. If Spenser's Fairyland is a land of fame, and not (outside the city of Cleopolis) exclusively a land of good fame, there is no reason why all its inhabitants should be virtuous, and, in fact, if the life of Fairyland is to exhibit virtue in action, and thus preserve the image of "former times," there must be evil there for the good to strive

---

[144] *Myreur,* V, 126–27.

[145] For example, in the romance of *Richard Coeur de Lion,* ll. 4883 *et sqq.* he appears in the midst of a battle, invisible to all but Richard, and from a great white horse slays a multitude of Saracens.

[146] *FQ,* III, III, xxvii, 9.

[147] *Ibid.,* xxvi.   [148] *Ibid.,* I, X, lxv, 8.   [149] *Fairy Mythology,* I, 96.

against. We have seen, however, that Spenser generally limits the term "fairy" to good characters, and perhaps for this reason he chose the epithet "false" for the beings who steal Artegall. "False fairies" might mean "fairies who were untrue to their nature." If the true fairies, in this sense, were the souls of heroes who continue to live in history as examples of virtue, these false fairies should represent the spirits of evil men, servants of the devil, who may still exert a malignant influence in human affairs.

Such an influence might well be symbolized by the stealing of St. George and Artegall, for it was certainly a work of the devil to withdraw True Holiness and Justice from Britain. As usual, however, the devil was foiled, for these virtues were not destroyed. They continued to live in memory and in idea, and were destined to return in due time through the influence of the two royal virgins, Una and Britomart, both of whom represent Queen Elizabeth. The Saxon kings submitted to Rome, and the Visible Church in England lost its humility and became corrupt.[150] It no longer resembled its true self; it was a changeling. Yet all the time the true Church was alive in Fairyland, in the England that had been and was to be. Similarly the withdrawal of Artegall from Britain coincided with a temporary eclipse of justice, when the legitimate British dynasty was threatened by Saxon and Roman usurpers. This situation ceased with the accession of Arthur, whose return foreshadowed the later triumph of justice under Henry VII and Elizabeth.[151]

[150] This interpretation was suggested by Howard, "Essay on the Historical Allusions of Spenser," quoted *Variorum*, I, 453. I have argued elsewhere (A New Source for Spenser's *Faerie Queene*, Bk. I, *SP*, XXXIII (1936), 175) that St. George in the political allegory stands for the English nation. According to Tudor ideas, this would be the same as the Visible Church in England. For the distinction between the Visible and Invisible Church, see Hooker, *Ecclesiastical Polity*, Bk. III, chaps. i–xiv, Everyman ed., Vol. I, pp. 283–97.

[151] For a fuller discussion of this point see below, pp. 224 *et sqq.*

The significance of St. George and Artegall in the moral allegory may thus explain the symbolic meaning which Spenser expressed through the familiar story of the fairy changeling. The early training of these two heroes in Fairyland, moreover, like the fairy adventures of Arthur, which form the main subject of the poem, may well symbolize the early training in virtue, acquired by a study of the past, which is necessary for an ideal ruler. So Jean Lemaire represents the early life of Paris, as a shepherd ignorant of his royal heritage, as symbolic of the "vie contemplative" of study and reflection which fits a noble youth for his later responsibilities.[152]

A similar interpretation of their sojourn in Fairyland is most probable for Arthur, Britomart, and Artegall, the three British characters in the *Faerie Queene* who are certainly destined to return to their native country and to repeat on earth the victories they have gained in Fairyland. The basis for Spenser's distinction between fairies and Britons has long been puzzling to students of the *Faerie Queene*. In the moral allegory, no distinction exists. The two cardinal virtues, Justice and Temperance, are represented by a Briton and a fairy, respectively. Nor does the historical allegory offer any basis for the distinction. Fairies and Britons alike have been identified with prominent Elizabethans, and Greenlaw's explanation that "by *Fairy* Spenser meant *Welsh* or more accurately *Tudor*,"[153] seems clearly untenable, since Arthur, Britomart, and Artegall, the ancestors of the Tudors, are not fairies at all. We are left with the alternative of assuming that Spenser's distinction between fairies and Britons belongs to his historical fiction. And if my view of the nature of Spenser's fairies be at all correct, we can easily see why they should be distinguished from Arthur, Britomart, and Artegall. For in Spenser's historical

[152] *Œuvres*, I, 5.   [153] *SP*, XV (1918), 120.

fiction these worthies belong not to the past or to the future, like the fairies, but to the present.[154] They are the living heroes, like Odysseus and Aeneas, who are permitted to visit the land of the dead and of the unborn. And, like Odysseus and Aeneas, they must return to earth, and win their right to a permanent dwelling in the heaven of heroes by their great exploits in their native countries, over which their "famous progenie" is to rule.

We cannot be quite sure that the same explanation holds in the case of St. George, the other one of Spenser's heroes who is definitely stated to be an Englishman and no fairy. To be sure, the fact that Spenser makes St. George descend from "Saxon kings" of England might lead us to make him also a contemporary of Arthur, since the Saxons first came to England in the reign of Vortigern, Arthur's great-uncle. It may possibly be for religious reasons, however, that Spenser insists so strongly that St. George is a "man of earth." Miss Tuve has suggested a connection between Spenser's insistence on St. George's mortal birth and the tradition that the fairies as fairies were shut out of heaven.[155] This idea, which in its origin is clearly connected with the belief that the fairies were devils, is not inconsistent with Spenser's more complimentary theory of their origin. For some of Spenser's original fairies were pagans, and their glory is an earthly glory. Gloriana's knights for the most part represent the moral, not the theological virtues. St. George is

[154] Against this point of view is Gough's comment on *FQ*, V, I: "The opening stanzas illustrate the fact that the action of the poem belongs to no age, but is purely ideal. The Knights of the Faerie Court lived when wickedness was beginning to raise its head and sully the innocence of the primitive world. Sir Artegall's childhood lay in the Golden Age itself. Spenser here completely ignores the semi-historical background, the age of Arthur in the sixth century." *Faerie Queene, Book V*, p. 165. But Artegall's childhood is passed in Fairyland, not in Britain.

[155] "The Red Crosse Knight and Medieval Demon Stories," *PMLA*, XLIV (1929), 706.

the link between the two. He has a place, not only in Cleopolis, but in the New Jerusalem.

Besides his use of the changeling motif, another inconsistent use of popular folklore with which Spenser has been charged is in the Sixth Book, where he tells us that the "ruder clown" dared not approach Mount Acidale, haunt of nymphs and fairies, and later that Calidore, himself a fairy, was unable to tell whether the dancing Graces were "Nymphes or Faeries, or enchaunted show,"[156] Keightley objects that the clown in question as an inhabitant of Fairyland should have been immune from fears that might be natural to an English rustic. But the common idea that Fairyland is a series of enchanted places on earth as well as a mysterious land under the earth or an island in the sea, would allow of the "ruder clown" being a mortal who had peeped into Fairyland, and been properly frightened. This view of Fairyland, though not essential to Spenser's conception, is perfectly compatible with it. In the second instance, however, Keightley's charge of inconsistency does seem to be justified. Spenser is apparently thinking of Sir Calidore as a man, and of the fairies as supernatural beings. This momentary confusion between the popular and the rationalized forms of the fairy mythology is quite understandable. The dancing fairies of folklore were so familiar to the Elizabethan imagination that it was natural for Spenser to think of them in describing the troop of dancing maidens who appeared to Calidore. The inconsistency is really only a verbal one, for the fairies appear in this passage as incidental imagery rather than as part of Spenser's general conception of Fairyland. In this passage, we may say with Keightley, Spenser momentarily "forgot himself."

A similarly inconsistent use of language occurs when

[156] *FQ*, VI, X, xvii, 6.

Merlin tells Britomart that Artegall is no kin to the fairies, but is "sprong of seed terrestriall."[157] If the latter phrase means "mortal" or "human," it clearly applies to Spenser's Elfin emperors, to whom Artegall must be related, since he is the half brother of Arthur, and ancestor of the succeeding British kings, all of whom claimed descent from Brutus. In explaining that Artegall is a Briton and no fairy, Merlin thus adopts phrasing which suggests the popular superstition which saw the fairies as members of a different race from men, instead of as members of the same race under different conditions. That the latter view of the basis for distinguishing fairies from Britons in the *Faerie Queene* represents Spenser's considered meaning is part of the hypothesis advanced in this book. In spite of the few verbal inconsistencies which may be alleged against it, the thesis that Spenser's fairies stand for famous men who in Arthur's day were either dead or unborn is too consistent with Spenser's meaning, and too clearly parallel with much that he would find in his probable sources and avowed models, to be lightly discarded. Spenser's Fairyland is a land of fame, which reveals the meaning of world history. In the preceding chapter we saw how this idea was expressed in the Renaissance understanding of ancient history, and in the classical myth of the Elysian Fields. The present chapter has added the evidence from Elizabethan fairy lore and from romance. From these sources Spenser must have drawn the materials for his mythical Otherworld, which is both a land of the gods and a land of the dead, which may be visited by great heroes like Odysseus, Aeneas, and Arthur as a preliminary to their completion of their earthly missions, and in which they are destined at last to enjoy the immortality which is the gift of Fame. In the *Faerie Queene*, the goddess

[157] *Ibid.*, III, III, xxvi, 5.

of fame is identified with the Fairy Mistress of Celtic myth and medieval romance. To elucidate the meaning which Spenser read into this most important figure in his fairy world will be our task in the following chapter.

IV
THE FAIRY QUEEN

The rugged forhead that with grave foresight
  Welds kingdomes causes, and affaires of state,
  My looser rimes (I wote) doth sharply wite,
  For praising love, as I have done of late,
  And magnifying lovers deare debate;
  By which fraile youth is oft to follie led,
  Through false allurement of that pleasing baite,
  That better were in vertues discipled,
Then with vaine poemes weeds to have their fancies fed.

Such ones ill iudge of love, that cannot love,
  Ne in their frosen hearts feele kindly flame:
  For thy they ought not thing unknowne reprove,
  Ne naturall affection faultlesse blame,
  For fault of few that have abusd the same.
  For it of honor and all vertue is
  The roote, and brings forth glorious flowres of fame,
  That crowne true lovers with immortall blis,
The meed of them that love, and do not live amisse.

Which who so list looke backe to former ages,
  And call to count the things that then were donne,
  Shall find, that all the workes of those wise sages,
  And brave exploits which great Heroes wonne,
  In love were either ended or begunne:
  Witness the father of Philosophie,
  Which to his *Critias,* shaded oft from sunne,
  Of love full manie lessons did apply,
The which these Stoicke censours cannot well deny.

To such therefore I do not sing at all,
  But to that sacred Saint my soveraigne Queene,
  In whose chast breast all bountie naturall,
  And treasures of true love enlocked beene,
  Bove all her sexe that ever yet was seene;
  To her I sing of love, that loveth best,
  And best is lov'd of all alive I weene:
  To her this song most fitly is addrest,
The Queene of love, and Prince of peace from heaven blest.
                     Faerie Queene, IV, Proem, i–iv.

AS ARTHUR'S fairy mistress, Gloriana is related to all the fairy queens of Celtic myth and medieval romance whose love was the crowning glory of "the best knight in the world." In particular, she is allied to the "queen of the privy isle" of Avalon, who is generally, though not always, identified with Morgan le Fay.[1] This lady, as we have already suggested, has some characteristics appropriate to a goddess of fame. In *Huon of Burdeux*, she wins the love of Julius Caesar by foretelling his victory over Pompey.[2] In *Ogier le danois,* she confers the gift of eternal youth.[3] In various versions of the Arthurian legend, she comes for Arthur in a magic boat, and carries him off to Avalon for the healing of his wounds.

This traditional healing and immortalizing power of the fairy queens of romance is particularly appropriate to fame, "Che trae l'uom del sepolcro e'n vita il serba."[4] Oberon's horn, which possessed the power of healing all wounds, was made " by iiii ladyes of the fayre in the yle of Chafalone."[5] One of these, who gave the horn its gift of healing, was named Gloriande. So far as I know, she has never been connected with Spenser's Gloriana. Yet the two fays resemble each other in more than name, as an examination of the stories about Gloriande will show.

In *Tristan de Nanteuil,* Gloriande bestows the gift of courage upon the erstwhile cowardly hero.[6] Through the inspiration of her beauty and the promise of her love,[7]

---

[1] They are distinct in *Huon,* I, Pt. 2, 536, and in *Prophecies de Merlin,* I, 415.

[2] *Huon,* I, Pt. 1, 73.

[3] So in all the summaries of the prose romance. Cf. Paton, pp. 75–80.

[4] Petrarch, *Trionfo della fama,* l. 9.   [5] *Huon,* I, Pt. 1, 66.

[6] *Histoire litteraire de la France,* XXVI, 246–47. Summarized also in P. Meyer, "Notice sur le roman de *Tristan de Nanteuil,*" *Jahrb. fur rom. und eng. Lit.,* IX (1868), 38 et sqq.

[7] *Ibid.,* pp. 39–40.

Tristan is enabled to vanquish a *luiton* in serpent form,
whom the fairy has brought to test his courage. She then
reveals her identity:

> Sachés que je sui fée, Gloriande ai à non;
> Je sui cousine Morgue et le roi Malebron.
> Mais ici sui venue pour vous doner le don
> D'avoir tel hardement que liepart ou lion.[8]

She then takes him to her fairy castle, where he finds Arthur,
Morgan, Oberon, and other fairies. Arthur gives Tristan a
horn which renders its owner invulnerable. Since Gloriande
has already given him courage, and has revealed to him the
secret of his birth, of which, like Spenser's Prince Arthur,[9]
he had previously been ignorant, Tristan leaves Fairyland
fully equipped for a life of ennobling adventure.

In *Tristan de Nanteuil,* Gloriande is a member of the
royal family of Fairyland. In another fourteenth-century
French poem, *Charles le chauve,* she appears as the Fairy
Queen.[10] The young prince Dieudonné is resting by a fountain when three fays arise from the water. They direct him
to the castle of their queen, Gloriande. At the bridge he is
challenged by a dwarf named Maufumé, who is five thousand years old, but who has only attained the stature of a
child of seven. Upon Dieudonné's refusal to fight with such
a puny opponent, Maufumé departs and reappears in the
form of a great knight, preceded by two lions. The two
champions fight, and Maufumé is overthrown. He then regains his original form, and tells Dieudonné that he is now
able to "passer en vaillance le plus hardi,"[11] and advises him
how to behave toward Gloriande.

Le château de la reine des fées n'est plus fermé pour toi; mais
je te donne un conseil: ne fais rien de ce que ma dame te de-

[8] *Hist. litt. de la France,* XXVI, 247.
[9] *FQ,* I, IX, iii, 3-4. Probably Arthur was to learn his parentage from
Gloriana.
[10] *Hist. litt. de la France,* XXVI, 103 *et sqq.*   [11] *Ibid.,* p. 104.

mandera, si tu ne veux demeurer constamment avec elle. Elle
s'est prise d'amour pour toi, prends garde de répondre à ses
avances.[12]

Dieudonné is then escorted into the castle, where he is
served with a sumptuous banquet. Gloriande appears to
him, first as a toothless crone wearing a golden crown, and
then as a surpassingly beautiful woman. She reveals to him
the secret of his parentage, and offers to share the throne of
Faerie with him. Although dazzled by her beauty, he refuses, since he has another love. Gloriande then magnani-
mously dismisses him with the parting gifts of a magic horn,
cup, and tablecloth, whose properties are similar to those of
Oberon's gifts to Huon. During his subsequent adventures,
Dieudonné is frequently assisted by Gloriande's knights.[13]

There is no proof that Spenser knew these fourteenth-
century French poems, and he may have promoted Gloriana
to the throne traditionally occupied by Oberon or Morgan
without knowing that a similar change in the sovereignty
of Fairyland had been made by the author of *Charles le
chauve*. We can hardly doubt, however, that Spenser's
Gloriana, Queen of Faerie and Goddess of Fame, owes something to the tradition of the fairy Gloriande, near relation
of Morgan and donor of courage, the essential virtue of a
famous knight. For these two characteristics of Gloriande,
her important position in the fairy world and her connection with knightly fame, are emphasized in the prose romance of *Ogier le danois*, which was easily available to
Spenser. Here Gloriande appears with five other fairy god-
mothers, presumably her sisters, at the cradle of the infant
Ogier. The episode is thus described in a passage quoted by
Le Roux de Lincy in *Le Livre des legendes:*

La nuit où l'enfant naquit, les demoiselles du château le
portèrent dans une chambre séparée, et quand il fut là, six belles

---

[12] *Ibid.*   [13] See especially *ibid.*, pp. 110–11.

demoiselles qui étaient fées se presentèrent: s'étant approchée de l'enfant, l'une d'elles, nommée Gloriande, le prit dans ses bras, et le voyant si beau, si bien fait, elle l'embrassa et dit: 'Mon enfant, je te donne un don par la grâce de Dieu, c'est que toute ta vie tu seras le plus hardi chevalier de ton temps. Dame, dit une autre fée nommée Palestrine, certes voilà un beau don, et moi j'y ajoute que jamais tournois et batailles ne manqueront a Oger. Dames, ajouta la troisième, nommée Pharamonde, ces dons ne sont pas sans péril; aussi je veux qu'il soit toujours vainqueur. Je veux, dit alors Melior, qu'il soit le plus beau, le plus gracieux des chevaliers. Et moi, dit Pressine, je lui promets un amour heureux et constant de la part de toutes les dames. Enfin, Morgues, la sixième, ajouta: J'ai bien écouté tous les dons que vous avez faits à cet enfant, eh bien! il en jouira seulement après avoir été mon ami par amour, et avoir habité mon château d'Avalon.' Ayant dit, Morgues embrassa l'enfant, et toutes les fées disparurent.[14]

In this passage the fairy gifts are divided between gifts of power which bring fame, and gifts of love, with Gloriande as principal donor of the first, and Morgan of the second. Spenser's Gloriana combines the two. Her love is both the inspiration and the reward of heroic action. In this dual character of her influence she differs from the typical fairy mistresses of romance. For these ladies, although they desire only famous men as their lovers, generally achieve their desires through enchantments which make the chosen knights forget the pursuit of glory, and sometimes their plighted troth to mortal maidens, for a life of ignoble ease in a paradise which has more in common with the land of

[14] *Livre des légendes,* pp. 178–79. All these fairies, except Pharamond, appear in other romances. Palestrine and Melior are sisters of Melusine. Melior is also the name of the fairy in *Partonope of Blois.* Pressine is Melusine's mother, sister of "the queen of the lost isle of Avalon." The story of the fairy gifts as given in the verse romance of *Ogier,* extracted in *Brun de la montaigne,* p. xi, has only four fairies, Gloriande, "soeur Anseris," Sagremoire, Faramonde, Beatrix, Morgue. Their gifts are substantially the same as in the version quoted in the text.

the Lotus Eaters or Circe's Aeaea than with Gloriana's Cleopolis. Thus, when Morgan sets the fairy crown on Ogier's head, he forgets his wife Clarice, his brother Guyon, and the wars of Christendom in which he has spent his life, and thinks only of Morgan and of the pleasures of Avalon, where the fairy damsels "toute jour chantoient, dansoient, et menoient vie tresjoyeuse, sans penser a nulle quelquonque meschante chose, fors prandre leurs mondains plaisirs."[15] As Ogier was by this time over a hundred years old, one might grant that he had earned his right to such a carefree existence. Besides, Morgan does send the rejuvenated hero back to France two hundred years later, when the national danger becomes acute. But Morgan is not always so altruistic. In Malory she is uniformly an evil character, hostile to Arthur and his knights, whose love is a destructive force to her lovers. In the *Prophecies de Merlin,* she is unfavorably compared with the Lady of the Lake by Merlin himself. I quote Miss Paton's paraphrase:

The Dame du Lac, he says, possesses greater natural gifts and a more subtle art than any woman in the world. Morgain is the child of passion and fire; the fair Dame du Lac was born near to Paradise. Morgain seeks to work evil, the Dame du Lac good. Morgain to kill knights, the Dame du Lac to help them. Morgain is the enemy of orphans; the Dame du Lac has nurtured Lancelot and his two orphan cousins.[16]

The Circe type of fairy mistress, who is led either by malice or by sensuality to lure her mortal paramour into a paradise which is also a prison, is particularly common in the Italian romance poems which Spenser imitated. In the *Orlando innamorato,* the fay Dragontina uses a magic cup to make Orlando and other knights forget their true ladies,

[15] Quoted by Keightley, I, 78–79.
[16] Paton, p. 195. Cf. *Prophecies de Merlin,* I, 122.

and become her lovers and prisoners.[17] In the same poem, Morgana, who is here represented as a sort of female Mammon, sends a white stag to Brandimarte, and by enchantment makes him forget his faithful Fiordelisa, and fall into Morgana's prison, a crystal palace at the bottom of a lake.[18] A similar under-water palace is the home of a troop of naiads, whose enjoyment of male society depends upon their skill in luring unwary paladins into their trap, a feat which they accomplish successfully with the future hero of Roncevalles himself, making him forget both Charlemagne and Angelica in a life of constant singing and dancing.[19] Ariosto's Alcina, who turns her lovers into trees,[20] also belongs definitely to the Circe type of enchantress. The Armida of Tasso begins as Circe,[21] and ends as Dido.[22]

The gardens of Armida, as every one knows, furnished the immediate model for Spenser's Bowre of Blisse, and Acrasia, the wicked fay who presides over that false paradise, is at the opposite pole from Gloriana. Just as Spenser splits up the conception of a goddess of fame into the sharply opposed figures of Lucifera and Gloriana, so he depicts the traditional fairy mistress of romance under the equally opposed aspects of Gloriana and Acrasia. Like Lucifera, Acrasia is a rival fairy queen, imitating the state of the legitimate sovereign, Gloriana. Like Gloriana, she is a "lady of the isle," who rears her throne "in widest ocean." Archimago, Phaedria, and Cymochles are her servants, the loyal subjects of Gloriana her enemies. She is overthrown by Gloriana through the agency of Guyon, one of the chief knights of Maidenhead.

[17] OI, I, VI, xliv et sqq.
[18] Ibid., I, XXII, lvii et sqq., I, XXV, v–xiii, II, VIII, xxxvi et sqq. Cf. also the gardens of Falerina, I, XVII, viii et sqq., destroyed by Orlando, II, IV, xv et sqq.
[19] Ibid., II, XXXI, xlv et sqq., III, VII, vi et sqq.   [20] OF, VI, l–li.
[21] GL, IV, lxxxvi, 5–8.   [22] Ibid., XVI, lvi et sqq.

This opposition between a good and an evil fairy queen has its counterpart in Arthurian romance, in which Morgan's evil deeds are frequently thwarted by the Lady of the Lake,[23] who, as we shall see later, was almost certainly one of the prototypes of Gloriana.[24] In Malory, for instance, Morgan sends Arthur a burning mantle, and the Lady of the Lake warns him not to put it on.[25] Similarly in the Italian *romanzi*, we find friendly as well as unfriendly fays, and mortal ladies are sometimes enabled to rescue the paladins from enchantments. So Fiordelisa plays a decisive part in rescuing Orlando from the *fiume del riso*,[26] and Ruggiero escapes from the gardens of Alcina by the help of the friendly enchantress, Melissa.[27]

In the *Faerie Queene*, the rival fays Gloriana and Acrasia are symbolic of two kinds of love, the love that immortalizes and the love that destroys. Arthur's love for Gloriana kindles "glorious fire" in his heart.[28] Verdant's love for Acrasia makes him forget glory altogether:

> His warlike armes, the idle instruments
> Of sleeping praise, were hong upon a tree,
> And his brave shield, full of old moniments,
> Was fowly rast, that none the signes might see;
> Ne for them, ne for honour cared hee,
> Ne ought, that did to his advauncement tend,
> But in lewd loves, and wastefull luxuree,
> His dayes, his goods, his bodie he did spend:
> O horrible enchantment, that him so did blend.[29]

Guyon takes Acrasia in the same net with which Vulcan trapped his unfaithful wife, and for this reason Acrasia has been identified with Venus Pandemos.[30] The parallel iden-

[23] Paton, p. 195.   [24] See below, pp. 231–32.
[25] *Morte d'Arthur*, Bk. V, chap. xv.   [26] *OI*, III, VII, xv, 5 *et sqq.*
[27] *OF*, VII, xli–lxxx.   [28] *FQ*, I, Proem, iii, 4.
[29] *Ibid.*, II, XII, lxxx.
[30] Greenlaw, "A Better Teacher Than Aquinas," *SP*, XIV (1917), 210.

tification of Gloriana with Venus Urania has become almost a commonplace of Spenser criticism. Nevertheless it may be questioned, or at least qualified.

Like all the virtuous female characters in the *Faerie Queene,* Gloriana certainly represents a type of Heavenly Beauty, but she is not therefore identical with the Sapience of the Fourth *Hymne,* or Heavenly Beauty in itself, as it appears in the Intelligible World. Rather she seems to represent that same beauty as it is manifested in the moral virtues which are the crown of the active life. The identification of Gloriana with Venus Urania has been supported by allegorical interpretations of the Virgilian Venus, particularly the mystical Neoplatonic commentary of Landino.[31] But though we may agree with Mr. Hughes that "in all her incarnations in the *Faerie Queene,* Elizabeth owes something to the tradition that made the Virgilian Venus into a kind of Beatrice,"[32] we cannot be sure that this identification should be pressed so far as to make Arthur's quest for Gloriana identical with the mystical pursuit of the *Visio Dei* which Landino reads into the *Aeneid.* Even though this may be Arthur's ultimate goal, it does not seem to be his immediate goal in the *Faerie Queene* nor in the projected sequel, both of which were to be concerned with "the Ethicke part of Morall Philosophy,"[33] or with the practice of virtue in the active life. Though Arthur's initial vision of the Fairy Queen may be in some sense a vision of Divine Beauty, which will lead him at last to heaven, his meeting with her in Cleopolis can hardly represent the complete actualization of that vision as expressed in the Fourth

[31] *Camaldulenses disputationes.*

[32] "Virgil and Spenser," *University of California Publications in English,* II (1929), 363.

[33] Bryskett, *Discourse of Civill Life,* quoted by De Selincourt, Introduction to *Oxford Spenser* (one vol. ed.), p. xxvii.

Hymne. For Cleopolis, as we have seen, is not heaven. Assuming that Spenser was influenced by Landino,[34] we might compare the end of Arthur's quest with the meeting between Venus and Aeneas before he goes to Carthage, which Landino interpreted as the active life. Hence Venus does not appear in her proper form but disguised as a huntress, and veiled in matter *(silva)*. Yet Aeneas catches a glimpse of her divine beauty before she departs,

Nam cum in vita civili quae recta & honesta sunt/ diu coluerimus ex illorum pulchritudine ad divina: quorum haec veluti simulacra sunt: erigimur.[35]

This passage makes Venus represent the beauty of moral ideals, a conception which is certainly primary for Spenser's Gloriana, queen of the moral virtues. Furthermore, as Mr. Hughes pointed out,[36] this passage in the *Aeneid* was twice applied to Elizabeth by Spenser, once in the *April Eclogue*,[37] and again in the description of Belphoebe.[38]

Another identification of the Virgilian Venus with the sum of the moral virtues appears in the *Dialoghi* of Speroni.[39] In answer to those critics who wished to expunge the lines in which Aeneas meets Helen in the temple during the sack of Troy, on the ground that it was a serious breach of decorum for a brave man to attack a woman, Speroni points out that Aeneas does not in fact kill Helen. He has an impulse to kill her:

questo è affetto si naturale, che nissuno habito virtuoso non può impedirli il camino, che suol condurlo da gli occhi al core; bene è possente di trarnel fuori; poi che vi entrò, sè con ragione non si accompagna; e cotale habito di fortezza, o di prudentia,

[34] Hughes admits that there is no proof of direct influence, *op cit.*, p. 402.
[35] *Camaldulenses disputationes*, p. Hvi verso.
[36] *Virgil and Spenser*, pp. 263, 360.
[37] Emblem and Glosse. *SC*, Renwick's ed., pp. 54, 59.
[38] *FQ*, II, III, xxxiii, 2–4.
[39] Hughes also mentions this passage, *Virgil and Spenser*, p. 405.

ò di temperantia volle Virgilio significare per la presenza di Venere, come altra volta per Pallade fù già da Homero significato, all'hor, che Acchille fu per uccidere Agamnenone.[40]

These two interpretations of the Virgilian Venus as representative of moral beauty, which stands midway between sensible and intelligible beauty, suggest Gloriana rather than Sapience. But if Gloriana is primarily moral beauty, she is certainly also a mirror of intelligible beauty, and possibly Spenser intended to symbolize this fact by making her appear at the close of the *Faerie Queene* as a veiled Venus, like Una[41] and the Nature of the *Mutabilitie Cantos*.[42] On the other hand he might plan to represent these two manifestations of the Venus principle under two different symbols. I raise this question not because I believe it can be answered, but because it suggests a caution against overemphasizing the identification between Gloriana and Sapience or Venus Urania.

Even though the identification stand, moreover, it does not completely explain Spenser's use of the fairy mistress motif in the contrasted figures of Gloriana and Acrasia. For Spenser's emphasis in the *Faerie Queene* as in the first two *Hymnes,* is not upon the metaphysical distinction between sensible and intelligible beauty but upon the moral distinction between love and lust.[43] Acrasia is an earthly Venus, but she is opposed on her own level of the Platonic "ladder" by another earthly Venus, who brings up Amoret in the Gardens of Adonis, which differ from the Bowre of Blisse precisely in being devoted to generation, the primary purpose of Christian marriage, for which Amoret is being trained. But Amoret has a twin sister, the virgin Belphoebe, representative of Elizabeth as woman, who inspires in gentle

[40] *Dialoghi*, p. 284.   [41] *FQ*, I, XII, xxii–xxiii.
[42] *Ibid.*, VII, VII, v–vi. Cf. Bennett, "Spenser's Venus and the Goddess Nature of the *Cantos of Mutabilitie*," *SP*, XXX (1933), 164.
[43] Cf. Renwick's ed. of *Daph.*, p. 211.

hearts the second type of "true love" recognized by Renaissance tradition, namely, the "Platonic" devotion which seeks only a marriage of twin souls, "a band of vertuous mind,"[44] "Through thoughts aspyring to eternall fame."[45]

It is this type of true love which Spenser chiefly celebrates in his Fourth Book, in the Proem to which he recommends Queen Elizabeth to Cupid "That she may hearke to love, and read this lesson often."[46] Since he can hardly have been recommending marriage to the Queen in 1596, this passage must refer to "Platonic love." Arthur takes part in the Fourth Book, while in the Third, which is devoted principally to married love, he practically disappears.[47] This suggests that his relation with his fairy mistress was to be Platonic, a perfect friendship between members of the opposite sex of the type imperfectly represented in the story of Timias and Belphoebe. Gloriana would thus bear the same relation to Britomart, mother of kings to be, as Belphoebe does to Amoret. The ideal princess, like the ideal lady, may be a votary of Diana or of Venus. In either case she will be loving and beloved. The contrast between Acrasia and Gloriana, then, is not simply or primarily the contrast between earthly and heavenly love or beauty, but the contrast between the perversion of earthly love from its proper end in marriage to that lust which makes men act as "brute beasts that have no understanding,"[48] and the sublimation of earthly love into friendship, that spiritual marriage which

> brings forth glorious flowres of fame,
> That crowne true lovers with immortall blis.[49]

This interpretation of the projected relation between Arthur and Gloriana is of some importance in view of Spen-

[44] *FQ*, IV, IX, i, 8.   [45] *Ibid.*, IV, IX, ii, 5.   [46] *Ibid.*, IV, Proem, v, 9.
[47] Though he assists Britomart in IV, IX.
[48] Marriage Service, *Book of Common Prayer* (Ed. VI). Cf. *HL,* ll. 99–105.
[49] *FQ*, IV, Proem, ii, 7–8.

ser's "particular intention." For Gloriana, he tells us, represents Elizabeth as Queen, and Arthur has been generally identified with the Earl of Leicester. Since a marriage between Elizabeth and her favorite was for some time extremely probable, and was presumably desirable to the poet who began his career under Leicester's patronage, a large number of scholars have assumed with some plausibility that Spenser's original intention was to celebrate this union by depicting the marriage of Arthur and Gloriana at the end of the *Faerie Queene*. This view was pushed to extremes by Mr. Cory,[50] who saw in Spenser's poem "an epic of the future," designed wholly to praise the present and future achievements of Leicester as accepted lover of Elizabeth and later as King-Consort. The failure of Leicester to marry the Queen, according to Cory, gave a deathblow to Spenser's whole scheme, and after Leicester's death, he practically abandoned the idea of giving any unity to his poem.

This extreme view was combated by Greenlaw, who pointed out that while Spenser might at one time have thought of celebrating the prospective marriage between Elizabeth and Leicester, he must have abandoned this purpose before he published the first installment of the *Faerie Queene*, since the *Letter to Raleigh*, in which we first hear of the proposed sequel dealing with Arthur as king, was not published, and presumably not written, until after Leicester's death.[51] Greenlaw also pointed out that while Arthur might in some parts of the poem represent Leicester, he certainly represented Arthur the Briton, and that therefore his marriage with Gloriana, and their subsequent joint rule over a Fairyland identified in Spenser's particular intention with Tudor England might fittingly symbolize the mystical

[50] In *Edmund Spenser: a Critical Study, passim.*
[51] "Review of Cory's *Edmund Spenser*," MLN, XXXV (1920), 168.

"return" of the ancient British dynasty in the person of Elizabeth, sprung "of Arthur's rase and lyne."[52] The importance of this "return motif" in determining Spenser's choice of Arthur as hero can hardly be exaggerated, and it is extremely probable that the genealogical connection between Elizabeth and Arthur had some influence upon their relationship in the *Faerie Queene*. But the common belief that the first poem was to end with their marriage, and the sequel to celebrate their joint rule over Fairyland seems to me incompatible with Spenser's "historicall fiction."

According to this, the action of the *Faerie Queene* takes place during the later years of Uther Pendragon's reign. It deals with the adventures of Arthur "before he was king." His later adventures "after he was king" must then take place during his own reign as king of Britain. Now Arthur's Britain is not identical with Fairyland, though Elizabeth's Britain may be. Both Arthur and Britomart pass from Britain into Fairyland. In order to become king then, Arthur must leave Fairyland at the end of the *Faerie Queene,* and return to Britain, where he is to be recognized as son of Uther, and to perform the actions to be celebrated in Spenser's second projected epic. That this was Spenser's intention is further indicated by the information he gives us about the future adventures of Artegall and Britomart (Book III, Canto III). There Merlin tells Britomart that Artegall is no fairy but a Briton, son of Gorlois and half brother to Arthur. Britomart is destined to bring Artegall back to his native country:

> From thence, him firmely bound with faithfull band,
> To this his native soyle thou backe shalt bring,
> Strongly to his aide his countrey, to withstand
> The powre of forrein Paynims, which invade thy land.

[52] *Ibid.*, pp. 168–69, and *SP*, XV (1918), 116–22.

Great aid thereto his mighty puissaunce,
And dreaded name shall give in that sad day:
Where also proofe of thy prow valiaunce
Thou then shalt make, t' increase thy lovers pray.[53]

Now the first event of Arthur's reign was an invasion of foreign Paynims, the Saxons, by Malory called Saracens, whom Arthur overcame in twelve great battles. Spenser could hardly avoid giving some account of this war in his projected epic on Arthur as king.[54] The passage just quoted suggests the way in which this later poem was to be linked with the *Faerie Queene*. Britomart and Artegall, "fast bound in faithfull band," that is after the celebration of either their betrothal or their marriage at the court of Gloriana, were to return with Arthur to Britain, and to share with him in the glories of his reign. In a sense, indeed, they should rule with him, for the virtues they exemplify were supreme in the Golden Age, which was to return to Britain, and indeed to Europe, as a result of Arthur's conquests.

The reign of Justice and Chastity in the Golden Age is mentioned by Jean Lemaire, who says of Noah (Janus) that the Golden Age "commença à faillir tantost apres sa mort: Et ce tesmoigne Ovid au premier liure des Fastes, disant en la personne dudit Ianus, que Iustice et Chasteté regnoient en son temps."[55] Similarly Spenser connects Artegall and Britomart, the incarnations of Justice and Chastity, with the Golden Age. Artegall is the representative of Astraea, the divine idea of Justice, who reigned on earth during the Golden Age, and then returned to heaven.[56] Britomart and Artegall are also reincarnations of Isis and Osiris,[57] founders of the first good empire on earth after the division of the world among the sons of Noah, and thus the first of the long

---

[53] *FQ*, III, III, xxvii, 6–xxviii, 4.
[54] Is there perhaps a reference to this intention in *FQ*, I, XI, vii, 1–4?
[55] *Œuvres*, I, 39.   [56] *FQ*, V, I, v–xi.   [57] *Ibid.*, V, VII, i–xxiii.

line of rulers who may be said to have restored the Golden Age in justice and equity. Last of these of course was Queen Elizabeth, the royal Virgin, of whom Astraea is the heavenly idea, and Isis and Britomart the earthly ancestresses and prototypes. But the reign of Elizabeth was foreshadowed also in English history by the great age of Arthur, of whom Britomart is the feminine counterpart. For Arthur and Britomart to bring Artegall back from Fairyland to Britain would be a means of symbolizing the return of justice which ushered in the new Golden Age when a prince and princess of the ancient Trojan blood restored to Britain the representative of Astraea, who since her withdrawal from earth was reflected only in the world of history, which Spenser calls Fairyland. The Fairy Queen, representing as she does the beauty of moral virtue, the idea of kingship, "mirrour of grace and maiestie divine," is in part identifiable with Astraea, and Arthur's mystical winning of her love would thus furnish another symbol for the revival of justice on earth.

> iam redit et Virgo, redeunt Saturnia regna;
> iam nova progenies caelo demittitur alto.[58]

The Augustan, Arthurian, and Tudor Golden Ages were alike ushered in by a struggle for the throne. The return of justice marks the triumph of the rightful claimant. We should therefore expect Artegall to play a decisive part in the battles which established Arthur in his father's kingdom. The parallel to Tudor times is obvious, and might apply both to Henry VII and to Elizabeth. The true Prince, whose claim has been denied, about whose birth there is a mystery, is restored to rule, and the Golden Age begins. The particular allusion to Elizabeth is emphasized in Artegall's

---

[58] Virgil *Eclogue* iv. 6–7.

destined function of establishing Britomart upon her father's throne. So the priest of Isis interprets her vision:

> That Knight shall all the troublous stormes asswage,
>   And raging flames, that many foes shall reare,
>   To hinder thee from the iust heritage
>   Of thy sires Crowne, and from thy countrey deare.
>   Then shalt thou take him to thy loved fere,
>   And ioyne in equall portion of thy realme.
>   And afterwards a sonne to him shalt beare,
>   That Lion-like shall shew his powre extreame.[59]

This son, as Miss Harper has pointed out,[60] is Aurelius Conan, who seized the crown from Arthur's successor, Constantine, and became the ancestor of the succeeding British kings. It is often assumed that Spenser represents Elizabeth as the direct descendant of Arthur. Miss Harper, for instance, says: "According to Spenser, she [Elizabeth] was the descendant both of Prince Arthur and of Britomart."[61] The descent from Britomart is of course clear. The descent from Arthur, however, implies either a marriage between Arthur and Gloriana, which we have already seen reasons to doubt, or a mystical identification between Arthur and Artegall. The latter alternative is suggested by Miss Harper. After quoting the stanzas in which Merlin tells Britomart of Artegall's identity, she says:

These three stanzas make the transition from romance to chronicle material. Arthegall, who is to be the husband of Britomart, is the son of Gorlois, and brother to Cador, king of Cornwall, who is, by inference, another of the sons of Gorlois. Arthegall, therefore, stands in the same relation to Cador that Arthur does both in Hardyng and in the *Brut Tysilio*. Arthegall, like Arthur, fights against the pagan and is

> Too rathe cut off by practise criminall
>   Of secrete foes.

[59] *FQ*, V, VII, xxiii, 1–8.   [60] Harper, pp. 145 *et sqq.*
[61] *Ibid.*, p. 181.

After a fashion, then, Arthegall takes Arthur's place in the chronicle.[62]

Later on she reiterates this theory, as follows:

Spenser does not say in so many words that after the death of Arthegall Constantine assumed the crown, but such was evidently the case, as Arthegall's son took from Constantine the "crown that was his father's right."[63]

Miss Harper's opinion is entitled to great respect. Nevertheless I believe there is a simpler explanation of the facts, more in accord with Spenser's method of dealing with historical material.

This view assumes no mystical identification between Arthur and Artegall, but takes at its face value Spenser's statement of the relationship between them. Artegall is Arthur's half brother, son of Gorlois and brother of Cador, who appears prominently in the chronicle tradition as a principal supporter of Arthur in all his early wars, and as the father of Constantine, who succeeded to Arthur's throne. In some versions of the story, Arthur names Constantine as his successor.[64] I suggest that the position which Spenser designed for Artegall in his second epic was partly to be modeled on the positions of Cador and Constantine in the chronicle tradition. This view fits in with the changes which Spenser made in the story of Constantine and Conan.[65]

After the death of Arthur, Constantine killed the sons of Modred, who claimed the throne, and was himself killed by Conan, who then further consolidated his position by murdering two of his cousins and imprisoning their father, who

[62] *Ibid.*, p. 144.   [63] *Ibid.*, p. 146.

[64] Fletcher, *Arthurian Material in the Chronicles*, pp. 64 (Geoffrey of Monmouth), 117 (*Brut Tysilio*), 230 (Jehan de Wavrin). Cf. Malory, Bk. V, chap. iii.

[65] The succeeding account of these changes is based on Harper, pp. 145 *et sqq.*

was the legitimate heir to Constantine. After a short and inglorious reign, Conan was succeeded by his son Vortipore, who won great victories over the Saxons. This is in substance the story as given by Geoffrey and Hardyng. Holinshed also relates it, but doubts its accuracy, and suggests that Conan, Vortipore, and Constantius all lived at the same time, and reigned in different parts of the kingdom.

Miss Harper has noted that Spenser seldom departs from Geoffrey's account without other authority. Holinshed's doubts as to the chronology of Arthur's immediate successors would furnish an excuse for the changes which Spenser's "historicall fiction" made necessary at this point. These changes, as Miss Harper points out, are all controlled by the desire to whitewash Conan, whom Spenser makes the son of Britomart and Artegall, and represents as Arthur's legitimate heir, making Constantine the usurper, and transferring to Conan the victories over the Saxons which were actually won by Vortipore.

Miss Harper attributes these changes to Merlin's desire to spare the feelings of Britomart by suppressing the unpleasant aspects of her son's career, and by glorifying him at the expense of her grandson.[66] This seems to me to miss the point. Spenser was concerned to show that Elizabeth Tudor was the rightful heir to Arthur's crown and empire.[67] From Conan on, as Miss Harper points out, Spenser could represent the crown as descending in direct line from father to son by suppressing all references to rival claimants or to contemporary Saxon kings.[68] The Tudor claim to Arthur's empire thus depended upon a chain of succession whose weakest link was Conan. For according to the chronicles he has no real claim to Arthur's kingdom. On the contrary he

[66] *Ibid.,* pp. 147 n. and 148.
[67] This has been emphasized by Greenlaw, *Studies in Spenser's Historical Allegory.* Cf. *Variorum,* II, 406, 408.
[68] Page 180.

wades through slaughter to the throne with all the ruthlessness of Richard III, and among the legitimate claimants whom he murders is the man whom Arthur himself designated as his successor. Nor does Conan, like Henry IV, justify his irregular method of obtaining the throne by exhibiting any signal qualities as a ruler. Instead his reign is marked by civil war, and the defeat of the Saxons, made bold by Arthur's death, is postponed until the next reign.

Spenser met this difficulty, as we have seen, by transferring to Conan both Vortipore's victories and Constantine's claim to the throne. Conan and Constantine stand in the same relationship to Arthur. Both are grandsons of Gorlois and Igrayne. Conan claims the throne as "his fathers right." Probably Spenser intended to make Arthur name Artegall as his successor. But Artegall was "too rathe cut off by practise criminall," perhaps murdered by Constantine, to whom Spenser might easily transfer Conan's murder of the unnamed uncle who should have succeeded to the throne. Conan would thus become the just avenger of his father and Arthur's rightful heir, a fact that is further emphasized by his repetition of Arthur's victories over the Saxons.

The idea that Artegall and his descendants were legitimate successors of Arthur seems more in keeping with Spenser's general purpose as a "poet historicall" than Miss Harper's theory that Artegall in some mystical way "takes Arthur's place in the chronicle." Nor need we postulate any more direct Arthurian descent for the Tudors than is implied in their descent from Artegall and Britomart. Spenser certainly states that Elizabeth is of "Arthur's rase and lyne":[69]

> Thy name O soveraine Queene, thy realme and race,
> From this renowmed Prince derived arre,
> Who mightily upheld that royall mace,

[69] Churchyard, *Worthines of Wales*, quoted Millican, p. 39.

> Which now thou bear'st, to thee descended farre
> From mightie kings and conquerours in warre,
> Thy fathers and great Grandfathers of old,
> Whose noble deedes above the Northerne starre
> Immortall fame for ever hath enrold.[70]

But this does not necessarily imply direct descent. The genealogies which trace the descent of the Tudors from Arthur,
do not, so far as I know, provide Arthur with a son, but
follow the chronicle tradition in representing Arthur as
succeeded by Constantine and Conan. Furthermore several
authorities explicitly state that Arthur had no legitimate
children.[71] In view of this well-known fact Spenser could
hardly make the Tudors descend directly from Arthur, but
he could invent an ancestry for Conan that would connect
him closely with Arthur and give him a right to the throne
superior to Constantine's. This would free the succeeding
kings from the charge of usurpation, a subject upon which
the Tudors were naturally sensitive.

The closeness with which Spenser has generally followed
the chronicles in working out the historical part of his poem,
as well as the generally accepted epic theory of his time,
increase the likelihood that his projected poem on Arthur
as king would have been in its broad outlines historical,
though for its detailed development he might have utilized
romance tradition as well as his own invention. How far he
had thought out this poem when he wrote the *Letter to
Raleigh* we cannot say, but the fact that Spenser mentions
it there as a sequel to the *Faerie Queene* indicates that he
had decided at least upon its main action and on the part
to be played in it by the leading characters of the earlier

[70] *FQ*, II, X, iv, 1–8.
[71] Fletcher, *Arthurian Material in the Chronicles*, pp. 140 (Wace), 155
(Layamon), 215 (large *Brut*).

poem. Of Britomart and Artegall we have already spoken. Arthur's role would largely be determined by tradition. What of Gloriana and her fairy knights?

I do not see how Gloriana could possibly appear in the second poem as Arthur's queen, but her knights might well assist him in his battles as the pagan gods assisted the heroes of classical epic, and as fairy knights assist Huon, Ogier, and Dieudonné in the romances. Such assistance would be appropriate also to Spenser's moral allegory, since it would mean that Arthur's victories were the result of his virtues. The Fairy Queen herself might well appear as a sort of Egeria whose presiding influence was responsible for Arthur's great achievements. Spenser himself calls Egeria a fay.[72]

There are some traces of a tradition that Arthur did obtain such assistance from a fairy mistress. In the *Petit Brut* prepared in 1310 for Henry de Lacy, Earl of Lincoln, Rauf de Boun, the author, says that Arthur's victories were known to be due to his love, "la dame de *faierie*."[73] According to Fletcher, this chronicle is "unique," containing much material based either on unknown sources or on the author's invention. It has never been printed, and there is no reason to assume that Spenser knew it directly, but it is not unlikely that he knew of the tradition it represents from some other source which is unknown to us. Miss Paton suggested that Morgan and Arthur were originally lovers, not brother and sister, and that Spenser may have had before him some tradition of Arthur's early winning of a fay, in which the original relationship between Arthur and Morgan was preserved. There is more evidence for a love affair between Arthur and the Lady of the Lake, who may originally have been identi-

[72] *FQ*, II, X, xlii, 7-8.
[73] Fletcher, *Arthurian Material in the Chronicles*, p. 211.

fied with Morgan.[74] In Drayton's *Poly-Olbion*, Song IV, the nymphs sing of Arthur, and of

> The feasts that under-ground the Faërie did him make,
> And there how he enjoyd the Lady of the Lake.[75]

The Lady of the Lake gave Arthur his sword, Excalibur,[76] which was the token enabling him to enter Fairyland after the last fatal battle near Glastonbury.[77] It is possible that in some versions of the story, known to the Elizabethans, but no longer extant, the gift of the sword was associated with an earlier visit of Arthur to Fairyland. Such a visit is described in an Italian poem published the same year as the first installment of the *Faerie Queene*. In *La caccia* of Erasmo di Valvasone, Arthur follows a golden stag to Morgan's palace, which is approached by a subterranean route, but is itself at the top of a hill from which all the stars are visible. There Morgan gives him a sword whose hilt is made of the cast horns of the golden stag, a magic animal which only appears to famous men. The sword confers the gifts of self-knowledge and self-control, without which no king can be truly great. The next morning Arthur awakens to find himself outside the hill into which he had followed the miraculous beast. He would have believed the whole experience a dream, did he not still have the sword by his side.[78] One wonders whether a similar legend had anything to do with the naming of Drake's ship, the Golden Hind. Certainly, unless Valvasone was inventing his story, which seems unlikely, it is probable that some version of this tale about Arthur's first visit to Fairyland entered into Spenser's conception of Gloriana.

In the chronicles, Arthur is represented as particularly

---

[74] See Loomis, *Celtic Myth and Arthurian Romance*, p. 193, for evidence that Morgan and the Lady of the Lake were originally the same person.
[75] Ll. 307-8.   [76] Malory, *Morte d'Arthur*, Bk. I, chap. xxv.
[77] *Ibid.*, Bk. XXI, chap. v.   [78] Valvasone, *La caccia*, IV, clxi *et sqq.*

devoted to the Virgin, whose picture he bears on his shield. In Alain Bouchart's *Grandes chroniques de Bretagne,* the Virgin intervenes to help the king in his fight with the giant Flollo, whom she blinds by covering Arthur's shield with her mantle.[70] This recalls the blinding radiance of Arthur's uncovered shield in the fight with Orgoglio, and suggests the possibility of later miraculous interventions on the part of Gloriana herself. Certainly we may assume that she was destined to come for him in the magic barge and take him back to Fairyland.

Not until this closing episode in his life could Arthur be permanently united to Gloriana. This union, therefore, must have been reserved for the conclusion of Spenser's second epic, sequel to the *Faerie Queene.* Only after his death, or disappearance from the earth, does Arthur become king of Fairyland.

The story of Arthur and Gloriana would thus run parallel to the story of St. George and Una. As St. George is led by Una to the House of Holiness and the Mount of Heavenly Contemplation, where he learns of his ancestry and of the bliss prepared for him in the heavenly city, so Arthur is led by Gloriana, first through her appearance in his dream, and then through his meetings with the knights who represent her virtues, to her dwelling in Fairyland, where he will presumably learn of his ancestry and future fame, and see the place prepared for him in Cleopolis, city of earthly glory. As St. George in Eden sees Una unveiled, so Arthur in Cleopolis will at last come face to face with that "excellent beauty" that he has hitherto seen only in a dream or vision. And as St. George must leave Una in Eden after their betrothal, and return to his militant labors in the service of Gloriana, so Arthur must leave Gloriana in Cleopolis, until he has set up the Round Table, defeated the Roman

---

[70] Fletcher, *Arthurian Material in the Chronicles,* p. 232.

Emperor, and made Britain the first nation of the world. This parallel between the stories of St. George and Arthur, the two heroes who represent most clearly the destinies of England, is symbolic of the likeness between heavenly and earthly glory as represented in the two cities of New Jerusalem and Cleopolis. The triumph of both heroes is postponed. Only after death is the saint secure in possession of divine truth and the hero of immortal fame.

True to his Platonic training, Spenser represents both Truth and Glory as forms of Beauty, and thus as objects of love. Both Una and Gloriana are "heavenly born," types of that Beauty which

> can not die,
> Being a parcell of the purest skie.[80]

And Una and Gloriana are alike also in that the love which they inspire is essentially spiritual, bringing forth the spiritual fruit of good works or the deeds appropriate to

> The noble hart that harbours vertuous thought,
> And is with child of glorious great intent.[81]

The consummation of this Platonic love of Arthur and Gloriana in their spiritual union in the land of fame after Arthur's death[82] is thus an appropriate symbol for Spenser's general intention, in which Arthur is the ideal hero, sum of all the virtues, and Gloriana the glory that inspires his deeds. The same spiritual union is an equally appropriate symbol for his particular intention, in which Gloriana is Elizabeth. If we take Greenlaw's view that Spenser wished primarily to praise the Queen by celebrating her virtues and by connecting her with Arthur, from whom her crown descended, we may interpret the union of Arthur and Gloriana in Spenser's particular intention as meaning that Arthur

[80] *HB*, ll. 104–5.   [81] *FQ*, I, V, i, 1–2.

and Elizabeth will live forever in song and story as the twin glories of English history, the two sovereigns whose reigns exhibit the ideal of kingship, and who are thus fittingly represent as joint rulers over the land of fame.

Gloriana's love for Arthur the Briton may also imply a compliment to Elizabeth as woman, for it may mean that no living man is worthy of her, because no living man is comparable to her in virtue. The acceptance of this view depends upon the belief that while Gloriana in Spenser's particular intention is always Elizabeth, Arthur is only secondarily and intermittently Leicester. This way of reading the poem is inconsistent with a thoroughly logical interpretation of the allegory on three mutually independent levels of historical fiction, general intention or moral allegory, and particular intention or political allegory. Nevertheless, the researches of Greenlaw and Millican suggest the possibility of such a mixing of allegorical levels in this particular case. Arthur the Briton was too solid a figure in sixteenth-century thought to be a mere label for an Elizabethan worthy, and Arthur's adventures probably contain complimentary allusions to other courtiers besides Leicester.

In fact, there is good reason to believe that Arthur, in his capacity of Spenser's principal hero, model of all the virtues, and chosen lover of Gloriana, was intended by 1590 to represent not Leicester, but Essex.[83] This identification was made in 1863 by Frank Howard, [84] but was rejected on the ground that in 1580, when Spenser had begun work on the *Faerie Queene,* Essex was only a boy.[85] There can be little doubt that the original Arthur was Leicester, and that his

[82] There is an interesting but probably accidental parallel to this situation in the relation between Connla and his mistress in the *imram* of Teague Son of Cian, *Silva Gadelica,* II, 392 *et sqq.*

[83] I suggested this in *SP,* XXXIII 180.

[84] "The Arcadia Unveiled," quoted *Variorum,* I, 452.

[85] C., "The Arcadia Unveiled," quoted *Variorum,* I, 453.

exploits are celebrated in the Belge episode in Book V. In 1589, however, when Spenser described the plan of his whole poem to Raleigh, Leicester was dead, and Essex was beginning to take his place, not only as the Queen's favorite, but as the leader of the "forward school" whose militant anti-Spanish imperialism had always enlisted Spenser's enthusiasm.[86] The position of Essex as successor to Sidney, Walsingham, and Leicester has recently been re-emphasized by Mr. Heffner in two articles identifying Essex with Artegall in the Burbon and Irena episodes of Book V,[87] and with Calidore in Book VI,[88] without denying Spenser's original intention of complimenting Grey and Sidney. If Spenser made such changes in the contemporary allusions behind the characters of Artegall and Calidore, there was every reason for a similar change in the case of Arthur, for Essex succeeded to Leicester's position as well as to Sidney's and Grey's. Mr. Heffner has shown that Essex was regarded, in 1590–97 as "the ideal courtier," and as the "hope of England for a great imperial policy." What Elizabethan after Leicester's death would be a better original for Spenser's Arthur, the allegorical "image of a brave knight" and historical founder of the British Empire? If Arthur is Essex, he may still be Calidore and Artegall as Mr. Heffner has maintained. Spenser presented Elizabeth herself "in mirrors more than one." There is no reason why he may not have done the same for her favorite, particularly since Arthur represents the all-inclusive virtue of Magnificence.

The theory that Essex had taken Leicester's place in the main action of the *Faerie Queene* would explain the other-

---

[86] See Greenlaw, "Spenser and British Imperialism," *MP*, IX (1912), 365–66.

[87] "Essex and Book V of the Faerie Queene," *ELH*, III (1936), 67–82.

[88] "Essex the Ideal Courtier," *ibid.*, I (1934). 7–36. The identification of Calidore with Essex was first made by Percy Long, "Spenser's Sir Calidore," *Englische Studien*, XLII (1910), 53 *et sqq.* For opposition to this view, see K. T. Rowe, "Sir Calidore: Essex or Sidney?" *SP*, XXVII (1930), 125 *et sqq.*

wise curious absence of any mention of Leicester in the
Letter to Raleigh or in the dedicatory sonnets. It also fits
the phrasing of the sonnet to Essex, who alone is addressed
as "magnificke," and whose virtues are emphasized:

> Magnificke Lord, whose vertues excellent
>   Doe merit a most famous Poets witt,
>   To be thy living praises instrument,
>   Yet doe not sdeigne, to let thy name be writt
> In this base Poeme, for thee farr unfitt.
>   Nought is thy worth disparaged thereby,
>   But when my Muse, whose fethers nothing flitt
>   Doe yet but flagg, and lowly learne to fly
> With bolder wing shall dare alofte to sty
>   To the last praises of this Faery Queene,
>   Then shall it make more famous memory
>   Of thine Heroicke parts, such as they beene:
> Till then vouchsafe thy noble countenaunce,
> To these first labours needed furtheraunce.[89]

Of this sonnet, Mr. Heffner says:

The dedicatory sonnet to Essex . . . indicates that Spenser was
looking to that nobleman to continue the patronage of Leicester and Sidney. It is certain evidence, too, that he intended
to place Essex in his great epic, though it seems equally certain
that it says that Essex has no place in the first three books of the
Faerie Queene.[90]

After suggesting that Essex has no part in the first three
books because they refer to events which preceded his rise
to power, Mr. Heffner goes on to say:

Spenser promises Essex, in no uncertain terms, that he shall have
a part in some future installment of the *Faerie Queene*. Whether
he is to be in the second three books or in the last six, we cannot
ascertain from this sonnet.[91]

[89] Howard's suggestion that Essex was Arthur is based principally on this
sonnet, particularly on the phrase, "Magnificke Lord," and on the promise
in ll. 11–12. *Variorum*, I, 452.
[90] *ELH*, III (1936), 67.   [91] *Ibid.*, p. 68.

There are several points in this statement with which I disagree. It does not seem to me "certain" that Essex does not appear at all in the first three books. Rather, the sonnet seems to imply that he does not play so large a part in the first installment as his fame deserves. This would fit the position of Arthur in the first three books, particularly if we assume, as I believe we must, that not all his adventures are to be referred to one Elizabethan worthy.[92] Mr. Heffner may be right in assuming that most of the events alluded to in the first three books took place in the earlier part of Elizabeth's reign, but this need not be true of the description of Arthur's vision of the Fairy Queen, which initiates the central action of the poem. This would fit Essex, who had succeeded to Leicester's position as the Queen's favorite,[93] and whose chivalric pursuit of personal glory would certainly suggest the character of the famous Briton Prince. Granting that specific achievements of Essex are celebrated in the deeds of Calidore and Artegall as Mr. Heffner suggests, we can hardly take these allusions as a complete fulfillment of Spenser's promise in the dedicatory sonnet. For "the last praises of this Faery Queene" must surely mean the last, not the second installment of the poem.

Since this last praise of Elizabeth and Essex was to constitute a "bolder" flight of the Muse than anything described in the first installment of the *Faerie Queene*, it probably refers to the epic conflict between the "great Faery Queene and Paynim King", to which Spenser alludes in strikingly similar terms in the invocation to the Muse preceding his description of the fight with the dragon:

> O gently come into my feeble brest,
>   Come gently, but not with that mighty rage,

[92] I have argued in *SP*, XXXIII, 177–79 for the identification of Arthur with Howard in *FQ*, I, VIII.

[93] Mr. Heffner reminds us that after 1590 Essex shared with Cumberland the position of Queen's champion. In the above mentioned article, I suggested that Cumberland might be Timias in parts of Book I.

Wherewith the martiall troupes thou doest infest,
And harts of great Heroës doest enrage,
That nought their kindled courage may aswage,
Soone as thy dreadfull trompe begins to sownd,
The God of warre with his fiers equipage
Thou doest awake, sleepe never he so sownd,
And scared nations doest with horrour sterne astownd.

Faire Goddesse lay that furious fit aside,
Till I of warres and bloudy *Mars* do sing,
And Briton fields with Sarazin bloud bedyde,
Twixt that great faery Queene and Paynim king,
That with their horrour heaven and earth did ring,
A worke of labour long, and endlesse prayse:
But now a while let downe that haughtie string,
And to my tunes thy second tenor rayse,
That I this man of God his godly armes may blaze.[94]

I have already suggested that this great battle was designed
for the climax of the poem.[95] Probably it was to take place
under the walls of Cleopolis, and was to enlist the service of
all Spenser's minor heroes after the completion of their several quests.[96] But the principal achievement, probably the
death of the Paynim King, would certainly be reserved for
Arthur, whose final triumph over the forces opposed to
Gloriana would thus form part of "the last praises of this
Faery Queene." In the historical allegory this victory would
certainly mean the final and decisive defeat of the Spanish

[94] *FQ,* I, XI, vi–vii. This passage has been thought to refer to the fight
with the Soldan in Book V. *Variorum,* I, 296. But the parallelism with the
sonnet to Essex suggests rather an epic conflict on a larger scale at the end
of the poem. There may possibly be an additional reference to the projected
sequel to the *Faerie Queene,* which would presumably contain an account
of Arthur's wars with the paynim.

[95] See above, p. 129.

[96] Cf. St. George's reason for leaving Una in Eden, *FQ,* I, XII, xviii. Such
a union of all the minor heroes would give an opportunity for the rehearsal
of antecedent material promised for the last book in the *Letter to Raleigh.*
A siege of Cleopolis, raised by Arthur, would have many parallels in Spenser's models. Cf. the siege of Albracca in *OI,* of Paris in *OF,* and the relief
of the Clere Toure in *Arthur of Little Britain.* In each of these a "great
Paynim King" plays a prominent part.

power, in which Spenser had every reason to hope Essex would play a leading role. As Mr. Heffner has shown, this hope was fed by the events of the next six years, and, in *Prothalamium*, Spenser reiterates his intention of celebrating Essex as the liberator of England from the threat of Spanish domination. Gloriana's war with the Paynim King, which withdraws St. George from the contemplation of Una's unveiled beauty in Paradise, is surely the Holy War for which Sidney died and Walsingham and Leicester intrigued.[97] The liberation of the Protestant states of the Continent and the innocent savages of the New World from the terrors of the Inquisition was the avowed object of these men, to whose policies Spenser early subscribed, and constantly adhered. The hero of the *Faerie Queene* was to be the man through whom these policies were to be carried out. in 1580, this was Leicester; in 1590, it could be no one but Essex.

The identification of Essex with Arthur in the central action of the poem increases the likelihood that the love between Gloriana and her chosen knight was to be Platonic, for there was no serious possibility of a marriage between Elizabeth and Essex, as there had been between Elizabeth and Leicester. The part played by Arthur in the "last praises" of Gloriana would symbolize the coöperation of Essex and Elizabeth in the upbuilding of the future British Empire, which was to revive, not only the golden age of Arthurian chivalry, but the older "Elfin" empire of Osiris and Hercules. When Spenser represented Elizabeth as Fairy Queen, he said in effect that she was a throw-back to the golden age of the early gods, the age whose glories were revived in Arthur's day. So Raleigh had described her in *Cynthia:*

> that nature's wonder, virtues choice,
> The only paragon of time's begetting,

[97] Cf. Harvey's commendatory verses to the *Faerie Queene*.

Divine in words, angelical in voice,
  That spring of joys, that flower of love's own setting,
The idea remaining of those golden ages,
  That beauty, braving heavens and earth embalming,
Which after worthless worlds but play on stages,
  Such didst thou her long since describe, yet sighing
That thy unable spirit could not find aught,
  In heaven's beauties or in earth's delight,
  In likeness fit to satisfy thy thought.[98]

Similarly Spenser celebrates the Golden Age with its true
understanding of love and its reverence for beauty, which
are rare in the degenerate times that follow:

But antique age yet in the infancie
  Of time, did live then like an innocent,
  In simple truth and blamelesse chastitie,
  Ne then of guile had made experiment,
  But voide of vile and treacherous intent,
  Held vertue for it selfe in soveraine awe:
  Then loyall love had royall regiment,
  And each unto his lust did make a lawe,
From all forbidden things his liking to withdraw.[99]

But these happy days were succeeded by others, quite different:

Then beautie, which was made to represent
  The great Creatours owne resemblance bright,
  Unto abuse of lawlesse lust was lent,
  And made the baite of bestiall delight:
  Then faire grew foule, and foule grew faire in sight,
  And that which wont to vanquish God and man,
  Was made the vassall of the victors might;
  Then did her glorious flowre wex dead and wan,
Despisd and troden downe of all that overran.

And now it is so utterly decayd,
  That any bud thereof doth scarse remaine,
  But if few plants preserv'd through heavenly ayd,

[98] *Tercentenary Selections from Raleigh's Works*, p. 34.
[99] *FQ*, IV, VIII, xxx.

> In Princes Court doe hap to sprout againe,
> Dew'd with her drops of bountie Soveraine,
> Which from that goodly glorious flowre proceed,
> Sprung of the auncient stocke of Princes straine,
> Now th' onely remnant of that royall breed,
> Whose noble kind at first was sure of heavenly seed.[100]

The "goodly glorious flowre" is of course Elizabeth, and the "royall breed" the Trojan line sprung from Osiris. If Spenser represents them here as "of heavenly seed," whereas previously he had insisted that they were "derived from earth."[101] he is not contradicting himself, but is expressing two sides of his attitude toward the pagan gods, and hence toward his fairies. The gods and fairies were derived from earth; that is, they were men and women, not angels or devils. Yet the good kings of old were truly divine, for they were exceptionally perfect mirrors of the heavenly ideas of goodness and beauty. For this reason they were exalted to heaven in the memory of after ages. A race of good kings might therefore be regarded as coming from heaven, a sort of emanation of the divine kingship: "nova progenies caelo demittitur alto." Or they might be thought of as rising to heaven, becoming the hypostases of the virtues which their lives had exemplified:

> Well therefore did the antique world invent,
>   That Iustice was a God of soveraine grace,
> And altars unto him, and temples lent,
>   And heavenly honours in the highest place;
> Calling him great *Osyris,* of the race
> Of th' old Ægyptian Kings, that whylome were;
>   With fayned colours shading a true case:
>   For that *Osyris,* whilest he lived here,
> The iustest man alive, and truest did appeare.[102]

Elizabeth Tudor is thus a goddess or fairy queen in the same sense that Isis was, but whereas Isis lived in the "an-

[100] *Ibid.,* xxxii–xxxiii.   [101] *Ibid.,* II, X, ii, 4.   [102] *Ibid.,* V, VII, ii.

tique times" which also produced an Osiris, Elizabeth has
no masculine counterpart in the degenerate sixteenth century. Thus although she loves all her subjects in the degree
to which they share her virtues, she cannot be completely
united in "band of vertuous mind" with any of them. Her
true spiritual mate is Arthur, inaugurator of the Britain's
first Golden Age, the very type of manly virtue.

All Spenser's true lovers express the Platonic identity of
the Good and the Beautiful. The man is drawn by beauty,
the woman by virtue. Una is in love with Holiness. Britomart, in many ways Spenser's ideal woman, is in love with
Artegall, knight of Justice, "most sacred virtue . . . of all
the rest." To gain Amoret, Scudamour has to pass through
the "Gate of Good Desert." And Gloriana seeks out Arthur,
in whom all knightly virtues are included, for the same reason, infinitely refined, that inspired every fairy mistress of
romance to seek out a mortal lover, because he was "the best
knight in the world."

If Queen Elizabeth loved the Earl of Leicester or the Earl
of Essex, Spenser would have said, it was for the same reason.
These men were mirrors of the ideal manly virtue perfectly
exemplified in Arthur the Briton. They were thus linked
to Elizabeth in the "band of vertuous mind," insofar as they
coöperated with her in those heroic acts which were to make
memorable the story of her reign. The final union of Gloriana and Arthur has therefore two explanations, which are
perfectly compatible. The fame of Elizabeth is indissolubly
linked with the fame of Arthur, since from them was born
the British Empire. But the fame of Elizabeth is equally
linked with the fame of "the worthy whom she loveth best,"
for from them was born the glory of the Elizabethan age.

A somewhat similar view of the relations between Elizabeth and her favorite is exhibited in Lyly's *Endymion:*

I favoured thee Endimion [says Cynthia] for thy honor, thy
vertues, thy affections: but to bring thy thoughts within the

compasse of thy fortunes, I have seemed strange, that I might have thee staied; and now are thy days ended before my favour begin.[103]

Later, when Cynthia asks Endymion whether it is true that he has loved her, he answers:

The time was Madam, and is, and ever shall be, that I honoured your highnesse above all the world, but to stretch it so far as to call it love, I never durst. Ther hath none pleased mine eyes but *Cynthia,* none delighted mine ears but *Cynthia,* none possessed my hart but *Cynthia.* I have forsaken all other fortunes to follow Cynthia, and heere I stande ready to die if it please *Cynthia.* Such a difference hath the Gods sette between our states, that all must be dutie, loyaltie, and reverence; nothing (without it vouchsafe your highnes) be termed love. My unspotted thoughts, my languishing bodie, my discontented life, let them obtain by princelie favour that, which to challenge they must not presume, onlie wishing of impossibilities; with imagination of which, I will spende my spirits, and to my selfe, that no creature may heare, softly call it love. And if any urge to utter what I whisper, then will I name it honor. From this sweet contemplation if I be not driven, I shall live of al men the most content, taking more pleasure in mine aged thoughts than ever I did in my youthful actions.

Cynth. Endymion, this honourable respect of thine shall be christened love in thee, and my reward for it favour.[104]

Lyly's Endymion is not a Platonic lover, and his excessive humility suggests Spenser's Timias in relation to Belphoebe rather than his Arthur in relation to Gloriana. The Platonic code allowed Spenser to represent Elizabeth as welcoming and even seeking the love of her favorite in a way that was suited to the characters under which he represents them. Arthur is not a mere courtier, but a famous prince, whose love leads him to embrace a life of strenuous action. Spen-

[103] IV, iii, 78 *et sqq.*   [104] *Ibid.,* V, iii, 162 *et sqq.*

ser's ideal knight is a patriot rather than a courtier. He seeks not merely present favor, but enduring fame.

Whatever may have been Spenser's original intention, it seems clear that in the *Faerie Queene* as he finally conceived it, he intended to represent the love of Elizabeth and her favorite as Platonic. But there is some reason to believe that his purpose may not have been immediately clear to his contemporaries. The second installment of the *Faerie Queene* begins with a very significant protest, which I have set at the head of this chapter. Some one, presumably Burghley, has misunderstood the purpose of the first three books:

> The rugged forhead that with grave foresight
>   Welds kingdomes causes, and affaires of state,
>   My looser rimes (I wote) doth sharply wite,
>   For praising love, as I have done of late,
>   And magnifying lovers deare debate.[105]

Professor Padelford objects that Spenser would not have applied the term "looser rimes" to the *Faerie Queene*,[106] but Spenser may be echoing the language of his critic. Mrs. Bennett thinks this passage refers to the *Amoretti* and *Epithalamium*,[107] but it is hard to see why they should be dangerous to "fraile youth," and even if the primary reference is to these shorter love poems, an additional reference to the *Faerie Queene* is still probable.

Spenser goes on to say that those who object to poems in praise of love do not understand it:

> Such ones ill iudge of love, that cannot love,
>   Ne in their frosen hearts feel kindly flame:
>   For thy they ought not thing unknowne reprove,
>   Nor naturall affection faultlesse blame,
>   For fault of few that have abusd the same.
>   For it of honor and all vertue is

---

[105] *FQ*, IV, Proem, i, 1–5. [106] *Variorum*, III, 304.
[107] *SP*, XXVIII (1931), 51.

> The roote, and brings forth glorious flowres of fame,
> That crowne true lovers with immortall blis,
> The meed of them that love, and do not live amisse.[108]

Now I do not believe that this bitter protest was called forth simply by personal dislike of Burghley or by disappointment over his hypothetical refusal of Spenser's pension. Spenser implies that Burghley had objected to the treatment of love in the first installment of the *Faerie Queene*. The lines just quoted reiterated the "proposition" of that poem, which was announced as dealing with love as well as war in the invocation to Cupid:

> And thou most dreaded impe of highest *Iove*,
> Faire *Venus* sonne, that with thy cruell dart
> At that good knight so cunningly didst rove,
> That glorious fire it kindled in his hart.[109]

Miss Tuell suggested that Burghley was shocked by the freedom of expression in Spenser's description of the reunion of Scudamour and Amoret in the original ending of Book III.[110] But though this may be so, it would not account for Spenser's subsequent praise of Platonic love—"Witnesse the father of Philosophy" nor for the appeal to the Queen,

> In whose chast breast all bountie naturall,
> And treasures of true love enlocked beene,
>
> . . .
>
> To her I sing of love, that loveth best,
> And best is loved of all alive I weene:
> To her this song most fitly is addrest,
> The Queene of love, and Prince of peace from
> heaven blest.[111]

---

[108] *FQ*, IV, Proem, ii.   [109] *Ibid.*, I, Proem, iii, 1–4.
[110] "The Original End of *Faerie Queene*, Book III," *MLN*, XXXVI (1921), 309–11.
[111] *FQ*, IV, Proem, iv, 3–9.

It seems to me extremely likely that this defense of love was called forth, at least partly, by the fact that Burghley and perhaps others had read the first installment of the *Faerie Queene* much as Cory did, and had seen in the love affair between Arthur and Gloriana a raking up of old scandal about Elizabeth and Leicester, or an encouragement of new gossip about her relations with Essex. If Burghley ever made such a charge, it is easy to understand the bitterness with which Spenser speaks of him here and in the *Ruines of Time:*

> O let the man, of whom the Muse is scorned,
> Nor alive, nor dead be of the Muse adorned.[112]

For not only would such a misunderstanding of Spenser's intention lay him open to considerable personal danger, and put an end to all his hopes of advancement, but it would also touch him most sensitively as an artist. We know how highly he conceived of the poet's mission. To class him with the base rhymers who used their talent for unworthy ends was to offer an insult not only to Edmund Spenser, but to the Muse herself. It is as an enemy of poetry, a foe to "learning," that Spenser attacks Burghley in the *Ruines of Time*.

Elizabeth herself apparently did not misunderstand Spenser's meaning. Perhaps she was assisted in interpreting it by the poet himself in the audience which Raleigh obtained for him. In the dedication to *Colin Clouts Come Home Againe,* Spenser acknowledges an "infinite debt in which I acknowledge my selfe bounden unto you, for your singular favours and sundrie good turnes shewed to me at my late being in England," and beseeches Raleigh to protect the present pastoral "against the malice of evill mouthes, which are alwaies wide open to carpe at and misconstrue my simple

[112] *RT*, ll. 454–55.

meaning." The poem thus introduced contains a long discourse on the nature of Platonic love, understood by shepherds, but unknown at court, which agrees with the account implied in the Fourth Book of the *Faerie Queene*.

If Spenser's interview with the Queen relieved him of the fear of a punishment which would certainly have included the suppression of the poem from which he hoped for immortal fame, it is easy to see why he should hail her with grateful affection as "The Queene of love, and Prince of peace from heaven blest." But apart from any personal gratitude he may have felt, Spenser was not talking idly when he called Elizabeth

> her that loveth best,
> And best is loved of all alive, I weene.

There was a personal bond between the Queen and her subjects. "I have desired," she said to her Parliament on one occasion, "to have the obedience of my subjects by love and not by compulsion."[113] In the religious struggles of the period, it was largely the personal devotion of all Englishmen to the Queen that averted the danger of civil war. Whatever may have been the tangled personal and political motives behind her long refusal to marry, her virgin state undoubtedly worked for the good of England, and emphasized her sole devotion to her people. She called her coronation ring her wedding ring, and declared that she would have no husband but England.[114] As head of the Church, she stood to Protestant Englishmen as the direct representative of God, and her marriage with her people might be considered symbolic also of the mystical union between Christ and his Church.[115]

---

[113] Quoted in Green, *Short History of the English People*, II, 384.

[114] Camden, quoted in *Shakespeare's England*, I, 6.

[115] This seems to be the implication in addressing her as "Queene of love and Prince of peace from heaven blest."

All these ideas entered into Spenser's conception of Elizabeth. Naturally he would represent her feeling for her people under symbols at least partly derived from the Italian Platonism that was a literary fashion in his day. Elizabeth as goddess of love is related to the Venus of Book IV, who presides over all the different kinds of "true love" in the earthly sphere. As mother of her people, the Queen inspires "naturall affection"; as a fair woman, she is a mirror of that Beauty which inspires, not only "Cupid's greater flame," but the Platonic love "that on chaste vertue groundeth its desires."

This last type of love, since it is based on likeness of soul, is preëminently a bond of union, not only between lover and beloved, but between different lovers, who, resembling their common beloved, must necessarily resemble, and hence love, each other. The beauty which inspires the highest type of love, is thus, like Concord, a "mother of blessed peace and friendship trew." This unifying power of love is particularly emphasized in Book IV, whose Proem hails Elizabeth as "Queen of love and Prince of peace." The three sons of Agape find their natural affection increased by their common love of Canace.[116] The false Florimell, like her prototype, Angelica, causes strife among her lovers, who are rebuked by the Squire of Dames in words that surely represent Spenser's own feeling.[117]

The lovers of the true Florimell, on the other hand, like the suitors of Helen,[118] are united by their common affection for their common mistress. When Satyrane finds Florimell's girdle, he is loath to arouse the envy of "full many knights,

[116] *FQ*, IV, II, liv, 4-5.
[117] *Ibid.*, IV, II, xxiv, 2-9.
[118] That Spenser's true and false Florimell are partly borrowed from the story of the true and false Helen has been often suggested. Another prototype of Florimell is Florence in *Arthur of Little Britain*. She also has a troop of devoted knights, who support Arthur, her chosen suitor.

that loved her like deare,"[119] and puts it up as prize in a tournament, in which the other Knights of Maydenhead (except Artegall, who comes in disguised on the other side) appear as members of Satyrane's party.[120]

That Gloriana's love was an even stronger bond of union between her knights is evidenced by the many examples of friendship and mutual assistance by which the minor heroes of the *Faerie Queene* are reciprocally linked with each other and with Arthur. The love of Gloriana represents both the "goodly golden chaine" which unites the virtues in the inclusive virtue whose meed is glory, and the patriotic devotion to the sovereign which creates a united nation. This twofold spiritual love, the ground of individual nobility and of public peace, is celebrated in the love story of Arthur and Gloriana, which Spenser designed for the central action of the *Faerie Queene*. Into the old tale of the fairy mistress and her mortal lover, Spenser poured a wealth of new meaning, in which the facile moral edification and elegant Platonic compliment of the typical Renaissance court poet are fused and vivified by the fire of a sincere personal emotion. For it was not only Prince Arthur or the Earl of Leicester who was moved by love of Gloriana to hunt with long labors after fame. The poet who undertook to write the great English epic, "a work of labour long and endless praise," was inspired by the same vision that drew Arthur upon his quest. Like his great disciple Milton, Spenser was at times oppressed by the loneliness of the artist in an unheeding world:

> Alas! What boots it with uncessant care
> To tend the homely slighted Shepherds trade,
> And strictly meditate the thankles Muse.[121]

This mood is perhaps more pervasive with Spenser. The note of weariness, the malaise of a sensitive man struggling, un-

---

[119] *FQ*, IV, II, xxvi, 2.   [120] *Ibid.*, IV, IV.   [121] *Lycidas*, ll. 64–66.

appreciated, as he imagines, with a mighty task, makes itself felt in many of the finest passages in the *Faerie Queene*. The strongest arguments of Despair, the most seductive temptations of the Bowre of Blisse are promises of rest, of forgetfulness. They offer the gift of the Lotus Eaters:

> O turne thy rudder hither-ward a while:
> Here may thy storm-bet vessell safely ride;
> This is the Port of rest from troublous toyle.
> The worlds sweet In, from paine and wearisome turmoyle.[122]

If Spenser shut his ears to this siren voice, he did so from a desire to reach his haven, to see the face of his goddess, Gloriana. This haven, for Milton, was heaven. "Fame is no plant that grows on mortal soil." For Keats, as for Shakespeare of the *Sonnets,* it was a purely pagan immortality, "Non omnis moriar." "I think that I shall be among the English poets after my death." But Spenser looked for part of his reward on earth. His Gloriana dwelt in a sort of halfway house between earth and heaven, the fairyland of fame in which Spenser was to have his place with Homer, Virgil, Ariosto, and Tasso. But equally she dwelt on earth in the person of that great queen whose love for her subjects was creating a new and greater England, whose service was the road to present advancement and enduring glory. It was no mere abstraction, but a living symbol, that Spenser saw at the end of Arthur's quest and of his own. For his name, too, was to be indissolubly linked with that of Elizabeth Tudor in the fairy city of Cleopolis, "to live with the eternitie of her fame."

[122] *FQ,* II, XII, xxxii, 6–9.

BIBLIOGRAPHY

THE FOLLOWING is a list of the principal works used in the preparation of this study. It should be consulted for the full titles of works cited in the text or in the footnotes. In view of the very full Spenser bibliographies now available in Carpenter's *Reference Guide,* Miss Atkinson's *Supplement,* and the volumes of the *Variorum Spenser,* I have included only those items of Spenser scholarship which are actually cited.

Annius, Johannes. Le antichità di Beroso Caldeo . . . et d'altri scrittori . . . tradotte . . . da Francesco Sansovino. Vinegia, 1583.
———Berosi . . . antiquitatum . . . libri quinque, commentariis Ioannis Annii illustrati . . . & reliquis eius argumenti authoribus. . . . Antwerpiae, 1552.

Ariosto, Ludovico. Orlando furioso . . . tutto ricorretto, et di nuove figure adornato. Con le annotationi . . . di Ieronimo Ruscelli. La vita dell' autore dal Signor Giovan Battista Pigna . . . di nuove aggiuntovi li cinque canti. Venetia, 1572.
———Orlando furioso. Con un discorso di Vincenzo Gioberti. Classici Italiani. Novissima bibliotheca, diretta da Fernando Martini. Seconda editione. 2 vols. Milano, n. d.

Aristotle. The Ethics. Chase's translation, newly revised. New York and Melbourne, n. d.

Arras, Jean d'. Melusine. Compiled by Jean d'Arras. Englisht about 1500. Ed. A. K. Donald. EETS, extra series, 68. London, 1895.

Atkinson, Dorothy. Edmund Spenser. A Bibliographical Supplement. Baltimore, 1937.

Auberon. I complementi della chanson d'Huon de Bordeaux . . . Publicata da A. Graf. 1: Auberon. Halle, 1878.

Augustine. De civitate Dei. Ed. J. E. C. Welldon. 2 vols. London, 1924.
———The City of God. Translated by J. Healey. 2 vols. Edinburgh, 1909.

Baskervill, C. P. The Genesis of Spenser's Queen of Faerie. MP, XVIII (1920), 49-54.

Becker, Ph. A. Jean Lemaire, der erste humanistiche Dichter Frankreichs. Strassburg, 1893.

Bellay, Joachim du. Œuvres poétiques. Édition critique publiée par Henri Chamard. Tome 2. Paris, 1910.

Bennett. Josephine Waters. Spenser's Muse. JEGP XXXI (1932), 200-19.

——Spenser's Venus and the Goddess Nature of the Cantos of Mutabilitie. SP XXX (1933), 160–92.

——The Theme of Spenser's Fowre Hymnes. SP, XXVIII (1931), 18–57.

Blandy, William. The Castle or Picture of Pollicy. London, 1581.

Blondus, Flavius. De Roma triumphante libri decem. Venetiis, 1511.

Boccaccio, Giovanni. Geneologia de gli dei. . . . Tradotti . . . per . . . Giuseppe Betussi. Vinegia, 1547

——Opere volgari . . .Ed. I. Moutier. 17 vols. Firenze, 1827–34

Bodin, Jean. Methodus ad facilem historiarum cognitionem. Geneva, 1595.

Boiardo, Matteo Maria. Orlando innamorato. Collezione Salani. 2 vols. Firenze, 1926.

Bouchet, Jean. Les Corectes et additionnees annales dacquitaine. Poitiers, 1531.

——Les Anciennes et modernes genealogies des roys de France. Paris, 1539.

Bourchier, John, Lord Berners. The History of the Valiant Knight Arthur of Little Britain . . . originally translated from the French by . . . Lord Berners. Ed. E. Utterson, London, 1814.

——The Boke of Duke Huon of Burdeux, done into English by . . . Lord Berners. Ed. S. L. Lee. EETS, extra series, 40, 41, 43, 50. 2 vols. in 3. London, 1882–87.

Brown, A. C. L. The Knight of the Lion. PMLA, XX (1905), 673–706.

Bruce, James D. The Evolution of Arthurian Romance from the Beginnings down to the Year 1300. 2 vols. Göttingen and Baltimore, 1923–28.

Brun de la montaigne: roman d'aventure publié . . . par Paul Meyer. Société des anciens textes français, 3. Paris, 1875.

Buchanan, George. The History of Scotland, translated from the Latin . . . with notes and a continuation to the union in the reign of Queen Anne. By James Aikman. 4 vols. Glasgow, Edinburgh, 1827.

Burckhardt, Jacob. Der Kultur der Renaissance in Italien: ein Versuch. Leipsig, 1869.

Burton, Robert. The Anatomy of Melancholy. Ed. A. R. Shilleto. 3 vols. London, 1896.

Bush, Douglas. Mythology and the Renaissance Tradition in English Poetry. Minneapolis, 1932.

Caius, John. The Works . . . Cambridge, 1912.

Calvin, Jean. Commentary on the Epistles of Paul the Apostle to the Corinthians . . . translated . . . by John Pringle. 2 vols. Edinburgh, 1848–49.

Camden, William. Annales rerum Anglicarum et Hibernicarum regnante Elizabetha . . . 2 vols. in 1. Londoni, 1615–27.
——Britain; or a chorographicall description of . . . England, Scotland, and Ireland . . . translated by Philemon Holland . . . revised . . . with additions by the author. London, 1610.
——Britannia, sive, florentissimorum regnorum, Angliae, Scotiae, Hibernae . . . chorographica descriptio. Nunc tertiò recognita, & magna accessione adaucta. Londini. 1590.

Carpenter, Frederick Ives. A Reference Guide to Edmund Spenser. Chicago, 1923.

Caxton, William, translator. The Recuyell of the Historyes of Troye . . . reproduced with a critical introduction . . . by H. O. Sommer. 2 vols. London, 1894.

Chambers, E. K. Arthur of Britain. London, 1927.
——The Fairy World. Appendix A. of Shakespeare's Midsummer Night's Dream. Warwick edition. London, 1911.

Chapman, George. The Works . . . Vol. 2. Poems and Minor Translations. London, 1875.

Chaucer, Geoffrey. The Complete Works. Ed. F. N. Robinson. Students' Cambridge edition. Boston, 1933.

Cicero, M. T. De finibus bonorum et malorum, with an English translation by H. Rackham. Loeb Classical Library. London. 1914.
———De natura deorum. Academica, with an English translation by H. Rackham. Loeb Classical Library. London, 1933.
———The Republic . . . reprinted and translated by G. G. Hardingham. London, 1881.

Coke, John. Le Débat des hérauts d'armes de France et d'Angleterre, suivi de The Debate between the Heralds of England and France by John Coke. Ed. L. Pannier et Paul Meyer. Société des anciens textes français, 8. Paris, 1877.

Comes, Natalis. Mythologiae sive explicationum fabularum libri decem. Parisiis, 1583.

Cory, Herbert E. Edmund Spenser: a critical study. Berkeley, 1917.

Cross, Tom Peete. The Celtic Elements in the Lays of Lanval and Graelent. MP, XII (1915), 585–644.

Dante Alighieri. Le opere . . . testo critico della società dantesca italiana. Firenze, 1921.

Delattre, Floris. English Fairy Poetry. London and Paris, 1912.

Dio Cassius. Dio's Roman History, with an English translation by E. Cary. Loeb Classical Library. 9 vols., London and New York, 1925.

Diodorus Siculus. Bibliothecae historicae quae supersunt ex nova recensione L. Dindorfii, Graece et Latine . . . 2 vols. Parisiis, 1843–55.
———The Historical Library . . . translated by G. Booth. 2 vols. London, 1814.

Douglas, Gavin. The Poetical Works. 4 vols. Edinburgh and London, 1874.

Drayton, Michael. The Poly-Olbion. Vol. 4 of Drayton's Works, tercentenary edition. Ed. J. W. Hebel. Oxford, 1933.

Dunlop, J. C. History of Prose Fiction. New edition revised . . . by Henry Wilson. 2 vols. London, 1896.

Estienne, Charles. Dictionarium historicum, geographicum, poeticum. Geneva, 1633.

Eusebius Pamphili. Chronicorum canonum quae supersunt. Ed. A. Schoene. Berolini, 1866.

Ferrario, Giulio. Storia ed analysi degli antichi romanzi di cavalleria e dei poemi romanzeschi d'Italia . . . 4 vols. Milan, 1828–29.

Firth, C. H. Sir Walter Raleigh's History of the World. Proceedings of the British Academy, VIII (1918), 427–46.

Fletcher, J. B. Dante's School of the Eagle. Romanic Review, XXII (1931), 191–209.
———Huon of Burdeux and the Faerie Queene. JEGP, II (1898), 203–12.

Fletcher, R. H. The Arthurian Material in the Chronicles, Especially Those of Great Britain and France. Boston, 1906.

Flores historiarum. The Flowers of History . . . collected by Matthew of Westminster, translated by C. D. Yonge. 2 vols. London, 1853.

Fordun, Johannis de. Scotichronicon cum supplementis . . . Walteri Boweri. 2 vols. Edinburghi, 1759.

Freymond, E. Artus' Kampf mit dem Katzenungetüm. In Beiträge zur romanischen Philologie. Festgäbe für Gustav Gröber. Halle, 1899.

Froissart, Jean. Œuvres . . . poésies publiées par M. Aug. Scheler. 3 vols. Bruxelles, 1870–72.

Fulgentius, Fabius Planciades. Opera. In Muncker, Thomas. Mythographi Latini. Vol. II. Amsterdam, 1681.

Gardner, Edmund. The Arthurian Legend in Italian Literature. London, 1930.

Gatfield, George. Guide to Printed Books and Manuscripts relating to English and Foreign Heraldry and Genealogy. London. 1892.

Gautier, Léon. Les Épopées françaises. 2me édition. 5 vols. Paris, 1878–97.

Geoffrey of Monmouth. The historia regum Britanniae. With contributions to the study of its place in early British history by Acton Griscom. . . . London and New York, 1929.

Gervase of Tilbury. Otia imperialia. Ed. F. Liebrecht. Hannover, 1856.

Giraldus, Lilius G., Opera omnia. 2 vols. in 1. Lugduni Batavorum, 1696.

Giraldus Cambrensis. De principis instructione liber. In Opera, Vol. VIII. Ed. G. F. Warner. Rerum Britannicarum medii aevi scriptores, 21. London, 1891.

Girault, François. The Tale of Gargantua and King Arthur. Ed. H. Brown. Cambridge, Mass., 1932.

Godfrey of Viterbo. Pantheon, sive universitatis libri, qui chronici appellantur xx. Basileae, 1559.

Golder, H. Bunyan and Spenser. PMLA, XLV (1930), 216–37.

Gordon, George. The Trojans in Britain. Essays and Studies by Members of the English Association, IX (1924), 9–30.

Graf, Arturo. Roma nella memoria e nelle immaginazioni del medio evo. 2 vols. in 1. Torino, 1882–83.

Green, J. R. A Short History of the English People. 4 vols. New York, 1878–80.

Greenlaw, Edwin. A Better Teacher Than Aquinas. SP, XIV (1917), 196–217.

——Britomart at the House of Busirane. SP, XXVI (1929), 117–30.

——Review of Cory's Edmund Spenser. MLN, XXXV (1920). 165–77.

——Shakespeare's Pastorals. SP, XIII (1916), 122–54.

——Spenser and British Imperialism. MP, IX (1912), 347–70.

——Spenser's Fairy Mythology. SP, XV (1918), 105–22.

——Studies in Spenser's Historical Allegory. Baltimore, 1932.

Guy, Henri. Histoire de la poésie française au XVIᵉ siècle. Tome 1. L'École des rhétoriqueurs. Paris, 1910.

Hakluyt, Richard. The Principal Navigations, Voyages, Traffiques and Discoveries of the English Nation. 8 vols. Everyman Library. London and New York, 1926.

Hardyng, John. The Chronicle of Iohn Hardyng . . . with the continuation of Richard Grafton. Ed. Henry Ellis. London, 1812.

Harper, Carrie A. The Sources of the British Chronicle History in Spenser's Faerie Queene. Bryn Mawr, 1910.

Hawes, Stephen. The Pastime of Pleasure. . . . Ed. W. E. Mead. EETS, original series, 173. London, 1928.

Heffner, Ray. Essex and Book V of the Faerie Queene. ELH, III (1936), 67–82.

——Essex, the Ideal Courtier. ELH, I (1934), 7–36.

Henley, Pauline. Spenser in Ireland. Cork, 1928.

Herodotus. Literally translated . . . by H. Cary. Bohn's Classical Library. London, 1894.

Hibbard, Laura. Mediaeval Romance in England. A study of the sources and analogues of the non-cyclic metrical romances. New York, 1924.

Higden, Ranulph. Polychronicon . . . together with the English translations of John Trevisa and of an unknown writer of the fifteenth century. Ed. C. Babington and J. R. Lumby. Rerum Britannicarum medii aevi scriptores, 41. 9 vols. London, 1865–86.

Histoire littéraire de la France. Ouvrage commencé par des religieux Bénédictins de . . . Saint-Maur, et continué par des membres de l'Institut. . . . Tome 26. Quatorzième siècle. Paris, 1873.

Holinshed, Raphael. Chronicles of England, Scotland, and Ireland. Ed. H. Ellis. 6 vols. London, 1807–8.

Hooker, Richard. Of the Laws of Ecclesiastical Polity. Everyman's Library. 2 vols. London and New York, 1925.

Horace. Opera. Recognovit. . . . E Wickham. Scriptorum classicorum bibliotheca Oxoniensis. Oxon., 1901.

Hughes, Merritt Y. Virgil and Spenser. University of California Publications in English II (1929), 263–418.

Huizinga, J. The Waning of the Middle Ages. London, 1924.

Huon, roy de fayerce. Ausgaben und Abhandlungen aus dem Gebiete der romanischen Philologie, XC (1892), 81–92.

Hyginus, C. J. Fabulae. Recensuit . . . H. I. Rose. Lugduni Batavorum, 1933.

Isidore of Seville. Etymologiarum sive originum libri xx. Recognovit W. M. Lindsay. Scriptorum classicorum bibliotheca Oxoniensis. 2 vols. Oxon., 1911.

Jack, A. A. A Commentary on the Poetry of Chaucer and Spenser. Glasgow, 1920.

Jacobus a Voragine. Legenda aurea . . . recensuit Th. Graesse. Editio tertia. Vratislaviae, 1890.

Jaffray, Robert. The Two Knights of the Swan. New York, 1910.

Jean d'Outremeuse. Ly Myreur des histors, chronique de Jean des Preis dit d'Outremeuse. Publiée par A. Borgnet et S. Bormans. Collection des chroniques belges inédites. 7 vols. Bruxelles, 1864–87.

Jones, H. S. V. A Spenser Handbook. New York, 1930.

Jordan, Heinrich. Topographie der Stadt Rom im Alterthum. 2 vols. in 4. Berlin, 1871–1907.

Keightley, Thomas. The Fairy Mythology. 2 vols. London, 1833.

Kelso, Ruth. The Doctrine of the English Gentleman in the Sixteenth Century. University of Illinois Studies in Language and Literature, XIV (1929), 1–288.

Kelton, Arthur. A Chronycle with a Genealogie. . . . Newly compyled in metre. London, 1547.

Kittredge, W. L., Sir Orfeo. American Journal of Philology, VII (1886), 176–202.

Lacombe, P. Cleopolis. Description et éloge de Paris par Stoa. Bulletin de la Société de l'histoire de Paris et de l'Ile de France, XVII (1890), 114–17.

La Coudrette. The Romans of Parthenay or of Lusignen: otherwise known as The Tale of Melusine: translated from the French . . . (before 1500 A.D.). Ed. W. W. Skeat. EETS, original series, 22. London, 1866.

Landino, Cristoforo. Christofori Landini . . . libri quattuor; primus de vita activa & contemplativa, secundus de summo bono, tertius & quartus in Publii Virgilii Maronis allegorias . . . typis Mathias Schürerius . . . in officina sua litteratoria Argentoraci, 1508. [Title in colophon: Camaldulenses disputationes.]

Latham, Minor White. The Elizabethan Fairies. New York, 1930.

Lemaire de Belges, Jean. Œuvres. Publiées par J. Stecher. 4 vols. Louvain, 1882–91.

Le Roux de Lincy, A. J. V. Le Livre des légendes. Introduction. Paris, 1836.

Long, Percy. Spenser's Sir Calidore. Englische Studien, XLII (1910), 53–60.

Loomis, Roger Sherman. Celtic Myth and Arthurian Romance. New York, 1927.
——Sir Orfeo and Walter Map's De Nugis. MLN, LI (1936), 28–30.
——Verses on the Nine Worthies. MP, XV (1917), 211–19.

Lotspeich, H. G. Classical Mythology in the Poetry of Edmund Spenser. Princeton, 1932.

Lucian. Selections from Lucian. Translated by Emily J. Smith. New York, 1892.

Lydgate, John. The Fall of Princes. Ed. H. Bergen. EETS, extra series, 121–24. 4 vols. London, 1924–27.
——The Temple of Glas. Ed. J. Schick. EETS, extra series, 60. London, 1891.
——Troy Book. Ed. H. Bergen. EETS, extra series, 97, 103, 106, 126. 4 vols. London, 1906–35.

Lyly, John. The Complete Works . . . Ed. R. Warwick Bond. 3 vols. Oxford, 1902.

Lyndsay, Sir David. The Works of Sir David Lindsay of the Mount. Ed. D. Hamer. Scottish Text Society, 3d series, 1–2, 6–8. 4 vols. Edinburgh and London, 1931–36.

Macarthur, J. R. The Influence of Huon of Burdeux upon the Faerie Queene. JEGP, IV (1902), 215–38.

Malory, Sir Thomas. Le Morte d'Arthur. Everyman's Library. 2 vols. New York, 1919.

Marchand, Jean. La Légende de Mélusine, selon le roman . . . par Jean d'Arras . . . renouvelé par J. Marchand. Paris, 1927.

Maury, L. F. A. Les Fées du moyen age. Paris, 1843.

Meyer, P. Notice sur le roman de Tristan de Nanteuil. Jahrbuch fur romanische und englische Literatur, IX (1868), 1–42.

Michie, Sarah. Celtic Myth and Spenserian Romance. University of Virginia Abstracts of Dissertations (1935), 11–13.

Millican, Charles Bowie. Spenser and the Table Round. Cambridge, Mass., 1932.

Milton, John. The Poetical Works. . . . Ed. H. C. Beeching. Oxford, 1925.
———Prose Works. 5 vols. London, 1868.

Mirabilia urbis Romae. The Marvels of Rome or a Picture of the Golden City. An English version . . . with a supplement of illustrative matter and notes by F. M. Nichols. London and Rome, 1889.

Mohl, Ruth. The Three Estates in Medieval and Renaissance Literature. New York, 1933.

Mort Artu: an Old French prose romance . . . being the last division of Lancelot du Lake. Ed. J. D. Bruce. Halle, 1910.

Neale, J. E. Queen Elizabeth. New York, 1934.

Neilson, W. A. The Origins and Sources of the Court of Love. Boston, 1899.

Nennius. Historia Brittonum. Translated by W. Gunn. London, 1819.

Nottcutt, Clement. The Faerie Queene and Its Critics. Essays and Studies by Members of the English Association, XII (1926), 63–85.

Nutt, A. The Fairy Mythology of English Literature: its origin and nature. Folklore, VIII (1897), 29–53.
———The Happy Otherworld in the Mythico-Romantic Literature of the Irish. In The Voyage of Bran. Ed. Kuno Meyer. Vol. I. London, 1895.

Orosius, Paulus. Historiarum adversum paganos libri vii. Ex recognitione C. Zangemeister. Bibliotheca scriptorum Graecorum et Latinorum Teubneriana. Lipsiae, 1889.

Osgood, Charles G. Boccaccio on Poetry. Princeton, 1930.

Parsons, A. E. The Trojan Legend in England. MLR, XXIV (1929), 253–64.

Parthenius. The Love Romances . . . with an English translation by S. Gaselee. Loeb Classical Library. London and New York, 1916.

Partonope of Blois. The Middle-English Versions of Partonope of Blois. Ed. A. T. Bödtker. EETS, extra series, 109. London, 1912.

Patch. H. R. Some Elements in Medieval Descriptions of the Otherworld. PMLA, XXVI (1918), 601–43.

Paton, Lucy Allen. Studies in the Fairy Mythology of Arthurian Romance. Boston, 1903.

Petrarch, F. Il canzoniere di Francesco Petrarca. Riveduto da . . . G. A. Scartazzini. Leipsig, 1883.
——Opera quae extant omnia. Ed. J. Herold. 4 vols. in 1. Basileae, 1581.
——Petrarch's Secret; or The Soul's Conflict with Passion. Translated from the Latin by H. Draper. London, 1911.

Plato. The Republic. Translated by J. L. Davies and D. J. Vaughn. The Golden Treasury Series. London, 1925.

Pliny the elder. Naturalis historiae libri xxxvii. Edidit C. May-hoff. Bibliotheca scriptorum Graecorum Teubneriana. 5 vols. Lipsiae, 1892–1909.

Plutarch. Plutarch's Morals. Theosophical Essays. Translated by C. W. King. Bohn's Classical Library. London, 1889.

Poliziano, Angelo Ambrogini. Rime. Raccolta nationale dei classici del Rinascimento del Libro. Firenze, 1929.

Prophecies de Merlin, Les, . . . Ed. L. A. Paton. 2 vols. New York and London, 1926–27.

Raleigh, Sir Walter. The Works of Sir Walter Raleigh . . . to which are prefixed the lives of the author by Oldys and Birch. 8 vols. Oxford, 1829.
——Sir Walter Raleigh, the Shepherd of the Ocean. Tercentenary edition of selections from his poetry and prose. Ed. F. C. Hersey. New York, 1916.

Rathborne, Isabel E. A New Source for Spenser's Faerie Queene, Book I. SP, XXXIII (1936), 166–81.

Read, Conyers. Mr. Secretary Walsingham and the Policy of Queen Elizabeth. 3 vols. Oxford, 1925.

Renwick, W. L. Edmund Spenser. An Essay on Renaissance Poetry. London, 1925.

Rhys, J. Lectures on the Origin and Growth of Religion as illustrated by Celtic Heathendom. 2d edition. London, 1892.

Richard Coeur de Lion. Der mittelenglische Versroman über Richard Löwenherz . . . ausg. von Karl Brunner. Wiener Beiträge zur englischen Philologie, 42. Wien und Leipzig, 1913.

Rowe, K. T. Sir Calidore: Essex or Sidney? SP, XXVII (1930), 125–41.

St. Brandan: a medieval legend of the sea, in English verse and prose. Ed. T. Wright. Percy Society. London, 1844.

Schofield, W. H. The Lays of Graelent and Lanval and the Story of Wayland. PMLA, XV (1900), 121–80.

Scott, Sir Walter. Minstrelsy of the Scottish Border. Ed. T. F. Henderson. 4 vols. Edinburgh, London, and New York, 1902.

Shakespeare, William. The Complete Dramatic and Poetic Works. Ed. W. A. Neilson. Cambridge edition. Boston and New York, 1906.

Shakespeare's England. An Account of the Life and Manners of His Age. 2 vols. Oxford, 1917.

Silius Italicus, C. J. Punicorum libri septemdecim. Ed. A. Drakenborch. Trajecti ad Rhenum apud G Vandewater, 1717.

Silvia Gadelica (I–XXXI). A collection of tales in Irish . . . ed. and translated by Standish O'Grady. 2 vols. London and Edinburgh, 1892.

Sir Orfeo. Ed. O. Zielke. Breslau, 1880.

Smith, Roland. Spenser's Irish River Stories. PMLA, L (1935), 1047–56.
——Una and Duessa. PMLA, L (1935), 917–19.

Spargo, J. W. Virgil the Necromancer. Cambridge, Mass., 1934.

Spens, Janet. Spenser's Faerie Queene. An interpretation. London, 1934.

Spenser, Edmund. The Axiochus of Plato. Translated by Edmund Spenser. Ed. F. M. Padelford. Baltimore, 1934.
——Complaints. Ed. W. L. Renwick. London, 1928.
——Daphnaida and Other Poems. Ed. W. L. Renwick. London, 1929.
——The Shepherd's Calendar. Ed. W. L. Renwick. London, 1930.
——A View of the Present State of Ireland. Ed. W. L. Renwick. London, 1934.
——The Faery Queene, Book I. Ed. G. W. Kitchin. New edition. Oxford, 1929.
——The Faerie Queene, Book II. Ed. L. Winstanley. Cambridge, 1922.
——The Faerie Queene, Book V. Ed. A. B. Gough. Oxford, 1932.
——The Poetical Works. Ed. J. C. Smith and E. de Selincourt. Oxford, 1916.
——The Works . . . variorum edition. Ed. E. Greenlaw, C. G. Osgood, F. M. Padelford. Vols. I–V. Baltimore, 1932–36.

Speroni, Sperone. Dialoghi. Venetia, 1596.

Stoa, J. F. Quintianus. De celeberrimae Parrhisiorum urbis laudibus silva cui titulus Cleopolis. Eiusdem Orpheos libri tres. Parisiis, 1514.

Tasso, Torquato. Opere . . . colle controversie sulla Gerusalemme . . . ricorette sull'edizione fiorentina ed illustrate dal Professore G. Rosini. 33 vols. Pisa, 1831–32. Vol. 1: Rinaldo; Vols. 24–26: Gerusalemme liberata.

Tatlock, J. S. P. Geoffrey and King Arthur in Normannicus Draco. MP, XXXI (1933), 1–18, 113–25.

Thaler, Alwin. Shakespeare and Spenser. SAB, X (1935), 192–211.

Thompson, Edward. Sir Walter Ralegh. London, 1935.

Thoms, W. J., ed. Early English Prose Romances. Second edition enlarged. 3 vols. London, 1858.

Tiraboschi, Girolamo. Storia della letteratura italiana. 9 vols. in 12. Roma, 1782–85.

Tuell, Anne K. The Original End of Faerie Queene, Book III. MLN, XXXVI (1921), 309–11.

Tuve, Rosamund. Spenser's Reading: The De Claris Mulieribus. SP, XXXIII (1936) 147–65.

——The Red Crosse Knight and Mediaeval Demon Stories. PMLA, XLIV (1929) 706–14.

Tyndale, William. Doctrinal Treatises and Introductions to Different Portions of the Holy Scriptures. Ed. H. Walter. Parker Society Publications, 32. Cambridge, 1848.

Urlichs, L., ed. Codex urbis Romae topographicus. Wirceburgi, 1871.

Valvasone, Erasmo di. La caccia. Classici italiani. Milano, 1808.

Varrerius, Gaspar. Censura in quendam auctorem qui sub falsa inscriptione Berosi Chaldaei circumfertur. In La Bigne, M. de. Bibliotheca maxima veterum patrum. Lugduni, 1677. Vol. II, pp. 529–44.

Vincent of Beauvais. Speculum historiale. Vol. IV of Bibliotheca mundi . . . 4 vols. Duaci, 1624.

Virgil. Virgil with an English translation by H. R. Fairclough. Loeb Classical Library. 2 vols. London and New York, 1930.

Ward, H. L. D., and J. A. Herbert. Catalogue of Romances in the Department of Manuscripts in the British Museum. 3 vols. London, 1883–1910.

Warner, William. Albion's England. In Vol. IV of Chalmer's English Poets. London, 1810.

Whitney, Lois. Spenser's Use of the Literature of Travel in the Faerie Queene. MP, XIX (1921), 143–62.

Williamson, G. Mutability. Decay, and Seventeenth Century Melancholy. ELH, II (1935), 121–50.

Xenophon. Memorabilia of Socrates. In Socratic Discourses by Plato and Xenophon. Everyman's Library. London and New York, 1923.

INDEX

Capalus, 187, 189, 197–200 *passim*
Caxton, William, 78, 114, 117, 187
Chapman, George, 4, 35, 162
Charles le chauve, 212, 213
Chaucer, Geoffrey, 5, 21, 41–48, 59,
    159, 162, 187
Churchyard, Thomas, 229
Cicero, 4, 11, 50, 94, 151
Cleanthes, 11
Cleopolis: allegorical meaning of, 18,
    19, 20, 22, 73, 75, 105–7, 112, 115,
    127, 153; sources and analogues of,
    23, 24, 26, 28, 29, 32, 33, 91, 111,
    112, 116, 117, 118, 149, 193–97 *pas-
    sim*
Coke, John, 5, 151, 174
Comes, Natalis, 8, 15, 71, 95, 96, 97,
    100, 103, 144
Copland, Robert, 174
Copland, William, 174
Cory, H. E., 222, 247
Court of Love, 48
Cumberland, Earl of, 238

Dante, vii, 26, 78, 104, 117, 127, 128,
    152, 154
Delattre, F., 158
Desperiers, Bonaventure, 164, 165,
    166
Diana, *see* Gloriana, sources and ana-
    logues of
Dictys Cretensis, 80
Dio Cassius, 124
Diodorus Siculus, 73, 74, 84, 90, 91,
    92, 94, 99, 106, 111, 117, 165
Douglas, Gavin, 48–52, 57, 161
Drake, Francis, 232
Drayton, Michael, 144, 232
Duessa, 32, 169, 173, 201
Dunbar, William, 120
Dunlop, J. C., 177, 188

E. K., 164
Elfin emperors, ix, 66–76 *passim*; 79,
    86, 92, 106, 130, 141, 142, 157, 192,
    200, 206; genealogy of, 77; identi-
    fication of, 107–28
Elizabeth, Queen, *passim*, 162, 222–
    23, 225, 228, 229, 235, 240, 242, 247,

Elizabeth.—*cont.*
    248. *See also* Gloriana, Belphoebe,
    Britomart
Elysian Fields, vii, 35, 144, 149, 150,
    152, 153, 154, 157, 162, 181, 186,
    187, 193, 199, 206
Essex, Earl of, 235–40 *passim*, 243
Estienne, Charles, 82, 111
Eusebius, 73, 74, 75, 81, 84

Fairies, distinguished from Britons,
    vii, 203–4, 206. *See also* Elfin em-
    perors, Fairy Queen, Fairyland,
    Fairy mistress, Fairy mythology
Fairyland, vii, 59, 65, 104, 141–43,
    148–49, 153, 157, 181–82, 191, 192,
    197, 202, 206, 223, 225, 251, *passim*.
    See also Avalon
Fairy mistress, viii, 143, 207, 211, 214,
    216, 221, 231–32
Fairy mythology, vii, viii, 106, 142,
    143, 150, 152, 157, 158, 164, 167,
    172, 185, 193, 197, 205
Fairy Queen, *see* Gloriana
Ferrario, G., 182, 188, 197
Fletcher, J. B., x, 26, 149, 193
Fletcher, R. H., 69, 115, 227, 230, 231,
    233
Flores historiarum, 74, 75
Florimell, 249
Freymond, E., 199
Froissart, 53
Fulgentius, 100

Gargantua, 186
Gatfield, G., 69
Geoffrey of Monmouth, 76, 85, 124,
    182, 191, 227, 228
Gervase of Tilbury, 179
Giants, 30, 86, 87, 88, 95, 98, 119, 146,
    148, 189, 200
Giraldus, Lilius, 96, 100, 101, 112,
    113
Giraldus Cambrensis, 178
Girault, François, 186
Gloriana: allegorical meaning of, 10,
    12, 14, 17, 18, 19, 20, 59, 145, 162,
    217, 218, 220, 222, 234, 235, 247,
    250, 251; antitypes of, 7, 8, 11, 12,